Assessing Language for Specific Purposes

THE CAMBRIDGE LANGUAGE ASSESSMENT SERIES

Series editors: J. Charles Alderson and Lyle F. Bachman

In this series :

Assessing Vocabulary *by John Read*
Assessing Reading *by J. Charles Alderson*

Assessing Language for Specific Purposes

Dan Douglas

CAMBRIDGE
UNIVERSITY PRESS

PUBLISHED BY THE PRESS SYNDICATE OF THE UNIVERSITY OF CAMBRIDGE
The Pitt Building, Trumpington Street, Cambridge, United Kingdom

CAMBRIDGE UNIVERSITY PRESS
The Edinburgh Building, Cambridge CB2 2RU, UK   http://www.cup.cam.ac.uk
40 West 20th Street, New York, NY 10011–4211, USA   http://www.cup.org
10 Stamford Road, Oakleigh, Melbourne 3166, Australia
Ruiz de Alarcón 13, 28014 Madrid, Spain

First published 2000

Printed in the United Kingdom at the University Press, Cambridge

Typeface Utopia (*The Enschedé Font Foundry*) 9/13 pt.   *System* 3B2 [CE]

A catalogue record for this book is available from the British Library

Library of Congress Cataloguing in Publication data applied for

ISBN 0 521 58495 7 hardback
ISBN 0 521 58543 0 paperback

To Matt and Ben

Contents

Series editors' preface

The field of Languages for Specific Purposes (LSP) is a lively, productive and at times controversial field. Until recently, there has been very little in the way of research or publications for those who need to assess language for specific purposes. Teachers and testers have had to take what has been produced for teaching purposes, and seek to convert and adapt it for assessment. There has been very little practical guidance for test development, and there has been no attempt to develop a theoretical framework within which the assessment of language for specific purposes might develop.

The author of this book, Dan Douglas, has long experience of teaching and assessing languages for specific purposes, and has formulated a theoretical framework that provides a basis for developing and using assessments of languages for specific purposes. This framework reflects the belief that language performance in individuals varies according to the context in which the language is used, and the psychological schemata which are engaged by the discourse.

Dan Douglas clearly discusses the practical implications for test development of his theory, within a framework of language ability, and the latest approaches to language test development. Moreover, he richly illustrates his discussion with examples from a range of assessment situations. This is a book not just for professional test developers, but also for classroom teachers, those who teach languages for specific purposes. The book includes very important descriptions and evaluations of a number of 'high stakes' specific purpose tests in widespread use, for which teachers may be preparing their students, or which may be used to evaluate their courses. Furthermore, the book discusses principles and procedures according to which tests can be developed for a range of 'low stakes' settings, from classrooms to the workplace.

A language test aims to elicit a person's language behaviour, and to provide for a means of describing and judging that behaviour. Language tests are needed by a whole range of professionals, from language teachers to speech therapists, from personnel recruitment agencies to college admissions officers and army officers: in short, anybody who uses language or needs to know how well somebody else uses language. The importance of the series, and Dan Douglas' volume in the series in particular, is that it combines different angles on language and language testing, bringing applied linguistic insights together with guidelines for test construction and test analysis.

This volume explores what language knowledge and language use are in the context of specific purposes for language; it derives principles for the design of assessment procedures from theories of language and from research in language use; and it shows how these principles can be applied to the design of good assessment instruments, appropriate for their contexts.

This book is unique in the two fields of languages for specific purposes, and of assessment, precisely because it brings them together. It combines in one volume theoretical and practical considerations for the assessment of languages for specific purposes.

J. Charles Alderson
Lyle F. Bachman

Acknowledgements

I am grateful to the series editors, Charles Alderson and Lyle Bachman, for the care they took in helping me get this book ready for publication. Their advice, suggestions, and occasional imperatives have contributed a great deal to whatever merits my book may have.

I must also thank a number of people who have read various parts of the manuscript and offered valuable advice: Carol Chapelle, Caroline Clapham, Andrew Cohen, Fred Davidson, Felicity Douglas, Tim McNamara, Margaret van Naerssen, and Larry Selinker.

I want to acknowledge and thank the members of my class in specific purpose language testing during the spring of 1997, who struggled through an early version of the book and offered many useful and insightful comments and suggestions: Roxanne Clemens, Beth Collins, Deb Crown, Louise Libby, Julio Rodriguez, Amy Waltman, and Christianna White.

I must also acknowledge generous support from the university departments I have been associated with during the writing of the book: the Department of Linguistics and Modern English Language at Lancaster University, the Department of English Language and Literature at Chukyo University, and the Department of English at Iowa State University.

Finally, thanks are owed to the editors at Cambridge University Press, Alison Sharpe and Mickey Bonin, for their wisdom and patience in helping me get the book ready for publication.

Whatever faults remain in the book are due entirely to my own stubbornness.

The publishers and I are grateful to the authors, publishers and others who have given permission for the use of copyright material identified in the text. It has not been possible to identify, or trace, sources of all the materials used and in such cases the publishers would welcome information from copyright owners.

University of Cambridge Local Examinations Syndicate. 1990. *International English Language Testing System. Module A Specimen Version* p. 2 with permission of UCLES: Cambridge; McNamara, T. 1990a. *Assessing the Second Language Proficiency of Health Professionals.* Doctoral Dissertation, University of Melbourne p. 454 and by permission of Addison Wesley Longman Ltd; OIBEC: *Executive Level Syllabus and Specimen Materials* 1990. University of Oxford Delegacy of Local Exams p. 3 by permission of UCLES: Cambridge; University of Cambridge Local Examinations Syndicate. 1994. *An Introduction to IELTS* p. 6 with permission of UCLES: Cambridge; McNamara, T. 1996. *Measuring Second Language Performance* by permission of Addison Wesley Longman Ltd; University of Cambridge Local Examinations Syndicate. 1995c. *International English Language Testing System: Specimen Materials. Listening* p. 8 and audio tape transcription with permission of UCLES: Cambridge; Northern Examinations and Assessment Board (NEAB). 19 June 1996. *University Entrance Test in English for Speakers of Other Languages. Listening Skills: Audio tape* Manchester: NEAB; Northern Examinations and Assessment Board (NEAB). 19 June 1996. *University Entrance Test in English for Speakers of Other Languages. Listening Skills: Answer Book* p. 10 Manchester: NEAB; National Languages and Literacy Institute of Australia Language Testing Centre. 1993. *Proficiency Test for Teachers: Italian. Draft Handbook for Candidates.* University of Melbourne pp. 4, 5 and 15 with permission of Department of Education Training and Youth Affairs: Australia; Iowa State University, Graduate College. *Instructions for Preparing for the TEACH Test* pp. 1–2; Iowa State University, Graduate College. Laboratory. *Exercise 11, Events in the Cardiac Cycle* p. 1; Iowa State University, Graduate College. *Guide for TEACH Test Student-Questioners* p. 3; Iowa State University, Graduate College. *TEACH Rating Sheet*; University of Cambridge Local Examinations Syndicate. *CEIBT Content and Administrative Information* pp. 14, 15, 20 and 21 with permission of UCLES: Cambridge; National Languages and Literacy Institute of Australia Language Testing Centre. 1992. *The Japanese Language Test for Tour Guides. Handbook for Candidates* University of Melbourne p. 6 with permission of Department of Education Training and Youth Affairs: Australia; Institute of Air Navigation Services: Luxembourg. 1994. *PELA: A Test in the Proficiency in*

English Language for Air Traffic Control. Information Package pp. 22, 23, 24, 29 and 30 with permission of EUROCONTROL Brussels; OIBEC: *Executive Level Syllabus and Specimen Materials* 1990. University of Oxford Delegacy of Local Exams. Sample case study pp. 2, 4, 8 and sample question paper pp. 2–3 by permission of UCLES: Cambridge; University of Cambridge Local Examinations Syndicate. 1995a. *International English Language Testing System. Specimen Materials: Academic Reading* pp. 17, 18 and 19 with permission of UCLES: Cambridge; University of Cambridge Local Examinations Syndicate. 1995b. *International English Language Testing System. Specimen Materials: Academic Writing* p. 23 with permission of UCLES: Cambridge; Northern Examinations and Assessment Board (NEAB). 28 February 1996. *University Entrance Test in English for Speakers of Other Languages. Written English: Question Paper* pp. 1 and 5. Manchester: NEAB; Northern Examinations and Assessment Board (NEAB). 28 February 1996. *University Entrance Test in English for Speakers of Other Languages. Written English: Answer Book* p. 13. Manchester: NEAB; Northern Examinations and Assessment Board (NEAB). 19 June 1996. *University Entrance Test in English for Speakers of Other Languages. Written English: Question Paper* pp. 4 and 5. Manchester: NEAB; Adult Migrant English Service. 1994. *Exemplar for ELSA Test.* Sydney: Australia pp. 4 and 5; Royal Society of Arts (RSA) Examinations Board. 1994b. *CBLC – German. Certificate in Business Language Competence. Sample Assessment Material* pp. 13 and 15 with permission of OCR: Coventry; Educational Testing Service. 1982 *Test of English for International Communication (TOEIC). Form 3EIC2* pp. 30, 42 and 43. Princeton; Fulcher, G. *Resources in Language Testing Page [On-line].* Available: *http://www.surrey.ac.uk/ELI.ltr.html* and Fulcher, G. *Thesis Writing: Quiz 6 [On-line].* Available: *http://www.surrey.ac.uk/ELI/sa/thesis6.html*; University of Birmingham. *MedWeb [On-line].* Available: *http://www.medweb.bham.ac.uk/cases.markcase.fcgi.* The TOEIC test directions are reprinted by permission of Educational Testing Service, the copyright owner. However, the test questions and any other testing information are provided in their entirety by Cambridge University Press. No endorsement of this publication by Educational Testing Service or The Chauncey Group International Ltd. should be inferred.

CHAPTER ONE

....

Why test language for specific purposes?

Introduction

Testing language for specific purposes (LSP) refers to that branch of language testing in which the test content and test methods are derived from an analysis of a specific language use situation, such as Spanish for Business, Japanese for Tour Guides, Italian for Language Teachers, or English for Air Traffic Control. LSP tests are usually contrasted with general purpose language tests, in which purpose is more broadly defined, as in the *Test of English as a Foreign Language* (*TOEFL*) (Educational Testing Service 1965). As you will see, it is important to note that tests are not either general purpose or specific purpose – all tests are developed for some purpose – but that there is a continuum of specificity from very general to very specific, and a given test may fall at any point on the continuum. I will argue later in this chapter that LSP testing is a special case of communicative language testing, since both are based on a theoretical construct of contextualized communicative language ability, and that LSP tests are no different in terms of the qualities of good testing practice from other types of language tests.

I should note that, over the years since its beginnings, specific purpose language testing has been criticized on a number of grounds: specific purpose language proficiency is really just general purpose language proficiency with technical vocabulary thrown in; we don't need specific purpose tests since, if we test general language knowledge, specific uses will take care of themselves; specific purpose

1

language tests are unreliable and invalid since subject knowledge interferes with the measurement of language knowledge; there is no theoretical justification for specific purpose language testing; and specific purpose language testing is impossible anyway, since the logical end of specificity is a test for one person at one point in time. In this book, I intend to refute these and other arguments in favor of the view that specific purpose language tests are indeed necessary, reliable, valid, and theoretically well-motivated.

Typically, LSP tests have been construed as those involving language for academic purposes and for occupational or professional purposes. Readers may wish to have a look at the following publications for further information on the field of language for specific purposes, of which LSP testing is certainly a part: Swales (1985) for a discussion of the development of the field, and Dudley-Evans and St John (1998) for a discussion of current developments. I will focus on two aspects of LSP testing that may be said to distinguish it from more general purpose language testing: **authenticity of task** and the **interaction between language knowledge and specific purpose content knowledge.** Authenticity of task means that the LSP test tasks should share critical features of tasks in the target language use situation of interest to the test takers. The intent of linking the test tasks to non-test tasks in this way is to increase the likelihood that the test taker will carry out the test task in the same way as the task would be carried out in the actual target situation. The interaction between language knowledge and content, or background, knowledge is perhaps the clearest defining feature of LSP testing, for in more general purpose language testing, the factor of background knowledge is usually seen as a confounding variable, contributing to measurement error and to be minimized as much as possible. In LSP testing, on the other hand, as you will see in Chapter 2, background knowledge is a necessary, integral part of the concept of specific purpose language ability.

LSP testing, like LSP teaching, has a relatively short history. A case could be made for the beginning of LSP testing as early as 1913, with the establishment of the University of Cambridge Local Examinations Syndicate's (UCLES) *Certificate of Proficiency in English*, a test designed for prospective English teachers to demonstrate their proficiency in the language (University of Cambridge Local Examinations Syndicate 1995). Another candidate for the title of first LSP test might be the College Entrance Examination Board's *English Competence* examination in the US, a test for international applicants to US colleges and universities introduced in 1930 (Spolsky 1995). Both of these tests have clearly defined purposes related to vocational and academic English, respectively, and thus in a sense qualify as examples of LSP tests. However, as I mentioned above, LSP testing requires first, an analysis of a target language use situation, from which characteristics of test content and method are derived, as well as an interaction between language knowledge and specific purpose content knowledge. Clearly, not all examples of what we call LSP tests manage to meet these criteria completely, but I will argue in this book that a theory of LSP testing establishes these two characteristics as fundamental goals. The UCLES and the College Board tests were not developed on the basis of analyses of language teaching or academic situations, nor did the tasks on the tests bear much relationship to the kinds of tasks required of either teachers or students (except when taking language tests!).

So, when might we say that true LSP testing began? A strong candidate is the *Temporary Registration Assessment Board* (*TRAB*) examination, a test introduced in 1975 by the British General Medical Council for the purpose of evaluating the professional and language abilities of physicians trained outside the UK applying for temporary registration to practice medicine in Britain (Rea-Dickens 1987). The examination consisted of an assessment of both professional competence and ability to communicate in English. The language component comprised a taped listening test, a written essay, and an oral interview in which both professional knowledge and language ability were assessed. The *TRAB* language component was based on an analysis of the language, both spoken and written, actually used by physicians, nurses, and patients in British hospitals. As I have discussed, this analytical approach is a critical feature of LSP test development. In addition, the language testing specialists who developed the language component of the *TRAB* test were not solely responsible for its development, but worked together with medical experts in constructing the tests. This is an important aspect of specific purpose test development. As Rea-Dickins (1987) put it in discussing the *TRAB* development process, collaboration with practitioners in the specialist area 'would seem to be a pre-requisite for the design of a "special purposes" test as the domains incorporated within the specialist area go beyond those in which the linguist – independently – is competent to make judgements' (p. 196). Thirdly, the *TRAB* developers attempted to promote the engagement of the test takers' language ability and background knowledge in the test tasks by providing appropriate and rich contextual features in the test material. For example, in the writing tasks, the test takers were presented with authentic information about a patient's case history, and the tasks were linked systematically to the problems presented. Typical writing tasks included the following:

> Write a letter to Dr Jones summarising the case and giving your recommendations for Mr Brown's after-care.
>
> Complete the x-ray request card for this examination.
>
> When the patient is admitted to hospital, what written instructions would you leave the night nurse in charge of the ward regarding management?
>
> Rea-Dickins (1987: 195)

We can see in this early example of an LSP test the embodiment of the critical features of LSP test development: analysis of the target language use situation, authenticity of task, and interaction between language and content knowledge. The *TRAB* was later revised (its name changed to *PLAB – Professional and Linguistic Assessment Board*), and is at present no longer in use, but it stands as a worthy prototype of the art of LSP test development. (Readers might also want to note another early LSP test, the *English Language Teaching Development Unit [ELTDU]* test, introduced in 1976 as an assessment of vocational English. See North 1994 for information.)

You might reasonably ask the question, however, as to why LSP testing is necessary, or even desirable. To consider this issue, let us imagine a typical language testing situation. As in all good language testing projects, LSP test development begins with a problem to be solved.

A problem

Suppose we want to determine whether people involved in international trade know English well enough to conduct their business. In such a situation, we might reasonably decide to devise a test of English for international business purposes. We would begin our task as test developers by interviewing experienced business people, as well as company supervisors, heads of international divisions, and an assortment of middle level managers who typically deal with international colleagues. We might observe actual negotiating sessions and business meetings, and tape record participants' use of English in the various situations they find themselves in: large meetings, one-on-one discussions in offices, individual and conference telephone calls, the ubiquitous business lunch and other business-related social occasions, and so on. Our goal would be to describe the situations in which international business people conduct their work, and the characteristics of the language they use and of the tasks they must perform in English.

We would need to make some decisions about the scope and content of our test. For example, how important is it to test ability to communicate about food or travel? Should we require the test candidates to demonstrate knowledge of their field of business as well as their abilities in English? Such decisions would have to be made in consultation with the sponsors of the test, for their purposes in wishing to give the test – and their willingness to pay for a longer and more varied test! – will help determine what aspects of the milieu of international business we will include in our test. Eventually, however, we would be in a position to produce **test specifications**, a blueprint of the test we intend to develop, including a statement of the purpose of the test, a description of what it is we intend to measure, a description of the contexts and tasks we intend to include in the test (based on our analysis of the features of the international business domain), details of how the test will be scored, and an indication of how scores on the test should be interpreted.

On the basis of these specifications, we would then actually produce test tasks and assemble a specific purpose test of English for international business. After trying the new test out, perhaps by giving it to a group of business people, and revising it, we would offer it to our target group of prospective international traders. We would interpret their performance on our test as evidence that they could, or could not, use English well enough to succeed in the tasks required of them in the marketplace.

Why bother?

But why go to all the trouble of devising a new test? Why spend the time, effort, and money to interview people, describe the language tasks of international business, devise the test, and pilot and revise it? Why not just turn to an existing test of English language ability, one such as the Educational Testing Service's *Test of English as a Foreign Language* (*TOEFL*), or the Cambridge University Local Examinations Syndicate's *Certificate of Proficiency in English* (*CPE*)? These, after all, are well-known international tests, with well-known measurement properties. The *TOEFL* is a multiple-choice test of listening, structure, reading comprehension, and writing, and is often taken by people who wish to demonstrate English language ability for international communication. *TOEFL* candidates can opt to take a speaking test as well, to further demonstrate their ability to use English. The *CPE* is a general test of English reading, writing, structure, listening, and speaking, and is used by many businesses to certify the English language skills of their employees, in addition to its main purpose for university admissions. So, why not use an existing, general purpose language test for our international business candidates?

Reason 1: language performances vary with context

One reason is that researchers are pretty much in agreement that language performances vary with both context and test task, and therefore our interpretations of a test taker's language ability must vary from performance to performance. For example, if we give test takers a reading test based on a passage about square-rigged sailing ships, followed by one based on a passage about micro-chips in computers, they will probably perform somewhat differently on the two tests, particularly if they are studying computer engineering! However, as you will see, it is not enough merely to give test takers topics relevant to the field they are studying or working in: the material the test is based on must engage test takers in a task in which both language ability and knowledge of the field interact with the test content in a way which is similar to the target language use situation. The test task, in other words, must be **authentic** for it to represent a specific purpose field in any measurable way. I will discuss the nature of authenticity in more detail below, but for now let us agree that LSP testing requires the use of field specific content in tasks which might plausibly be carried out in those fields. Returning to our business English example, it would not be enough, in this view, to provide test takers with listening texts about the work of international commerce, but rather it would be necessary to provide test tasks that share similar characteristics with the tasks that international traders actually perform in their work, both in the processing of information and in responding to it. Thus we must keep in mind that an important reason for using specific purpose measures is that if we wish to interpret a person's test performance as evidence of language ability in a specific language use situation, we must engage the test taker in tasks which are authentically representative of that situation.

There is quite a bit of research which suggests that this interaction between the test taker's language ability and specific purpose content knowledge and the test task is a necessary condition in LSP tests. It has been found, for example, that when test takers have some prior knowledge of the topic of a reading passage, they have an advantage in responding to comprehension questions based on that passage. This suggests that there may be no such animal as a pure language test. Measures of language ability are always colored by such factors as background knowledge and test method. It has also been found, however, that the advantage due to specific purpose content knowledge may be quite negligible unless the passage and tasks are sufficiently specific to engage the test takers in authentic language use. I will discuss evidence for this claim in some detail in Chapter 2.

Reason 2: specific purpose language is precise

A second reason for preferring LSP tests over more general ones is that technical language – that used in any academic, professional or vocational field, including cooking, law, physics, chemistry, air traffic control, scuba diving, religion, stamp collecting, or language teaching – has specific characteristics that people who work in the field must control. What we often refer to as jargon or even gobbledygook has a specific communicative function within that field, namely **precision**. There are lexical, semantic, syntactic, and even phonological characteristics of language peculiar to any field, and these characteristics allow for people in that field to speak and write more precisely about aspects of the field that outsiders sometimes find impenetrable. It is this precision that is a major focus of specific purpose language use and is a major factor arguing in favor of specific purpose language tests. A classic example of the need for precise, specific purpose language comes from the field of law. We frequently deplore what we call legalese, the arcane lexis, the convoluted syntax, the use of Latin terminology, and the interminable cross-references to previous laws and cases in legal texts. Yet, legal language was purposefully developed and is used dynamically by members of the legal profession to communicate among themselves the precise meaning of the law. A good example can be found on the back of any airline ticket:

Conditions of Contract

> 1   As used in this contract, 'ticket' means this passenger ticket and baggage check, of which these conditions and the notices form part, 'carriage' is equivalent to 'transportation,' 'carrier' means all air carriers that carry or undertake to carry the passenger or his baggage hereunder or perform any other service incidental to such air carriage, 'WARSAW CONVENTION' means the Convention for the Unification of Certain Rules Relating to International Carriage by Air signed at Warsaw, 12th October 1929, or that Convention as amended at The Hague, 28th September 1955, whichever may be applicable.   Ref. 1293 ATB (REV. 6–89)

This statement, not among the most opaque of legalese, but nevertheless quite recognizable as such, was clearly written not by the airline's public relations officer for the traveler who bought the ticket, but rather by lawyers for other lawyers, and is a good example of the legal profession's demand for precision in language. If, for whatever reason, we wanted to measure a lawyer's control of English to conduct the business of law, it would not seem to be sufficient to use texts and tasks which were not specific to the legal profession. There may be perfectly good reasons to include language and tasks not so strictly related to the legal register in the test, but certainly if our goal is to measure a test taker's ability to use language within a specific vocation, profession, or academic field, and that is the focus of this book, then specific purpose texts and tasks will be needed.

How are specific purpose language tests related to other types of language tests?

Speaking of precision, it is, of course, necessary to be more precise about the nature of specific purpose language tests than I have been so far. For the moment, let us agree to define our object of interest as tests which attempt to measure language ability for specific vocational, professional, and academic purposes. I will suggest a more precise definition later in this chapter, but before we can arrive at a useful definition of specific purpose language testing, we need to discuss a number of related concepts in language testing that form the background to LSP testing. These include **communicative testing**, **general proficiency testing**, **criterion-referenced testing**, and the notion of **authenticity**.

Communicative tests

Particularly since the publication in 1978 of Widdowson's book, *Teaching language as communication*, and in 1980 of Canale and Swain's paper, 'Theoretical bases of communicative approaches to second language teaching and testing,' the related fields of language pedagogy and language assessment have been characterized by the communicative paradigm, the communicative approach, and communicative language teaching. But even before the publication of Hymes's (1972) classic paper, 'On communicative competence,' which provided much of the impetus for the communicative approach, language testers were discussing 'productive communication testing' (Upshur 1971), and teachers and testers have been fascinated with the notion for over a quarter of a century now. As you will see below, specific purpose language tests are by definition communicative. Indeed, Sajavaara (1992), in a discussion of LSP test design, assumes from the outset that 'It is impossible to distinguish LSP testing theoretically from communicative language testing' (p. 123).

In his book *Communicative language testing*, Weir defines his topic as follows:

> In testing communicative language ability we are evaluating samples of performance, in certain specific contexts of use, created under particular test constraints, for what they can tell us about a candidate's communicative capacity or language ability.
>
> Weir (1990: 7)

In his definition, Weir employs a number of key terms: **communicative language ability**, **specific contexts of use**, **test constraints**, and **capacity**. Since specific purpose language testing involves all these concepts, we will conceive of it as a special case of communicative language testing. The first of Weir's terms, communicative language ability (CLA), was introduced by Bachman as a framework for describing language knowledge and the capacity for implementing it 'in appropriate, contextualized communicative language use' (Bachman 1990: 84). This leads us to Weir's second key term, specific contexts of use, requiring us to take account of the many features of context that influence communication, features such as the physical and temporal setting, the role(s) of the test taker and the interlocutor(s)/audience, the purposes of the communication, the topic and content of the message, its tone and manner, and the channels, codes, and genres being employed (cf. Hymes 1974). The third key term in Weir's definition, test constraints, reminds us that the methods we employ in eliciting a language performance will influence the nature of the performance and thus the interpretations we might make on the basis of it. Tests are, after all, contrived language use events, and even the most cleverly contrived test tasks limit to some degree the generalizability of our interpretations concerning the test takers' specific purpose language abilities.

Finally, Weir refers to capacity, a term employed by Widdowson (1983), as 'the ability to use knowledge of language as a resource for the creation of meaning' (p. 25), and is intended to be understood from the perspective of the language user rather than that of the language analyst (or, indeed, the language tester). In this book, I will use the term **communicative language ability** (and later, **specific purpose language ability**) to capture the notion of capacity as Weir and Widdowson use the term. The point that is crucial in the testing of language ability in specific purpose contexts is understanding that ability from the perspective of the language user. That is, not only are we interested in measuring communicative language ability rather than language performances *per se*, but we are called, in LSP testing, to interpret test performance from the point of view of language users in the specific purpose situation of interest. Thus, specific purpose language testing, as Widdowson points out with regard to specific purpose language teaching, is essentially an exercise rooted in an understanding of human activity from the point of view of the participants in the activity. In this regard, in Chapter 2, I will explore the concepts of grounded ethnography and indigenous assessment, as useful approaches for understanding the nature of LSP test performance from the point of view of the language users.

General purpose tests and specific purpose tests

Defining purpose

Widdowson (1983) points out that although, as I said above, all language courses (and tests) are purposeful, there is a difference in how purpose is defined. He suggests that in general purpose language courses, a distinction is made between **aims**, the eventual target behaviors of the learners, and **objectives**, pedagogical constructs which, it is believed, will enable the learners to achieve the behavioral targets. The goal, he says, of general purpose language courses, is to provide learners with an ability to solve on their own the profusion of communication problems they will encounter when they leave the language learning classroom. On the other hand, designers of specific purpose language courses, Widdowson suggests, often collapsed the distinction between aims and objectives, so that descriptions of target behaviors, usually derived from a needs analysis of a specific purpose language situation, become the course content. In other words, Widdowson argues, specific purpose language teaching suffered from a lack of theoretical motivation for course design, and became a very narrowly focussed training exercise in which learners were taught specific behaviors but not strategies enabling them to adapt to new, unspecifiable situations. Although many LSP courses are nowadays more strategically oriented, language teachers can tell anecdote after anecdote about learners who demonstrate an ability to perform the required language functions in the context of the classroom, but as soon as they walk out of the door, fail miserably to transfer the skills to the requirements of communication outside the classroom. There seems often to be a gap between what students can do in the classroom and what they can do in the real world.

In discussing the issue of a lack of theory in LSP testing, Davies (1990) argues that 'Tests of LSP/ESP are indeed possible, but they are distinguished from one another on non-theoretical terms. Their variation depends on practical and ad hoc distinctions that cannot be substantiated' (p. 62). It is one of the purposes of this book to provide some theoretical justification and frameworks for LSP testing that will take it out of the realm of narrowly focussed behavioral assessment and bring it more in line with the theoretical underpinnings of communicative language testing. Such an approach will lead to the assessment of the abilities that underlie communicative performance which will be generalizable from one situation to the next and from the test situation to non-test target situations. For example, if test takers demonstrated in a test that they could successfully read a patient's case history and then could use that information to write a letter of referral to another physician, we want to be certain that they could carry out a similar task in a non-test situation. More importantly, we must ask how many different communicative situations might the test takers potentially need to deal with in their work as physicians which need to be tested in a test of medical English. However, it is practically impossible not only to sample the variety adequately, but even to list all the possible permutations of communicative events that language users must cope with. The problem of generalizing to real life is a central one in LSP testing. We wish to avoid the potential problem of producing a test on which performance is interpretable only in terms of that test. This situation can come about when we equate target behaviors with test content without noting the features of the target situation that are shared by the test tasks. As I will discuss below, it is only by taking note of the features of the target situations and comparing them with those of the test task, that we can make that inference with any certainty. In this discussion, and, indeed, in the rest of the book, I will draw heavily on Bachman and Palmer's book *Language testing in practice* (1996), for their approach to test design and development is one that is useful in informing and carrying out any LSP testing enterprise.

Generalizing to real life

It has proven very difficult, and may eventually prove to be impossible, to make predictions about non-test performance in the real life target situation on the basis of a single test performance, no matter how true to real-life the test tasks might be. This is so because language use, even in highly restricted domains, such as taxi-driving, accounting, welding, biochemistry, or waiting tables, is so complex and unpredictable that coverage, or sampling of tasks, will be inadequate. Skehan (1984), for example, writing about the problems of testing English for specific purposes, notes that 'Merely making an interaction "authentic" does not guarantee that the sampling of language involved will be sufficient, or the basis for wide ranging and powerful predictions of language behaviour in other situations' (p. 208).

Spolsky (1986) agrees, and reminds us that how speech acts are realized is the result of a complex interaction among many contextual variables, and although we might study pragmatic values and sociolinguistic probabilities of various forms appearing in different contextual environments, 'the complexity is such that we cannot expect ever to come up with anything like a complete list from which sampling is possible' (p. 150). Bachman (1990) points out that now that it has become commonplace to recognize that language use takes place in contexts, and must be interpreted with reference to the context, and since the domain of language use consists of a potentially infinite number of unique instances, the assumption that we will be able to predict future communicative performances on the basis of a single test performance becomes untenable. He offers an example of attempting to produce a test of English proficiency for taxi-drivers in Bangkok by making lists of actual utterances the drivers might be expected to control. It soon became clear that the complexity involved in negotiating meaning even in this relatively narrowly defined context meant that 'there was probably an infinite variety of conversational exchanges that might take place' (p. 312). Skehan hypothesizes a similar problem in another domain, that of a waiter in a restaurant:

> Although at first sight 'waiter behaviour' might seem to be a straightforward affair, we soon need to ask questions like: what range of customers needs to be dealt with? What range of food is to be served? Once one probes a little, the well-defined and restricted language associated with any role is revealed to be variable, and requiring a range of language skills.
>
> Skehan (1984: 216)

Tests developed in the real-life mold, which equate language ability with a specific language performance, are analogous to the training courses criticized by Widdowson, above, as failing to test the ability of the learners to deal with new, unexpected, unique communication problems. This is a real problem for specific purpose language testing. Tests might contain tasks that mirror faithfully those of the target situation, and these tasks might meaningfully engage the test takers' language ability, and yet the test overall might not be truly representative of the target situation, since there are simply too many possible variations of target situation to cover adequately in a test.

I will consider this problem in more detail in the discussion of authenticity later in this chapter, but for the moment let us agree that what is required in LSP testing is not the holistic replication of a specific purpose domain, but rather the use of features or characteristics of tasks in specific purpose language use situations in the construction of test tasks. This leads us to a view of LSP testing in which test tasks are developed on the basis of an analysis of characteristics of context and tasks in target language use situations. It is this analysis of target language use task characteristics which will allow us to make inferences about language ability in the specific purpose domain. The distinction between ability and performance is an essential one in the approach to language testing advocated in this book. The interaction between ability and task characteristics leads to authenticity, which I will interpret as the extent to which the test does in fact engage the test takers in tasks characteristic of the target language use situation. It should be clear from this discussion, too, that language tests are not either specific purpose or general; rather, there are degrees of specificity, which can be described along two dimensions: the amount of content or background knowledge required for carrying out test tasks, and the narrowness of interpretations which may be made on the basis of test performance about language use in real-life contexts. In other words, language tests will be more or less specific purpose in relation to the degree to which they require the engagement of specific purpose content knowledge in responding to the test tasks and the degree to which they allow generalizations about language use in specific situations. For example, the *Test of English as a Foreign Language* (*TOEFL*) is a test intended to measure English proficiency broadly interpreted, without the engagement of any special background knowledge or specific reference to use (Educational Testing Service 1965), and would thus be considered a more general purpose language test. On the other hand, a test such as the *Proficiency Test in English Language for Air Traffic Controllers* (*PELA*), a language test for trainee air traffic controllers in Europe (Institute or Air Navigation Services 1994), requires a large amount of specialized knowledge about air traffic control, and interpretations of language use are specifically limited to the work of air traffic control officers. The *PELA* is therefore a prototypical example of a highly specific purpose language test. Between these two extremes is a test such as the *Test of English for Educational Purposes* (*TEEP*), intended as a test of academic English skills (Associated Examining Board 1984), though not related to any specific field, and the *Taped Evaluation of Assistants' Classroom Handling* (*TEACH*), a test of instructors' ability to present information to students in specific academic fields (Abraham and Plakans 1988). I will return to discussion of the characteristics of target language use situations and language test tasks in Chapter 5 and will consider these and other tests in Chapters 6 and 7 in light of such characteristics. For now, I will merely emphasize that test developers must always take both test purpose and task characteristics into account when setting out to measure communicative language ability.

Criterion-referenced tests and norm-referenced tests

A very important concept for specific purpose language testing is that of **criterion-referenced** (CR) testing. Usually contrasted with **norm-referenced** (NR) language testing, CR testing differs from NR tests both in design and in the interpretation we make of performance on them. NR tests are designed to maximize distinctions among test takers so as to rank them with respect to the ability being tested; CR tests, on the other hand, are designed to represent levels of ability or domains of content, and performance on them is interpreted with reference to the criterion level (Bachman 1990). In other words, on NR tests, passing would be determined by relative ranking within the population of test takers, while on CR tests, test takers might all achieve the criterion and so pass. As an example of CR test use, suppose we wanted to test prospective candidates for certification as scuba divers to see whether they knew certain essential diving terminology, such as bc jacket, pony bottle, and regulator. Scuba divers use this terminology in pre-dive checks, so it is essential to know whether candidates can carry out a pre-dive check using the appropriate vocabulary. We are not interested in discovering who knows the most terms; we want to know which candidates know all the essential terms. Our performance criterion, then, is whether the candidate can use all the terms appropriately. On the other hand, continuing with the scuba diving example, as a way of motivating students to learn the various concepts associated with diving, such as the relationship between depth and pressure, and the different types of equipment, an instructor might offer a weekly prize to the five students who get the highest scores on quizzes. In this case, the aim would be to rank the students against each other so that the top five could be identified – a norm-referenced use of the tests. Both types of test uses are relevant to LSP testing; however, the development process associated with CR testing, which involves a detailed analysis of the target language use situation, is of most direct relevance in LSP testing, particularly with regard to a fundamental concept in specific purpose testing, authenticity.

It is important, therefore, to note that specific purpose language tests might be developed as either CR or NR tests, but CR testing offers an important perspective to LSP testing: the necessity of specifying precisely the level of ability or the domain of content that is to be the criterion for performance. Thus, the process of developing a CR test, requiring as it does the precise, detailed specification of not only the features of the specific purpose target language use situation, but also the criteria for evaluating performance, is extremely useful in LSP test development. In fact, the development of evaluation criteria, or rating scales, is perhaps the most important, and also the most vexing, problem in LSP test development (McNamara 1990, 1996). Until very recently, the task of developing assessment scales has been left to test developers and other applied linguists, and, not surprisingly, the scales they have come up with reflect a linguistic orientation, so that such categories as grammar, cohesion, vocabulary, fluency, intelligibility or comprehension are commonly employed. I will discuss problems with this approach in Chapter 5, and suggest a possible solution, but for now, let us simply note that a precise definition of assessment criteria is an essential part of the LSP test development process, and CRT procedures offer a systematic approach to specifying these criteria.

Authenticity

Since authenticity is such an important concept in specific purpose language testing, it is necessary to consider its meaning in some detail and with some precision. Kramsch (1993) points out that the term has been used to indicate a reaction against the often artificial language of language textbooks and tests; it refers to the way language is used in non-pedagogic, non-test, natural communication. Since the publication of Widdowson's *Explorations in applied linguistics* (1979), many language teachers and testers have come to view authenticity as a property not of spoken and written texts themselves, but of the uses people put them to:

It is probably better to consider authenticity not as a quality residing in instances of language but as a quality which is bestowed
upon them, created by the response of the receiver. Authenticity
in this view is a function of the interaction between the reader/
hearer and the text which incorporates the intentions of the
writer/speaker . . . Authenticity has to do with appropriate
response.

Widdowson (1979: 166)

For example: a set of instructions for conducting a chemistry laboratory exercise may be a perfectly authentic piece of material, but when
used in a multiple-choice language test as a vehicle for testing knowledge of vocabulary or the use of imperatives, it is not being used for
the purpose intended by the author of the chemistry lab manual, or in
the way lab supervisors would use it. A key concept in Widdowson's
formulation above is that of interaction between the language user
and the text, and I will make use of this notion in my characterization
of authenticity in specific purpose language testing.

In response to this problem for language teachers, Widdowson
(1979, 1983) notes that there is often a confusion between the use of
'authentic' to refer to examples of language actually produced by
users in a communicative situation versus reference to the activities
and procedures that language users engage in, in association with the
forms of language produced. He suggests a distinction between the
terms **authentic** and **genuine**: the former referring to activities or
processes associated with instances of language use, and the latter for
the actual spoken or written texts produced by the users. Thus, our
use of a set of instructions from a lab manual for the purpose of
testing an instructor's ability to understand and use imperatives
would be the use of a genuine text for a purpose other than that for
which it was intended. Bachman (1991) reminds us of Widdowson's
point, quoted above, that authenticity is a function of an interaction
between a language user and a discourse, and proposes two aspects
of authenticity: **situational** and **interactional**. The first aspect is composed of authentic characteristics derived from an analysis of tasks in
the target language use situation, the features of which are realized as
test task characteristics. Thus, situational authenticity can be demonstrated by making the relationship between the test task characteristics and the features of tasks in the target language use situation
explicit. The second aspect of authenticity, interactional, is closely
related to Widdowson's definition above, and involves the interaction

of the test taker's specific purpose language ability with the test task. The extent to which the test taker is engaged in the task, by responding to the features of the target language use situation embodied in the test task characteristics, is a measure of interactional authenticity. It is important in specific purpose language tests that both these aspects of authenticity are present. It is quite possible, for example, that a test task may be perceived by test takers as having nothing whatever to do with their field of study, but which they nevertheless find quite interesting and which engages their communicative language ability interactively. Performance on the task would be interpretable as evidence of their communicative language ability, but not in the context of the target language use situation. By the same token, a test task may contain all the contextual attributes of the target situation and yet fail to engage the test taker meaningfully in communicative language use. Mere emulation of a target situation in the test is not sufficient to guarantee communicative language use, and, as Lewkowicz (1997) has pointed out, the focus on the interaction between the test taker's language ability and the situational characteristics of the test task is a strength of this dichotomous view of authenticity in specific purpose language tests.

I will develop these concepts more fully in Chapter 3, but for now, I propose to employ this dual notion of authenticity in specific purpose language testing. In LSP test development, what we must do is first describe a target language use situation in terms of features of context and task; we must then specify how these characteristics will be realized in the test so as to engage the test taker in test tasks, performance on which can be interpreted as evidence of communicative language ability with reference to the target situation. Building on the work of Bachman and Palmer (1996), Bachman *et al.* (1991), and Davidson and Lynch (1993), I will develop a 'means of classifying test tasks on the basis of dimensions . . . that we abstract from authentic language use' (Bachman 1990: 317) in the construction of specific purpose language tests.

Specific purpose language tests

I am at last ready to propose a more precise definition of specific purpose language tests than that I suggested at the beginning of the discussion.

> A specific purpose language test is one in which test content and
> methods are derived from an analysis of a specific purpose target
> language use situation, so that test tasks and content are authenti-
> cally representative of tasks in the target situation, allowing for an
> interaction between the test taker's language ability and specific
> purpose content knowledge, on the one hand, and the test tasks
> on the other. Such a test allows us to make inferences about a test
> taker's capacity to use language in the specific purpose domain.

This definition has emerged from the discussion of a number of concepts in this chapter. I have discussed reasons for wishing to develop
specific purpose language tests, and noted first that language performance varies with both context and test task, and that therefore our
interpretations of a test taker's language ability must vary from situation to situation. Second, we have seen how technical language – that
used in any academic, professional or technical field, including
cooking, law, physics, chemistry, air traffic control, scuba diving,
religion, or stamp collecting – has specific purpose characteristics
that people who work in the field must control. What we commonly
refer to, often disparagingly, as jargon has a specific communicative
function within that field, namely precision.

In considering how specific purpose language testing is related to
other types of and approaches to language testing, I discussed the
distinction between so-called general tests and LSP tests and we saw
that while all tests have purposes, in LSP testing, the notion of
purpose is typically more narrowly focussed than in more general
language testing. There is a problem inherent in this focus, however,
since there is in principle no way of determining how specific specific
needs to be. A criticism of specific purpose testing has been an
assumption that if a test taker could perform the real-life test task, he
or she would be able to perform in the target language use situation.
However, there are serious problems in demonstrating this to be the
case. It is impossible, except in the most restricted language use
situations, to specify with any completeness the range of language
forms that will be required. This is so because language use, even in
relatively specific domains, is so complex and unpredictable that
coverage, or sampling of tasks, will be inadequate.

As a way out of the dilemma of never-ending specificity on the one
hand and non-generalizability on the other, I have referred to context
and task characteristics, which are drawn from an analysis of a target
language use situation, and which will allow us to make inferences

about language ability in the specific purpose domain. In specific purpose language test development, what we must do is first describe a target language use situation in terms of characteristics of context and task, then specify how these characteristics will be realized in the test so as to engage the test taker in test tasks, performance on which can be interpreted as evidence of language ability with reference to the target situation.

I should discuss briefly here a concept that I have used a number of times in this chapter but have not yet defined precisely: **inference**. A central goal in language testing is making judgements about test takers on the basis of their performance on a test. That is, we give tests to elicit performances which we can observe so that we can make inferences about qualities of test takers which we cannot observe. A fundamental question involves what we wish to make inferences about. We might want to make inferences just about a person's language ability; for example, this candidate is able to write business letters in English, using correct syntax, vocabulary, and spelling. Alternatively, we might want to make a statement not only about language ability, but also, particularly in LSP testing, about specific purpose background knowledge; for example, this candidate is able to write business letters in English, incorporating appropriate types and amounts of information from material provided. Inferences of this type would be more complicated, since we would need not only a measure of language ability, but also one of background knowledge, so as to be able to disentangle the two types of knowledge and understand, for example, whether a candidate's failure to incorporate appropriate types and amounts of information was due to a lack of language ability or a lack of background knowledge. Finally, we might wish to make inferences about a candidate's specific purpose language ability, in which case, language and background knowledge would be left intertwined. The type of inference we want to make would depend on the purpose for which we were giving the test, but in specific purpose language testing, the first type of inference, that about a decontextualized language knowledge, is probably not very useful. The second type, where we want to separate out language knowledge from background knowledge, would be most useful when, for example, the test takers were trainees in the specific purpose field, and we needed to know if their low test performance was the result of problems with the language or a lack of background knowledge, so we could offer appropriate remediation. The final possibility, inferences about the dual component specific purpose language ability, would be most useful in situations where we could take the test takers' specific purpose background knowledge for granted, as in the case of qualified doctors who wish to demonstrate their language ability for purposes of licensure.

Making appropriate inferences is a crucial aspect of specific purpose language testing, and I want to discuss it just a bit more deeply. McNamara (1989, 1996) has distinguished between making inferences on the basis of LSP test performance about ability to do future tasks or jobs in the target language use situation, on the one hand, versus making inferences about ability to use language in specific future tasks or jobs, on the other. This seems a subtle distinction, but it is of extreme importance for the theoretical foundations of LSP testing. McNamara cautions against the first type of inference since job performance is influenced by a number of factors, such as personality characteristics, that are independent of language ability. He makes a theoretical distinction between a strong performance hypothesis, about an individual's ability to perform target tasks successfully, and a weak performance hypothesis, about ability to use language in the target situation, and prefers the latter. I will argue in Chapter 2 that we are not attempting to measure communicative success in LSP tests, but rather the knowledge and abilities that underlie communicative performances, and this point is related to McNamara's. I have asserted that it is practically impossible not only to sample the variety of tasks in a target domain adequately, but even to list all the possible types of communicative events that language users must cope with. Thus, I agree with McNamara that we should restrict ourselves in LSP testing to making inferences about language ability and not about job performance. However, I have also tried to establish a case for making inferences about specific purpose language ability, a construct defined on the basis of an interaction between language knowledge and specific purpose background knowledge. This departs somewhat from McNamara, who would include job-related background knowledge in his list of factors essentially unrelated to language knowledge. I will also argue later that language knowledge must be interpreted differently from one domain of use to another, since as Chapelle (in press) points out, context constrains language choice, and if we are interested in making inferences about test takers' abilities to use language in specific situations, then background knowledge associated with those situations must be a part of the construct we wish to measure with our tests.

Bachman and Palmer (1996) suggest that there are three possibilities for defining the relationship between language ability and background knowledge (which they call topical knowledge): first, making inferences only about language knowledge in situations where test takers vary widely in background knowledge; second, including both language knowledge and background knowledge in situations where there is minimal variety among test takers; and third, defining language knowledge and background knowledge as separate constructs in cases where the test developers and score users are uncertain about the relative strength of test takers' background knowledge. I have taken the view in this book that the first scenario is not relevant to the LSP testing enterprise, and will discuss both of the remaining possibilities in relation to test purpose in Chapter 2. For a detailed discussion of inferences in communicative language tests, see Bachman and Palmer (1996), Chapter 6.

We have also seen that specific purpose language tests are by definition communicative. The definition of communicative language testing employs a number of key terms: communicative language ability, specific contexts of use, and test constraints. As a special case of communicative language testing, specific purpose language testing encompasses these concepts.

Finally, I have discussed how authenticity does not lie in the mere simulation of real-life texts or tasks, but rather in the interaction between the characteristics of such texts and tasks and the language ability and content knowledge of the test takers. In other words, authenticity is not a property of spoken and written texts themselves, or even of the tasks associated with various professions, vocations, and academic fields. As you will see in the next two chapters, authenticity is only achieved when the properties of the communicative situation established by the test instructions, prompts, and texts is sufficiently well-defined as to engage the test takers' specific purpose language ability.

Overview of the book

In the remainder of this book, I will take up a number of issues concerning the theory and practice of testing language for specific purposes. In Chapter 2, I will consider in more detail the concept of specific purpose language ability, including the relationship between specific purpose background knowledge and language ability, and I will develop a framework for describing language in specific purpose situations that will form the basis of specific purpose language tests. The nature of specific purpose contexts, the important concept of discourse domain, and the analysis of the characteristics of language use tasks are the topics of Chapter 3. Again, I will develop a framework for describing features of target situations and tasks that will be employed in specific purpose tests. In Chapter 4, I will focus on the relationship between specific purpose background knowledge and language knowledge, which are internal to the language user, and the external features of context to which the language user responds in communication. I will develop the concept of strategic competence as a mediator between the external situational context and internal content and language knowledge. Chapter 5 contains a discussion of the important issue of making the transition from the analysis of language use in target specific purpose situations to test tasks, developing guidelines and techniques for investigating and describing language use situations and constructing specific purpose language tests. Chapters 6 and 7 provide numerous examples of specific purpose language test tasks, along with descriptions of their features, employing the frameworks developed in Chapters 2, 3, and 5. Finally, Chapter 8 will touch upon a number of issues in specific purpose language test development, including operationalization, piloting, revising, and validation, as well as issues concerning the use of technology in the development, delivery, and analysis of LSP tests. I conclude the book with a brief discussion of the future of specific purpose language testing.

CHAPTER TWO

....

Specific purpose language ability

Introduction

In this chapter I will review research on the nature of communicative language ability, and summarize our current best understanding of this complex concept, including a discussion of background knowledge in specific fields of interest. The goal is to work toward a clearer understanding of the construct of **specific purpose language ability**, for that, of course, is what we are attempting to measure with LSP tests. I will especially consider the relationship between language ability and specific purpose background knowledge. This is an important issue, for if language is learned in communicative contexts – and there is much evidence to suggest that this is so – then it follows that those contexts must affect the very nature of the language that is thus acquired. Chapelle (1998) points out, in an elaboration of what she calls an **interactionist view** of construct definition, that merely taking into account both the traits of the language user and the features of the context is not enough; rather, we must allow for the interaction between the two. This inevitably means that the quality of each changes: 'Trait components can no longer be defined in context-independent, absolute terms and contextual features cannot be defined without reference to their impact on underlying characteristics' (p. 43). This notion suggests that there is such a thing as specific purpose language knowledge, and that the nature of language knowledge may be different from one domain to another. However, this is a strong claim, and a contentious one, and it is not the purpose of this book to become embroiled in the issue of whether there are multiple competencies, each associated with a particular context, or whether there is one competence, variably drawn upon in different contexts.

I will take the position, again following Chapelle (1998), that what is required is a theory of 'how the context of a particular situation within a broader context of culture, constrains the linguistic choices a language user can make during a linguistic performance' (p. 15). I will discuss the features of context that influence linguistic choices in more detail in Chapter 3, but for now I will consider how language ability and specific purpose background knowledge interact with each other, bearing in mind that external context is a major factor in the engagement of specific purpose communicative language ability.

Communicative language ability

What does it mean to know a language? Bernard Spolsky asked this fundamental question more than a quarter of a century ago (Spolsky 1973), and researchers have been working to answer it ever since. We know more now about the nature of communicative language ability than we did then, but we are still far from understanding with any precision what language knowledge consists of and how the various bits and pieces work together to produce communicative utterances and written text.

As has become clear in recent years through empirical studies conducted by language testers and others, language knowledge is multi-componential; however, what is extremely unclear is precisely what those components may be and how they interact in actual language use. As Alderson (1991) has pointed out, the answer to the question of what it means to know a language, 'depends upon why one is asking the question, how one seeks to answer it, and what level of proficiency one might be concerned with' (p. 12). In the case of LSP testing, we will want to add, 'and in what specific situational context one is interested.'

In attempting to make sense of the various models of communicative competence and communicative language ability, Henning and Cascallar turn to the field of cartography for a metaphor:

> Various kinds of two-dimensional maps have been devised as aids
> to navigation. Some maps are useful geographical models for

> ocean navigation, others for automobile navigation, and still others for wilderness trekking . . . none of these two-dimensional maps provides a completely accurate representation of three-dimensional reality, nor does any one kind of two-dimensional map serve every navigational purpose equally well.
>
> Henning and Cascallar (1992: 4)

So it is with models of language ability. The framework I will develop in this chapter is not offered in opposition to any others; I will try to design a map to help achieve a particular purpose: navigating in the realm of specific purpose language use, and understanding the abilities that underlie it. Let us begin with the notion of communicative competence.

Communicative competence

The term **communicative competence** has been invoked for nearly three decades now to encompass the notion that language competence involves more than Chomsky's (1965) rather narrowly defined linguistic competence. As Hymes (1971, 1972) originally formulated the concept, communicative competence involves judgements about what is systemically possible (in other words, what the grammar will allow), psycholinguistically feasible (what the mind will allow), and socioculturally appropriate (what society will allow), and about the probability of occurrence of a linguistic event and what is entailed in the actual accomplishment of it. It is important to remember, as I noted above, that for Hymes, competence is more than knowledge: 'Competence is dependent upon both [tacit] *knowledge* and [ability for] *use*' (Hymes 1972: 282; brackets and emphasis in original). Hymes's formulation that communicative competence consists of language knowledge and ability for use has become something of a classic in the field of applied linguistics. However, it is important to note early in the discussion that communicative competence is not to be confused with communicative success: ability for use is not the same as use. Speakers may have sufficient knowledge to address a communicative task and yet, for reasons of their own, or perhaps owing to factors outside their control, choose not to address the task or not accomplish their communicative goal. This is pointed out by Hornberger (1989), who recounts the story of her use of her Spanish communicative competence to get a driver's license renewed in Peru.

She was in fact successful in getting the license, despite many set-backs and frustrations, but makes the following observation:

> it should be pointed out that my communicative competence in these events resides not in the fact of my obtaining the license I set out to get (which would be a kind of performance criterion), but rather in the knowledge and ability that allowed me to suit my language use to the events in which I found myself. Even if my goal of obtaining the license had not been achieved, it would not necessarily have meant that I was not communicatively competent for those events, but rather that . . . one or more of the external factors were insurmountable.
>
> Hornberger (1989: 228–229)

This is an important point for specific purpose language testing. For example, if we wanted to develop a test to measure the level of an air traffic controller's English ability, it may be possible to simulate the environment of the air traffic control room to a very high degree indeed, and that the radar screens and voice communication with the pilots of airliners would provide the test taker with a very realistic atmosphere. However, it must remain clear that what is being tested is not the success of the performance as air traffic control officers, but rather the underlying traits that produced the performance, i.e., communicative competence, or, as I will argue later, specific purpose language ability. In the particular case of the test of air traffic controllers, then, the raters would not be interested in whether or not the test taker was able to prevent a mid-air collision, which might be outside his or her control, owing to pilot error, for instance; rather, they would be interested in what the performance could tell them about the nature of the language ability underlying it.

I discussed this issue briefly in Chapter 1 in the sections on generalizing to real life and authenticity. The point I made was that if we do not distinguish between a language performance and the abilities that underlie it, it will make generalizing from performance in one context or situation to any other situation problematic. In tests, we observe performances which we elicit under controlled conditions and make inferences about the abilities that produced the performances. In Chapter 3 I will discuss a framework for controlling the conditions of the test tasks. For the present, simply bear in mind that failure to succeed in a test task does not automatically indicate a lack of communicative competence; it may indicate an impossible situation set up by the test developer. By the same token, it may also be true that success in accomplishing a test task does not automatically guarantee that the test taker possesses communicative competence, since it is possible to accomplish certain tasks by bringing other types of knowledge, such as background knowledge, to bear on the problem. The key point to remember is the importance of distinguishing performance on tasks from the abilities that make the performance possible.

Others have since reformulated Hymes's notion of communicative competence, and the current, most well-known, framework is that of Bachman (1990), recently elaborated by Bachman and Palmer (1996). They postulate two components of communicative language ability: **language knowledge** and **strategic competence**. Strategic competence serves as a mediator between the internal traits of background knowledge and language knowledge and the external context, controlling the interaction between them. The engagement of strategic competence, then, is of central concern in LSP testing, for this cognitive aspect is responsible for assessing the characteristics of the language use situation (including the language user's own background and language knowledge, as well as, subsequently, assessing the success of the communicative response to the situation), setting communicative goals, planning a response in light of the goals, and controlling the execution of the plan. This is the essence of an interactionist perspective (Chapelle 1998) on defining the construct of communicative language ability: an authentic language performance is the result of an interaction between internal traits of the language user and the external characteristics of the situational context.

The framework which I will present for communicative language ability combines Bachman and Palmer's formulation of the components of language knowledge with a modified formulation of strategic competence (Chapelle and Douglas 1993). In this framework, language knowledge consists of **grammatical knowledge** (knowledge of vocabulary, morphology, syntax, and phonology), **textual knowledge** (knowledge of how to structure and organize language into larger units: rhetorical organization; and how to mark such organization: cohesion), **functional knowledge** (knowledge of the ideational, manipulative, heuristic, and imaginative functions of language), and **sociolinguistic knowledge** (sensitivity to dialects, registers, naturalness, and cultural references and figures of speech). (See Bachman and Palmer, 1996, Chapter 2, for a fuller discussion of the components of communicative language ability.) Strategic competence comprises the processes of **assessment** (evaluating the communicative situation and engaging a discourse domain, a cognitive interpretation of the context, to be discussed in Chapter 3), **goal setting** (deciding whether and how to respond to the situation), **planning** (deciding what elements of language and background knowledge are required), and **control of execution** (organizing the required elements to carry out the plan). From the perspective of the LSP tester, such a framework can be employed in two ways: in defining the construct to be measured, and in interpreting test performances as evidence of specific purpose language ability.

Language knowledge and background knowledge

The distinction between language knowledge and background knowledge has long been a problem for language testers, since there is the difficulty of distinguishing between them in interpreting test results. There are a few studies which suggest that, under some conditions, background knowledge does not influence language test performance to any significant degree, but, on the other hand, several other studies have found significant interactions between background knowledge and language test performance. Thus, it appears that, under some conditions at least, background knowledge makes a difference to language test performance.

Since we are most interested in specific purpose background knowledge related to academic, professional or vocational contexts, we will be particularly concerned to know what the conditions are in which specific purpose background knowledge and language knowledge will interact, resulting in a performance that can be interpreted as a measure of specific purpose language ability. As you will see below, specific purpose language ability is most likely to be engaged when test content and tasks are sufficiently specified, and when subjects' levels of language knowledge are sufficiently high to enable them to make use of the situational information. A problem for specific purpose language testers is to understand the conditions that influence test performance. Until such features are understood and controlled, true LSP test development, authenticity in test performance, and valid interpretation of language test results will be elusive goals. In other words, if there is to be a congruence between the elicitation of language performances and the interpretation of those performances, there needs to be a congruence between the types of knowledge and tasks the test requires and the types of knowledge and tasks demanded by the situation for which the test results are to be interpreted, the target language use situation. Specific purpose language test developers need to be aware of this aspect of the relationship between background knowledge and language knowledge. I will begin by considering an important study of the relationship between specific purpose knowledge and language ability.

Caroline Clapham's study

In the most thorough study of the relationship between specific purpose background knowledge and language ability to date, Clapham (1996) studied performance on the reading modules of the *International English Language Testing System (IELTS)*. The *IELTS* is a test of academic English ability that contained (until its revision in 1995) reading sub-tests that were related to moderately specific fields: biological sciences, physical sciences, and humanities and social sciences (University of Cambridge Local Examinations Syndicate 1994). Although Clapham's study focussed on reading tests, her results have important implications for all types of tests in which background knowledge is intended to play a role in test performance and in the interpretation of scores.

In her study, Clapham made a number of important findings. First, students achieved significantly higher scores on the reading sub-test in their own subject area than on the sub-test outside it. However, in a pilot study (Clapham 1993), using a different set of passages, no significant differences were found. This suggests that the passages in her two studies varied significantly in their degree of specificity, but that if passages were sufficiently specific, test takers did better at tests in their own subject area.

Second, Clapham found that there was no significant subject area effect for the undergraduate students in her study, but there was a subject effect for the postgraduates in her test population. This finding indicates that the test takers' level of specific purpose background knowledge may have had an effect on their language performance. Additionally, Clapham found that test takers with scores of less than 60% on a grammar sub-test did not appear to profit from their background knowledge: there were no significant subject area effects; while students with grammar scores above 60% did show highly significant subject area effects. Thus, it appears that level of language knowledge, and specifically structural knowledge, had an influence on the effect of background knowledge on test performance. At the same time, however, there was no steady increase in the effect of background knowledge as students' level of proficiency rose; rather, there seemed to be a threshold below which students were not able to make use of this knowledge and above which they were.

Third, Clapham found that when scores were analyzed on the reading sub-tests containing texts of widely varying specificity, language proficiency accounted for 44% of the variance while the addition of background knowledge variables added only 1%. This finding suggests that what really counted in the test takers' performance was their language ability and not their background knowledge. This result agrees with that of Tan (1990), who found that comprehension of a discipline-related text could be predicted both by knowledge of the subject area and by language level, but that language level was the better predictor. Clapham went a step further, however: she removed the least field specific texts from her data and carried out her analysis a second time. When the less specific texts were excluded, the contribution of language proficiency, though still strong, was less marked: 26% of the variance was due to language ability; adding background knowledge raised the figure to 38%. It thus seems likely that as the modules become more subject specific, background knowledge will have a proportionately stronger effect on test scores.

Finally, though, Clapham looked at the performance of those test takers who scored very highly on the grammar module: she found, in addition to the threshold between low and intermediate proficiency readers, that readers above 80% on the grammar test were less affected by subject area than were the intermediate readers. Thus, it seemed that readers with a high level of language competence were so proficient that they could compensate for a certain lack of background knowledge by making fuller use of their language resources. The pattern of the relationship between language competence and specific purpose background knowledge, as suggested by Clapham's data, is shown in Table 2.1 below.

Much more research is needed before we can understand clearly the relationship between language knowledge and specific purpose background knowledge, but Clapham's study suggests that, at least for intermediate level students, background knowledge did make a

Table 2.1. *Variable effects of background knowledge on reading test performance*

Low language competence	Intermediate language competence	High language competence
Little effect of background knowledge on performance	Strong effect of background knowledge on performance	Little effect of background knowledge on performance

difference in their reading test performance. One might argue that, if general language knowledge were high enough, as indicated, for example, by a test of general grammatical knowledge, then specific purpose testing would be unnecessary since language knowledge would compensate for a lack of background knowledge. However, it seems likely, given Clapham's finding regarding the stronger effect on test performance of the more field specific texts, that highly specific texts would have a significant background knowledge effect even among the most highly proficient test takers, but we certainly need more research directed specifically at this question.

What makes a text highly field specific?

An important question for specific purpose language test development is, given that the specificity of texts varies so widely, what are the factors that contribute to it? Clapham found that the amount of field specific vocabulary did not affect the degree of specificity of the text so much as whether the vocabulary was explained or not. She also found that the source of the text did not seem to matter as much as the rhetorical functions of various sections of an article; for example, the introductions to research papers tended to be less subject specific, whereas the descriptions of processes tended to be more so. The section of an academic article from which a passage is selected will therefore have an effect on the suitability and difficulty of the passage for various readers. Similarly, the more academic a passage was, the more highly specific its subject matter tended to be, as it was aimed at more specialized audiences. However, it is not clear that there is any agreement about what academic means. Furthermore, Clapham found that cohesive devices, such as referring to a ship variously as the vessel, the craft, or she, in the more highly field specific texts tended to be lexical rather than explanatory, making this aspect of comprehension more difficult for the less nautical readers. The specificity of a text was also likely to depend on the extent to which comprehension of the text required knowledge of subject specific concepts which were not explained in the text. It thus appears that the amount of context-embedded information in a text or prompt affected field specificity.

There is clearly a problem here for LSP testers: texts, and even parts of texts, vary greatly in their specificity and this variation is not necessarily obvious to test developers. In fact, Lewkowicz (1997) found that it was not easy for either native speakers or non-native speakers of English to distinguish real-life texts from testing texts. Therefore, the LSP test writer must employ what Selinker (1979) has called **subject specialist informant** (SSI) techniques, which entail the involvement of practitioners from the specific purpose field in question to work with the test development team on the selection and use of appropriate texts. SSI techniques will be discussed in detail in Chapter 5. The immediate lesson is one that echoes advice given by Davidson and Lynch (1993): test development is best carried out as a collaborative effort involving a wide range of people for whom the test is important. In the case of LSP testing, as Rea-Dickins (1987) reminded us in Chapter 1, this range includes experts in the vocational, technical, professional, and academic fields that are the target language use domains of interest.

The construct of specific purpose language ability

To summarize the discussion so far, in the beginning of this chapter I took the position that what is required in specific purpose language testing is an understanding of how specific purpose background knowledge interacts with language knowledge to produce a communicative performance in specific purpose contexts. In considering what it means to know a language, I accepted Hymes's view that both knowledge and the ability to use it are essential requisites for communication (Hymes 1972) and modified the Bachman and Palmer framework, which hypothesizes two interacting components, language knowledge and strategic competence, to describe communicative language ability. Strategic competence serves as a link between the external situational context, or the specific purpose language use situation, and the internal knowledge that forms the wherewithal for communication, and I have explained how it plays a central role in communicative performance in assessing the situation, setting goals with respect to the situation, planning the response by deciding what elements of knowledge – both background knowledge and language knowledge – will be needed for meeting the goal, and controlling the execution of the plan by retrieving and organizing the language elements. Most importantly for specific purpose language testing, I examined the relationship between specific purpose background knowledge and language test performance, noting that research has suggested that under some conditions, namely a high level of specificity in a text and an intermediate level of language ability, background knowledge makes a difference to language test performance. The problem for specific purpose language testers is to understand the conditions that influence test performance. Table 2.2 below summarizes the construct of specific purpose language ability in the terms I have discussed. This formulation includes, importantly, specific purpose background knowledge as a component of communicative language ability, and gives a central role to the cognitive construct of discourse domain since this is where the language user interprets what I will refer to in Chapter 3 as **contextualization cues** – the features of the external communicative context that language users attend to in determining where they are and what type of communicative activity they are engaged in.

The discussion of the relationship of specific purpose knowledge to test performance provided a number of insights, and forms the basis for some preliminary guidelines for LSP test development:

1 If the nature of the input in a test is sufficiently field specific, test takers will do better at tests in their own subject area.
2 It is likely that as field specificity increases, background knowledge will have a proportionately stronger effect on test scores. In other words, when test content is highly specialized, and is based on complex concepts which are familiar to only a limited group of language users, good language proficiency alone will no longer be sufficient for effective performance.
3 However, there appears to be a non-linear relationship between the specificity of the input and the communicative language ability of the test takers: there seems to be a language proficiency threshold

Table 2.2. *Components of specific purpose language ability*

Language knowledge

Grammatical knowledge
  Knowledge of vocabulary
  Knowledge of morphology and syntax
  Knowledge of phonology

Textual knowledge
  Knowledge of cohesion
  Knowledge of rhetorical or conversational organization

Functional knowledge
  Knowledge of ideational functions
  Knowledge of manipulative functions
  Knowledge of heuristic functions
  Knowledge of imaginative functions

Sociolinguistic knowledge
  Knowledge of dialects/varieties
  Knowledge of registers
  Knowledge of idiomatic expressions
  Knowledge of cultural references

Strategic competence

Assessment
  Evaluating communicative situation or test task and engaging an appropriate discourse domain
  Evaluating the correctness or appropriateness of the response

Goal setting
  Deciding how (and whether) to respond to the communicative situation

Planning
  Deciding what elements from language knowledge and background knowledge are required to reach the established goal

Control of execution
  Retrieving and organizing the appropriate elements of language knowledge to carry out the plan

Background knowledge

Discourse domains
  Frames of reference based on past experience which we use to make sense of current input and make predictions about that which is to come

below which test takers are unable to make effective use of background knowledge, and a higher proficiency threshold above which a lack of relevant background knowledge could be compensated for by test takers making fuller use of their language resources.

4 The degree of specificity of input materials is not easily determined by test developers: such features as rhetorical function and the amount of context-embedded information appear to affect field specificity more than the source of the material or even the amount of field specific vocabulary. Therefore, LSP test writers must turn to what Selinker has called subject specialist informants (SSI) for help in selecting and using field specific materials.

Construct definition

At some point in the test design process, we will need to finally decide precisely what components of specific purpose language ability we will attempt to measure. This is the task of **construct definition**. There are four aspects we will need to consider: the level of detail necessary in the definition, whether to include strategic competence or not, the treatment of the four skills of reading, writing, listening, and speaking, and whether to distinguish between language knowledge and specific purpose background knowledge. It is important to note that in LSP testing, we need to make a distinction between the construct of specific purpose language ability as it is analyzed in the target language use situation and as it is realized in an LSP test: language ability is far richer and more complex than can be effectively measured in our tests. Actual language use in specific purpose contexts involves a complex interaction among the components of specific purpose language ability – all the features of language knowledge, strategic competence, and background knowledge – but it is not possible to actually score or rate all these components in a test. Therefore, while a communicative performance, whether in a target situation or in a test, may require a wide range of linguistic, strategic, and content knowledge, in assessing the performance in the test situation, we normally focus on only a small set of features. For example, we will see later in this book that an Australian test of English in a number of medical contexts actually elicits a rich sample of language and background knowledge, but only a narrow set of linguistic features – overall communicative effectiveness, intelligibility, fluency, comprehension, appropriateness of language, and resources of grammar and expression – are rated. This is an aspect of the dilemma in LSP testing of making the transition from the target language use situation to test tasks: constraints on the test development process, such as time, money, personnel, and what information the test sponsors want to get from the test, have a strong influence on what features of specific purpose language ability can be measured effectively. Thus in the discussion that follows, I will refer to the construct to be measured when I want to distinguish between the full description of specific purpose language ability in the abstract and those aspects of it that can or will be effectively measured in a specific purpose language test. I will begin by considering the level of detail required in defining the construct to be measured.

Level of detail

There are situations where a broader, less detailed definition will be sufficient: if the purpose of the test is to determine whether candidates' English language ability is sufficient for them to be admitted to a medical residency program, then a broad definition of language ability, which may simply be called, for example, communicative ability, without distinguishing its components, will be enough for test users to interpret the results. On the other hand, if the situation calls for a profile of component abilities as input to a remedial course of instruction, then a more detailed specification of the construct will be necessary. For example, the definition of the construct to be measured in the *TEACH* test mentioned in Chapter 1 includes grammatical knowledge, familiarity with the cultural code, rhetorical development, listening ability, and question handling and responding, in addition to other, non-language performance characteristics. The scores on these components can serve as input to the instructors in an instructional program for trainee teachers.

Strategic competence

As I noted earlier in this chapter, strategic competence serves as a mediator and interpreter between the external situational context and the internal language and background knowledge required to respond to the communicative situation, and its engagement in test tasks is central to the LSP enterprise. As a link between context and language knowledge, strategic competence is assumed to operate in all communicative situations. However, it may not be necessary for certain testing purposes to measure strategic competence. If all test users want to know is whether candidates for certification as air traffic controllers have adequate English skills to perform the job, for example, then the definition of the construct to be measured may well include only the language ability components and it can be assumed that strategic competence is implicitly a part of the performance. However, if the test users want to know how well candidates for certification as, say, international travel consultants can adjust to changing situational conditions, such as various interlocutors, topics, tones, and media, then strategic competence would be a relevant focus of the measurement. I have already noted the distinction between what components of specific purpose language ability may be described in a construct definition and what aspects of it are actually scored separately. For example, it may be that strategic competence, while a part of the theoretical construct of language ability in a specific purpose test, may not be given a separate score since the test users are not interested in receiving one. The scoring or rating of test performances will be discussed in more detail in Chapters 3 and 5.

The four skills

It has been traditional in language testing to categorize tests and subtests according to the four skills of reading, writing, listening, and speaking. We also find reference to tests of reading ability or listening ability, which would seem to merge the concepts of skill and ability. I do not want to get involved in the theoretical issues of untangling the notions of skills and abilities, but it is important to discuss the viewpoint I will take in this book concerning the treatment of the four skills. Clearly, what I have been referring to in this chapter as specific purpose language ability must be manifested in the performance of tasks involving reading, writing, listening, or speaking, or some combination of these, but that is precisely the point I wish to emphasize: the four skills will not be considered to be a part of specific purpose language ability, but rather the means by which that ability is realized in the performance of tasks in actual language use situations, including LSP tests. Therefore, I will try to avoid using terms such as speaking ability or reading ability, but rather focus on the interaction between specific purpose language ability and the characteristics of the tasks in which that ability is engaged. In Chapter 3, I will develop a framework for describing tasks in target language use situations and LSP tests, and the task characteristics will include the format of the input, which may be visual or auditory, and of the response to it, which may be spoken, written, or physical. For example, a test task may involve visual input in the form of a written text while the response will require a spoken summary of the text; the input may be in the form of a listening text while the response involves the written completion of a table. Thus, while the four skills are obviously an important consideration in language use, and for convenience we continue to use such terms as speaking test and reading test, the primary focus in LSP testing that I wish to convey in this book is the interaction between specific purpose language ability and the characteristics of language use tasks in specific purpose situations.

Specific purpose background knowledge

A final aspect in the definition of specific purpose language ability is that the construct contains, by definition, specific purpose background knowledge. The very essence of specific purpose language tests is that they require the test takers to engage themselves authentically in test tasks that are demonstrably related to the target language use situation, and, therefore, relevant background knowledge will necessarily be called upon in the interpretation of the communicative situation and in the formulation of a response. A question that needs to be considered in this regard is whether it will be necessary to distinguish between the two types of knowledge – language knowledge and specific purpose background knowledge. In some testing situations it may be, while in others it may not. For example, when test takers are known to possess a high level of expertise in the specific field, as in the case of applicants for doctoral studies, or when the evaluation of specific purpose knowledge is a part of the overall testing program, as in the case of candidates for medical licensure, then it will not be necessary to disambiguate language and background knowledge. On the other hand, when expertise in the field cannot be taken as given, as in the case of trainees, for example, it may be desirable to devise a test of specific purpose knowledge as a way of determining the source of a poor performance on the language test, so that, if necessary, appropriate technical training can be provided. See Bachman and Palmer (1996) for further discussion of the issues involved in deciding whether to include or not to include background, or topical, knowledge in the test construct.

Conclusion

In sum, the measurement of specific purpose language ability depends on the interaction between the language knowledge of the test taker and the specificity of the test input. This in turn depends on providing a sufficient number of specific cues in the test input to enable the test taker's strategic competence to engage a specific purpose discourse domain, set a communicative goal appropriate to the specific purpose area, and assemble relevant specific purpose background information and language knowledge to achieve the goal.

I can now define specific purpose language ability in LSP testing as follows:

> Specific purpose language ability results from the interaction between specific purpose background knowledge and language ability, by means of strategic competence engaged by specific purpose input in the form of test method characteristics.

In order for LSP testers to provide the essential field specific contextual signals in the test, we need a clear understanding of the nature of context, discourse domains, and the characteristics of language use tasks. These are the topics of discussion in Chapter 3.

....

CHAPTER THREE

Context, discourse domains, and task characteristics

Introduction

As I proposed in Chapter 1, in specific purpose language testing, we want to make inferences about individuals' abilities to use language in specific academic, professional, or vocational fields on the basis of their performance on a language test in which the characteristics of tasks in the target language use (TLU) situation, or context, are incorporated into the test tasks. Clearly, to produce such tests, we need an understanding, first, of the context and tasks in the specific field we are interested in, and second, of how to translate these features into test tasks. In this chapter I will first discuss the notion of **context** in language use, what I mean by the term, and what features characterize it. Next, I will consider the interesting idea that contexts change all the time – sometimes several times in a few minutes – so we need to understand how it is that we recognize contexts and how we signal to each other that a change is about to take place. Then, I will discuss the notion that what really matters in working with contexts is not so much what the external, situational features of them might be, but how language users interpret contexts. In Chapter 2 I discussed strategic competence, and in this chapter we will see how the external context is internalized by our strategic competence to engage a **discourse domain**, a key concept in specific purpose language use. Next, I will come to the nub of the matter: the elaboration of a framework for describing tasks in both the specific purpose TLU situation that we are interested in and the specific purpose language test we wish to develop. I will focus most of my attention on what it is we need to know about target specific purpose language use situations so that our test tasks will reflect their essential features, enabling us to make inferences about test takers' language abilities with regard to the TLU situation.

What (and when) is a context?

What is a context? Like communicative competence, the term context is one that has been much bandied about, and consequently suffers from a lack of precision. Without detailing the various usages of the term we might find in the literature (see Ellis and Roberts, 1987, for a discussion), we can observe that the most common references to it are either talking about the language addressed to, or used in the presence of, the language user – linguistic context – or the social, physical, and temporal situation the language activity is taking place in – situational context. In recent years increasing attention has been paid to the role of interaction and discourse in studies of context, and I will focus on the influence of interaction in the next section.

In attempting to define context, researchers over the years have listed a number of features, such as those suggested by Hymes in his well-known SPEAKING mnemonic: Setting, Participants, Ends, Act sequence, Key, Instrumentalities, Norms, and Genres. In his effort to come up with an easily memorable acronym, Hymes was forced into some rather opaque terminology which isn't intuitively meaningful, in my opinion, to most readers. In my discussion of context, and eventually in a framework for describing tasks in TLU situations and LSP tests, I have replaced some of Hymes's terms with ones which are more applicable to the LSP testing enterprise and, it is hoped, more meaningful, if not more memorable, as below (for readers' information, Hymes's original terms are provided in square brackets):

> Setting: physical and temporal setting
> Participants: speakers/writers, hearers/readers
> Purposes [Ends]: purposes, outcomes, goals
> Form and content [Act sequence]: message form (how something
>   is said/written) and message content (what is said/written,
>   topic)
> Tone [Key]: manner

Language [Instrumentation]: channels (medium of communication – face-to-face, telephone, handwritten, computer printout, electronic), codes (language, dialect, style, register)

Norms: norms of interaction (relative status, friendship, intimacy, acquaintance as these affect what may be said and how), norms of interpretation (how different kinds of speech/writing are understood and regarded with respect to belief systems)

Genres: categories of communication (e.g., poems, curses, prayers, jokes, proverbs, myths, commercials, form letters)

Adapted from Hymes (1974)

(Readers will note that this results in the unpronounceable acronym SPPFTLNG, but so be it.)

It seems clear that such situational factors as those set out by Hymes derive from a number of different sources: societal and community values, social situations, role relationships, personal interactions, and linguistic resources, and the list reminds us that the notion of context is grounded in a complex interaction of physical, social, and psychological factors. It is important to keep in mind, as Hornberger (1989) argues, that 'the very essence of a communicative event [is] that it is situated in a real, physical, cultural, historical, and socio-economic context' (p. 228). This is certainly an essential point for LSP test developers to bear in mind.

Context as a social/psychological construct

A context is not simply a collection of features imposed upon the language learner/user, but rather is constructed by the participants in the communicative event. A salient feature of context is that it is dynamic, constantly changing as a result of negotiation between and among the interactants as they construct it, turn by turn. It must be constantly borne in mind that context is not an object, but a dynamic social/psychological accomplishment, and that therefore, as Erickson and Shultz (1981) put it, in a paper instructively titled 'When is a context?':

> The production of appropriate social behavior from moment to moment requires knowing what context one is in and when contexts change as well as knowing what behavior is considered appropriate in each of those contexts.
>
> (p. 147)

In considering context and its effect upon LSP test performance, we need to take account of those features of external context that participants attend to in constructing, as I will argue below, an internal context (with the proviso that we may never be able to know with any precision what those features are because such assessment is dynamic, internal, highly personal, and to some degree unconscious).

Recognizing contexts

How do we recognize contexts? What sorts of information in the specific purpose environment do we pay attention to? I have already considered Hymes's eight features that form a framework for describing context, but, since context is a dynamic concept, not a static one, we need to be able to tell, as Erickson and Shultz point out, when features of context change. For example, in a chemistry lab, if two colleagues are discussing an experiment involving catalysts, and, in the casual give and take of discussion, one of them is reminded of an incident that occurred in a previous experiment, how can she signal that she is about to move the discussion from the present experiment to a past one? How will her colleague recognize the change? Probably, she will raise the pitch of her voice slightly, perhaps also the volume, and say something like 'Remember that titration experiment Bill did last week?' Such techniques as raising pitch and volume are ways we have of signaling changes in the context.

Gumperz (1976) refers to these signals as **contextualization cues**, culturally conventional, highly redundant signals that interactants attend to in their mutual construction of context. They include such signals as changes in voice tone, pitch, tempo, rhythm, code, topic, style, posture, gaze, and facial expression. For example, a study of contextualization cues used, and not used, by an elementary school teacher (Dorr-Bremme 1990) suggested that the pupils attended to the teacher's use of explicit formulations (such as 'Now, let's put today's date on our calendar'), shifts in speech rate and volume (such as slowing down for emphasis and speaking louder to get attention), and framing words (such as 'OK' or 'Good!'), and that when the teacher employed such cues (largely unconsciously), the transition from context to context occurred smoothly – in other words, the kids behaved themselves! However, in the instances where the teacher failed to employ such cues, the context remained unestablished for some period and the interactions were marked by uncertainty, confusion, and chaos on the part of the children.

It will be difficult to determine which cues language users are actually attending to in a communicative event for two reasons: there is variation in attention both between and within individuals from moment to moment, and different individuals have differing expectations and interpretations of the salient features of a communicative event owing to differing background knowledge. Thus, we can never be sure that individuals are all attending to the same cues, or that the presence or absence of any one type of cue is the factor that leads to particular observed twists and turns of discourse. For this reason, the cuing system is highly redundant. Erickson and Shultz (1981) suggest that redundancy makes it more likely that interactants will get the message that something new is happening, in spite of 'differences in interactional competence, whether due to difference in culture, to personality, or to level of acquisition of competence . . . and despite differences in individual variation in focus of attention at any given moment . . .' (p. 150). The redundancy in contextual cues means it will be difficult to determine exactly what features of a context are critical; there is a threshold, a cumulative effect of cues, that determines for an individual what is going on, and this will vary both from individual to individual and from time to time. Thus, in LSP tests, we can never be sure which of the contextual signals that we put into the test material test takers will attend to. That is why it is important for test developers to include a number of different types of contextual cues in the test material to help ensure that the intended domain is engaged. If the test takers don't know where they are, their performance on the LSP test tasks will be very difficult to interpret as evidence of language ability in specific purpose contexts.

Discourse domains

A further aspect, and a crucial one, of the notion of context is the following: what really counts in the communicative performance of a language user is how that individual interprets whatever contextualization cues are present in the communicative event. Thus, we are compelled, as I discussed briefly in Chapter 2, toward an internal view of context as a cognitive construct created by language users for the interpretation and production of language. Douglas and Selinker (1985) use the term **discourse domain** to refer to the internal interpretation of context, and I will employ it here in developing a theoretical framework for LSP testing.

Douglas and Selinker define discourse domain as a cognitive construct created by a language learner as a context for interlanguage development and use. Discourse domains are engaged when strategic competence, in assessing the communicative situation, recognizes cues in the environment that allow the language user to identify the situation and his or her role in it. If there are insufficient cues, if they are unrecognized by the language user, or if they are contradictory or ambiguous, the result will be uncertainty and stumbling around. In order to communicate, a language user has to know what's going on, where he or she is, who he or she is communicating with, what his or her role is, what the topic is. In specific purpose language testing, we must be careful to ensure that the intended discourse domain, that of the target language use situation, is well signaled in the test.

Douglas and Selinker argue that when test takers approach a test, there are three possibilities with regard to the interpretation of the context: (1) they will engage a discourse domain that already exists in their background knowledge if they recognize a sufficient number of cues in the test context; (2) they will create a temporary domain to deal with a novel situation, based on whatever background knowledge they can bring to bear in interpreting the situation; or (3) they will flounder, unable to make sense of a context that provides insufficient or ambiguous information for interpretation. Each of these possibilities has consequences for the interpretation of LSP test performance: if the cues provided in the test are sufficient to engage the intended discourse domain in test takers, then interpretations of test performance as indications of specific purpose language ability will be more likely to be valid; if the cues are insufficient, inappropriate, or unclear, and the test takers interpret the context in unintended ways, or simply flounder, then it will be difficult for test users to make valid interpretations of performance since they will not know with any certainty how the test takers were interpreting the contextual cues in the test. Thus, providing clear, appropriate, and sufficient contextualization cues to help ensure the engagement of the intended discourse domain is of paramount importance in specific purpose language testing. It is important to note, though, that the engagement of an appropriate discourse domain does not mean that the test taker will necessarily produce a better or more target-like performance: both Douglas and Selinker (1993) and Lewkowicz (1997) have found empirical support for the notion that it does not. The discourse domain is but one, though necessary, aspect of communicative language use, and weaknesses elsewhere in the strategic component can influence production and comprehension. For example, students, when challenged to carry out a language task in their own field, may tense up, hoping not to commit an error of fact or logic in their handling of content they are supposed to be familiar with. The result may be a performance that is flawed in grammatical or textual aspects, for example. So, the key point concerning the engagement of appropriate discourse domains in LSP testing is not that it will result in a better performance, but that it will produce a performance more easily interpretable as evidence of specific purpose language ability.

Task characteristics in specific purpose TLU situations and LSP tests

In the introduction to this chapter, I noted that what we need is a framework for describing the features of tasks in both the specific language use situation we are interested in and the language test we wish to develop. This is because we have to be certain that the specific purpose context and the test share essential characteristics so that test takers' performances on the test tasks can be interpreted as evidence of their ability to perform tasks in the non-test TLU situation. Bachman (1990) developed the notion that the correspondence between the TLU contexts and the methods used to measure language ability would directly affect the authenticity of performances on the test:

> In general, one would expect that the closer the correspondence between the characteristics of the test method and the essential features of language use contexts, the more 'authentic' the test task will be for test takers.
>
> Bachman (1990: 112)

I will follow Bachman's notion in attempting to develop a framework for making the correspondence between the TLU situation and the LSP test, but first I will briefly clarify my use of a crucial term, **target language use situation**. I have used the term a number of times so far in this book, echoing that used by Bachman and Palmer (1996), target language use domain, who define it as follows:

> a set of specific language use tasks that the test taker is likely to encounter outside of the test itself, and to which we want our inferences about language ability to generalize.
>
> Bachman and Palmer (1996: 44)

In this book, I will follow Bachman and Palmer in the essentials of the definition above, but I will continue to use the term target language use situation in order to distinguish it from the notion of discourse domain that I discussed earlier in this chapter.

Building on earlier work by J. B. Carroll (1968) and Clark (1972), Bachman (1990) developed the framework for describing context and test method characteristics that form the basis of my discussion in this book. Bachman originally organized the characteristics, which he referred to as facets, into five categories: the testing environment, the rubric, the input, the expected response, and the interaction between input and response. Bachman and Palmer (1996) have since revised the details of the 1990 framework somewhat, but the overall outline remains much the same. The framework that follows is thus based heavily on Bachman and Palmer, adapted to the particular case of LSP testing. I will use the concepts discussed here to develop a framework for evaluating TLU situations and tasks in terms of a set of characteristics which I can then use to develop test tasks. There are five categories of characteristics: four of those described by Bachman and Palmer – the rubric, the input, the expected response, and the interaction between input and response – and one other which I have added, assessment. In addition, I have incorporated what Bachman and Palmer call characteristics of the setting into my characteristics of the input.

Before beginning the discussion, I should note that some of these characteristics, particularly those of the input and the expected response, are more relevant to the LSP testing enterprise than others, but I will take the view that, at least potentially, all the test characteristics are derivable from the target specific purpose language use situation. For example, characteristics of the test rubric include the objective, procedures for responding, structure of the test/task, time allotment, and evaluation. On the surface, it would appear that a TLU situation would very rarely include such characteristics; however, it is certainly true that in real life, tasks are structured, operate with time constraints, and are evaluated, and we do have objectives and follow procedures for responding, even if these are heuristically derived from our own experience. Frequently, the difference between TLU situations and test situations lies not so much in the existence of such characteristics as in their explicitness or overtness in the situation: in real life, instructions, structure, timing, and scoring/rating criteria are often implicit and reside in the background knowledge of the language users; in test situations, these features are usually made as explicit and clear as possible, to prevent any test candidate from performing below his or her ability simply because he or she was not sufficiently familiar with the procedures for responding to the tasks, or because he or she misunderstood the criteria on which his or her response would be judged. As should be clear from my discussion of the construct of specific purpose language knowledge in Chapter 2, however, there may be occasions in LSP testing when such implicit appeals to background knowledge of procedures and criteria for assessment will be relevant to the test purpose. In such cases, we may very well want to ascertain whether the test takers can assess the communicative situation and respond appropriately.

Now, it is also true that very often in test situations such features as these are imposed somewhat artificially because of constraints not related at all to the TLU situation. For example, it may be that the test sponsors simply cannot afford to pay for development of a test that lasts for more than one hour, or that test candidates cannot devote more than an hour of their work schedules for testing purposes. Moreover, evaluation of test performances must be carried out efficiently and consistently, and these requirements will impose limitations on scoring methods and criteria. Finally, even in specific purpose test situations, candidates probably come from differing cultural and educational backgrounds and, therefore, care must be taken that all of them follow the same procedures for responding to the test tasks. The point is that the extent to which characteristics of test tasks are derived from and reflect characteristics of tasks in the TLU situation will depend on the purposes of the test, the characteristics of the test takers, and the resources available for developing and administering the test. To summarize, while it is true in principle that all the characteristics of test tasks are derivable from the specific purpose TLU situation, the degree to which this is true in practice will vary with external considerations often unrelated to the target situation.

A framework for analyzing TLU and test task characteristics

In the next sections, I will outline a framework of task characteristics in language use situations and LSP tests that will allow us to analyze a TLU situation and to develop test tasks that reflect the characteristics of the target situation. These characteristics will include features of the rubric, the input, the expected response to the input, the interaction between input and response, and assessment criteria. Table 3.1 summarizes the various features of the framework, which I will discuss in detail in subsequent sections.

So, to begin a consideration of the characteristics of TLU and test tasks, let us look first at characteristics of the rubric.

Characteristics of the rubric

The term **rubric** is a somewhat obscure one, originally used in Christian prayer books to refer to procedural information about the form of worship, separate from the religious content. In testing, the term has been defined by Bachman (1990) as characteristics 'that specify how test takers are expected to proceed in taking the test' (p. 118), and include the instructions, time allocation, and test organization. I will continue to use the term here, since I want to clearly separate purely test-related procedural information from specific purpose contextual information in the test input. However, in this discussion of specific purpose language testing, I will make some changes in the characteristics of the rubric from the Bachman framework, mainly to emphasize some aspects of the rubric over others. Thus, in this book, the characteristics of the rubric relate to the nature of the communicative event, whether in the target language situation or the language test, including its **objective**, **procedures for responding**, **structure**, **format**, the **time** available for completing it, and **evaluation** criteria and procedures.

The term objective here is more or less interchangeable with the more common usage, test purpose, but I do not want to confuse this meaning of purpose with contextual purpose in the characteristics of the input that I will discuss below. Thus, in non-test TLU situations, objectives might be to review problems in preparation for an exam, or to inform a pilot of weather conditions, or a customer about shipping costs; in LSP tests, objectives might be to assess speaking in the

Table 3.1. *Overview of target language use and test task characteristics*

Characteristics of the rubric

Specification of objective

Procedures for responding

Structure of the communicative event
  Number of tasks
  Relative importance of tasks
  Distinction between tasks

Time allotment

Evaluation
  Criteria for correctness
  Rating procedures

Characteristics of the input

Prompt
  Features of the LSP context
    Setting
    Participants
    Purpose
    Form and content
    Tone
    Language
    Norms of interaction
    Genre
    Problem to be addressed

Input data
  Format
    Visual
    Audio
    Vehicle of delivery
    Length

  Level of authenticity
    Situational
    Interactional

Characteristics of the expected response

Format
  Written
  Oral
  Physical

Table 3.1. *(cont.)*

Type of response
  Selected
  Limited production
  Extended production
Response content
  Nature of language
  Background knowledge
Level of authenticity
  Situational
  Interactional

Characteristics of the interaction between input and response

Reactivity
  reciprocal ⟷ non-reciprocal
Scope
  broad ⟷ narrow
Directness
  dependent upon input ⟷ dependent upon background knowledge

Characteristics of assessment

Construct definition
Criteria for correctness
Rating procedures

context of chemistry teaching, knowledge of vocabulary in the context of air traffic control, or knowledge of politeness forms in the context of international business. Procedures for responding include information about how the language users are to respond to the task: in non-test situations, this will usually be implicit in the situation, and participants will know that they must fill in forms, speak on the telephone, or take notes in a meeting. In test situations, this information must usually be given explicitly, and test takers are told that they should respond by checking boxes, writing terms in a table, or striking computer keys, for example. Structure refers to information on the number of tasks in the communicative event, their relative importance, and the degree of distinction among them. Again, this information is often explicit in TLU situations but must be provided explicitly in tests. Time allotment is information about how much time the language users have to perform the given tasks. In test situations, and often in non-test situations, this information is given explicitly: 'You will have 35 minutes to complete this section of the test'; or 'John, please have that report on my desk by 5:00.'

The characteristic of evaluation requires some discussion since it will be contrasted with another term, assessment, later on. In the rubric, evaluation refers strictly to what the language users or test takers are explicitly told about criteria by which their language performances will be judged and the procedures used to carry out the evaluation, the rating or scoring procedures. In non-test situations, participants are often given explicit information about these criteria, as, for example, when they are submitting manuscripts for publication; however, frequently the criteria are not explicitly stated but are rather an implicit part of the culture of profession, vocation, or academic field. In language tests, the evaluation criteria will need to be spelled out for the test takers to ensure that they are all equally aware of them as they plan their responses to the test tasks. The term assessment, as one of the five major categories of task characteristics, refers to a fuller, more technical description of the criteria by which language users and test takers are judged, based on an analysis of the TLU situation, as well as procedures for rating the performance and a description of the construct. On the one hand, the distinction between evaluation and assessment criteria is unimportant since there must be a complete match between the two – language users, and test takers in particular, cannot be told they will be evaluated on one set of criteria while those judging their work have a different set in mind! However, I believe the distinction is important in helping us understand the process of LSP test development: assessment features, called criteria for correctness in the framework, represent a full description of the criteria, both implicit and explicit, by which performances on tasks in professional, academic, and vocational contexts are judged. Such analyses may be extensive, technical, and complex, and the criteria need to be summarized, simplified, and interpreted so that the test taker will have a clear understanding of the grounds upon which the test performance will be judged, and this is the function of the feature of evaluation in the rubric. Both criteria for correctness and the procedures for rating the responses must be outlined.

As I suggested above, in non-test language use, characteristics of the rubric are usually implicit, residing in specific purpose background knowledge: language users who are in familiar situations can make rapid, often unconscious judgements about what type of communicative event they are about to engage in. However, the characteristics may also be more explicit, in the form of instructions from a supervisor, a lab manual, or a self-improvement video, for example. In test situations, the rubric will usually be explicit, since a test is, as I observed in Chapter 1, a focussed procedure whose express purpose is the elicitation of language performances from which inferences can be made about characteristics of the test takers. It is incumbent upon the test developers to make it as clear as possible to the test takers exactly what types of inferences will be made on the basis of each task and what the criteria are upon which their performances will be evaluated.

Extract 3.1 is an example of a rubric from the *IELTS*.

Extract 3.1

SECTION 1: READING

PART 1: LIFE WITHOUT A SUNSCREEN

You are advised to spend about 15 minutes on Questions 1–11.

Questions 1–3

Answer these questions, using Reading Passage 1, 'Life Without a Sunscreen', on pages 3–4.

Make sure your answers reflect the author's views, not your own.

Write your answers beside the questions. The first one has been done as an example.

University of Cambridge Local Examinations Syndicate (1990: 2)

Notice that this example gives the test takers information about the structure of the test (Section 1 Part 1), the skill being tested ('Reading'), the time allotted ('about 15 minutes'), how to record their responses ('write answers beside the questions'), and, less directly, how the responses will be evaluated ('reflect the author's views, not your own'). There is very little specific purpose information in this rubric.

As I said above, in a test, the rubric will usually be explicit; however, in LSP tests sometimes the test situation can be set up so realistically that some aspects of the rubric can be more implicit, just as it is in non-test situations. For instance, employing the example of a test of air traffic controllers' English ability, it would probably be the case that the input itself, in the form of an airport ground chart and tape-recorded voice communication from pilots, would provide sufficient information to the test taker about the nature of the task at hand – leading the pilot to a safe landing – and what type of response was required. However, it would still be necessary to provide the test taker with explicit information about what was being measured and how the performance would be evaluated. Such is the function of the rubric in LSP tests.

Characteristics of the input

Input is the specific purpose material in the TLU situation that language users process and respond to. In test situations, the input is the means by which features of context are established and controlled. As Bachman (1990) points out, 'The characteristics of test methods can be seen as restricted or controlled versions of [non-test] contextual features . . .' (p. 112). Remember that features of the context and contextualization cues are realized in language tests as task characteristics, and that it is by means of information contained in the test input that test takers are able to orient themselves and engage an appropriate discourse domain. Input material may be visual, or aural, or both, and may even be a physical object, as I will discuss below.

It is necessary to clarify the distinction between aspects of the rubric and input. It is usual in language testing to think of the rubric as separate from input, rubric being the specification of procedures, while the input is the material contained in the test task for the test takers to respond to. As I discussed above, the rubric gives the test taker explicit information about the nature of a test, sub-test, or task, as a measurement device. The rubric is not specific purpose, except to the extent that the criteria for correctness may reflect criteria used in the TLU situation to evaluate language performances. As you will see below, input does closely reflect the specific purpose context.

In LSP testing, we will make a further distinction between rubric, and two aspects of input: **prompt** and **input data**. I will use the term prompt to refer to specific purpose contextual information necessary for the language user to engage in a communicative task: establishing the setting, participants, purpose, and other features of the situation. The prompt may be intended to elicit an extended response, such as a written essay or an oral discussion. The term input data refers to the authentic aural or visual material which the language user must process in performing the task. Input data may include text and visuals such as tables, charts, graphs, diagrams, drawings, or photographs, delivered in print format or by means of computer/CD, movies or videos. Input data may also be actual objects and devices such as tools, machinery, or laboratory equipment. Input data may also include aural input, such as from audiotape, CDs, and computers, or from live interaction. Input data can serve as a resource for test tasks, as in the case of a summary task, for example, or can itself be manipulated to produce tasks, as, for instance, in cloze tests.

Prompt

The prompt may include information about procedures similar to that of the rubric, but in a specific purpose context. It may also include identification of the LSP context in terms of setting, participants, purposes, form and content, tone, language, norms of interaction, and genre, and a clear statement of the problem to be addressed. As I have discussed, some of the information in the prompt may be implicit, derivable from specific purpose background knowledge. As an example of a prompt, consider Extract 3.2, taken from a veterinary version of the *Occupational English Test*.

Extract 3.2

Setting:	Suburban clinic
Client:	Owner of a large male pet dog. The dog has been hit by a car and has some minor lacerations (cuts) on the body and leg.
	You want to give the dog a general anaesthetic while you attend to the lacerations. You feel you need protection and the dog must be still. It is a large, strong dog.
Task:	Persuade the owner to allow you to give the dog a general anaesthetic. Explain why you feel this is necessary.

McNamara (1990a: 454)

In this example of a prompt for a roleplay, we see that there is explicit contextual information about setting, participants, purpose, content, and language functions. The problem is clearly outlined: the test taker is a bit nervous about the behavior of the dog, and wishes to give a general anaesthetic. The norms of interaction are implicit, being defined by the veterinary/client relationship. Furthermore, unbeknown to the test taker prior to the test, the interlocutor in the roleplay task has been instructed to strongly oppose the use of a general anaesthetic on the grounds that it is dangerous and also that it is expensive, so, in this case, the tone of the communicative event will be established in the interaction of the roleplay itself.

Input data

The input data consists of visual and/or aural material to be processed during a communicative task. Such data may include text and visuals in the form of video, print, computer screen, photographs, charts, gestures, live actions. Input data may also include physical objects such as tools or equipment that the test taker is to describe or manipulate in some way to demonstrate communicative language ability. Much recorded visual data will be accompanied by audio data, but the input may be only aural, either live or reproduced on audio-tape or CDs, or by computers, including talk and natural or human sounds (such as the sound of traffic or machinery, or background talk, for example). The characteristic of length, relevant to spoken and written textual input, may be stated in terms of either number of words or time.

An important concern in selecting input data for an LSP test is the degree of authenticity and specificity of the material. The characteristic of level of authenticity in both input data and expected response, to be discussed below, is a bit different from the other situational and test task characteristics: data and responses to it in target language use situations are by definition authentic, whereas, when we incorporate them into a language test, thus divorcing them from their situational and interactional context, they potentially lose their authenticity (recall Widdowson's distinction between genuine and authentic texts, which I discussed in Chapter 1). It is only by taking stock of the situational and interactional features that the input data and response in the tests share with the target situation that we can ensure their authenticity. As I discussed in Chapter 2, the features of authenticity are not always apparent to the test developers, since such factors as the source of the material and amount of technical vocabulary may be misleading. The advice of experts in the specific purpose field must be sought in determining the degree of specificity of the input data. In considering the authenticity of input data, we need to evaluate both the situational characteristics and the interactional characteristics of the material, as I discussed in Chapter 1. In other words, the input data will usually be genuine in Widdowson's sense of an actual spoken or written text (or sometimes a physical object) produced by the users in the target language use situation. I say usually because input data may be manipulated or even created by the test developers for various purposes: the test may be intended for test takers of lower proficiency levels and a given input text may be simply too complex, or it may be that the text contains culturally or ethnically sensitive material which is deemed inappropriate for the test purpose. However, an important distinction between a prompt and input data is that while input data in a test represents genuine material imported from the target language use situation, the prompt will nearly always have been produced by the test developers specifically for the test itself. The prompt is used to set up a specific purpose situation in cases where there is no separate input data, or where the data alone do not provide enough contextual cues.

It should be remembered, too, that the characteristic of input data that I have called *level of authenticity*, comprising both situational and interactional authenticity, is actually a characteristic dependent not solely on features of the input data itself but of the interaction between the input and characteristics of test takers, as I discussed in Chapter 1. Input must not only display situational characteristics of target language use situations, but also interactional characteristics, and must therefore be *engaging* to test takers. Again, these characteristics may not be obvious to test developers, and that is the reason level of authenticity must always be considered when selecting input data for incorporation into an LSP test.

Returning for just a moment to the distinction between rubric and prompt, while it is true that the rubric generally contains non-specific purpose information about the test and the task, and the prompt contains specific purpose contextual information, the two will sometimes, perhaps even often, overlap. For example, consider how the writing task in Extract 3.3 is set up.

Extract 3.3

> Using the material in the accompanying information packet, write an introduction to a research report, including a title, a brief review of previous research, a statement of the research problem, and an outline of the present research procedure. Your introduction will be evaluated for completeness, organization, and appropriate terminology. A separate evaluation will be given for understanding of the research problem and procedure. You must hand your introduction in to the department secretary by 4:00 p.m. on Friday.

Note that this example contains features of both a rubric and a prompt. The distinction between the two is intended to be useful for reminding test developers of the types of procedural and contextual information they need to provide to test takers. A prompt may also be the lead-in to input data, as, for example, in a listening task where the prompt instructs the test takers to listen to a passage and respond to it by completing an incomplete diagram. Thus, it is important to remember that the distinctions among rubric, prompt, and input data may not always be clear in practice. I have distinguished the three types of characteristics, however, in trying to clarify the complexity of LSP test development, and test developers should interpret and apply the distinctions in light of the specific testing project they are engaged in and the types of interpretations they wish to make on the basis of test performance.

Providing rich input

The prompt and input data are clearly very important aspects of an LSP test in establishing the specific purpose context for the test taker. The information provided in the prompt and the features of the input data need to be as rich and engaging as possible. The following are some ideas for enriching and deepening the contextual parameters of LSP tests, using as a framework the features of communicative situation set out by Hymes (1974). Some of these suggestions are based on Kramsch (1993: 94ff.), and readers might also want to consult Brown and Yule (1983: 50ff.) for more discussion of contextual enrichment.

1 *Setting:* The tester can engage the test taker in appropriate specific purpose settings by means of detailed descriptions in the prompt, realistic drawings or photographs, and even sound effects. Smells might be going a bit too far, but perhaps not – Bachman and Palmer (1996) suggest the smell of chemicals and exhaust fumes as part of the setting in a hypothetical test for trainee auto mechanics! The temporal setting can be signaled by providing information about the time of day (or night), day of the week, season, and so on, in the prompt and in input data.

2 *Participants:* The test developer must identify the participants clearly and in some detail as professor, fellow student, close friend, colleague, etc. Information about age, gender, and personality might also be relevant, depending on the type of inferences one wishes to make about language ability. The behavior of the interlocutor(s) can be varied, as well. For example, the test task can be addressed to a listener who constantly asks for clarification, one who shows interest by asking questions, one who shows boredom, and so on. The number of participants is relevant, since performances will vary depending on whether an individual or a large group is being addressed, for example.

3 *Purpose:* A key aspect of specific purpose language use is the establishment of a clear purpose for communication in the context of the TLU situation, in addition to the obvious testing purpose of eliciting a performance for evaluation. The psychometric purpose, the objective, of the task will be made clear in the rubric, but a specific purpose reason for carrying out the task needs to be made clear in the prompt and the input data. For example, the test taker can be instructed to explain a term in his or her field in order to convince the interlocutor of its crucial importance to that field, to correct a misunderstanding, to solve a problem he or she is having, and so on. The goal of identifying purpose here is not to try to make the test taker forget that he or she is engaged in a language test, but to add another ingredient to the richness of the specific purpose context, increasing the likelihood that the test takers will engage their specific purpose language ability.

4 *Form and content:* That the topicality of the input should be clearly derived from the specific purpose language use situation almost goes without saying, but as I have noted a number of times in this book, providing an appropriate topic is just one factor in addressing the problem of establishing the specific purpose context. The topic

may be explicitly presented in a title or heading, but may often be implicit in the input data. Similarly, in LSP testing, the rhetorical form of the message is often as important as the content, and should reflect the norms of the target language use situation.

5 *Tone:* At least since Johns and Dudley-Evans (1980) suggested that the problem second language students have is not so much listening to lectures as listening to lectur*ers*, we have been aware that specific purpose talk and writing is not the unemotional, dry, objective discourse that idealists imagine. In LSP tests, irony, humor, sarcasm, and so on play a role in specific purpose discourse in addition to the matter of fact that many see as the norm. Depending on the objective of the test, sensitivity to tone may be an important object of measurement.

6 *Language:* Input can vary in channel (aural or visual) and responses in modality (written or spoken), and both can vary in vehicle (live or taped), language/dialect (target or native), and register (technical or non-technical). For example, test takers can be asked to carry out the same or similar tasks in two modalities so as to get a fuller picture of their abilities. In addition, language features can be combined in tasks: test takers can be instructed to read a passage out loud and then to summarize it in their own words, to write a report and then present it orally from notes, or to transfer information from a chart or table to a written report.

7 *Norms of interaction:* These vary somewhat automatically with the choice of setting and with the status and roles of the participants. For example, test takers should perform differently, in terms of forms of address, topic choice, turn taking routines, interruptions, and politeness forms, when the interlocutor is a professor than when it is a fellow student, or when speaking to a medical colleague as opposed to a patient. It is therefore doubly important for the test developers to provide sufficient information about setting and participants so that test takers will be able to make appropriate decisions about norms of interaction. It may be, too, that for some test purposes, norms of interaction will be specified, as, for example, 'Make a formal invitation to your supervisor to attend a conference presentation you are giving.'

8 *Genre:* The test input may be a monologue, an interview, a lecture, an advertisement, a panel discussion, etc. The objective of the test will help determine whether sensitivity to genre will be an important object of the assessment. For example, test takers could be

presented with a number of definitions in their field and asked to distinguish those which meet formal criteria for definitions from those which do not. Or they might be given certain information presented in a rather formal lecture, and other, related information in a conversation between the lecturer and an audience member, and asked to integrate the two sets of material.

With regard to these suggestions for enriching the context in LSP tests, the guiding principle for any of them should always be the objective of the test and characteristics of the activities that take place in the target language use situation. It will not make sense to manipulate, say, modalities, if the target situation doesn't involve information transfer from one modality to another, or if the purpose of the test is to measure language ability by means of speaking only, for example.

Characteristics of the expected response

The **expected response** refers to what the test developers intend that the test takers do in response to the LSP situation they have attempted to set up by means of the rubric and input. We do our best to provide rich enough information to the test takers about what they are to do and why, so as to elicit a certain response. However, the actual response the test takers produce may not be the one the test developers intended. Test takers have minds of their own, and may decide to respond in a way we simply did not anticipate; or perhaps they may not pay as close attention to the information we provided as we intend that they should, or the information may not have been as clear as we thought it was. For whatever reason, the expected response may not occur. Nevertheless, test developers must be as clear as possible in their own minds, and in the test specifications, about what sort of response they expect, and what effect various characteristics of the expected response will have on their interpretations of the test takers' performance.

The format of the expected response might vary in much the same ways as that of the input: it may be spoken or written, recorded on audio or video tape, or typed on a computer keyboard, written on a blackboard or overhead projector, or some combination of these. The expected response may be a physical action, a gesture, or a procedure.

It may be a selected response, as in a multiple-choice format (and these do occur in non-test communicative situations), or involve producing a word, phrase, or sentence – a limited production response – or a paragraph or longer written or spoken text – an extended response.

A key aspect of the expected response is the nature of the language and specific purpose background knowledge that the language user is expected to produce. The category of response content is intended to make these features explicit, and must reflect the construct to be measured, as discussed below. They are included in the characteristics of the expected response to help ensure that the response elicits the necessary aspects of specific purpose language ability, including features of language and background knowledge, so that the intended construct may be adequately measured. Finally, it is important that the format and content of the expected response be as plausible as possible in the context of the target language use situation, so level of authenticity, both situational and interactional, is also a consideration.

Characteristics of the interaction between input and response

In a normal language use situation, input and responses interact along at least three dimensions: reactivity, scope, and directness (Bachman and Palmer 1996). I will consider each of these dimensions as they apply to LSP testing.

Reactivity

Reactivity refers to the degree to which the input can be altered in light of the responses of the language user, and ranges on a continuum between **reciprocal** and **non-reciprocal**. In non-test language use, for example in a conversation, the interaction between the input and the response is often highly reciprocal. The speaker receives feedback from the listener about the effectiveness of his or her utterance in the form of facial expression or verbalization, and he or she can adjust his or her subsequent utterances, perhaps by speaking louder, using simpler, less technical terminology, simplifying syntax, and so on. In other situations, for example that of a lecture to a large audience, the speaker will be able to adapt his or her message to audience reaction only in general terms, since there are many levels of comprehension in a large audience and the speaker can attend to only a few quizzical looks or nods of agreement as representative of the group response. There are also situations when feedback is not available at all, as when speaking into a telephone answering machine, when writing a message, or when reading a text or listening to a taped message. In such cases, the interaction between the input and response is closer to the non-reciprocal end of the reactivity continuum.

In LSP tests the degree of reactivity also varies. In an interview, for example, the interviewer can provide feedback to the test taker, and the test taker's ability to adjust his or her responses in light of feedback can be a focus of the assessment. In such a highly reciprocal test, both input and response constantly change as a result of the interaction. The reciprocal interaction between input and response is a necessary condition for eliciting the dynamic, always changing context I discussed earlier in this chapter, as the interlocutors construct the context in real time. Reciprocal test formats usually require a live interlocutor or audience, but it is becoming more and more possible to simulate feedback using computer programs so that test takers can adjust their responses on the basis of feedback from the program, and the program itself can adjust input to match. Computer adaptive test (CAT) formats, which are discussed in Chapter 8, also simulate to some extent a reciprocal interaction, in that the presentation of test items or tasks differs in terms of difficulty depending on the correctness of previous responses. CATs have the advantage of efficiency of measurement over paper and pencil tests, since candidates can be presented with only those items that are near their level of ability, rather than items that are too easy or too difficult. The main disadvantage of CATs is that they are at present restricted to multiple-choice formats, which are usually not very attractive to LSP testers. Note, in this regard, that Bachman and Palmer (1996) also distinguish an adaptive relationship between input and response, referring specifically to the CAT format, in addition to reciprocal and non-reciprocal. Their distinction between reciprocal and adaptive rests on whether the test taker receives feedback (reciprocal) or not (adaptive). Since both relationship types affect the nature of the input as the communication progresses, and since adaptivity is really more of a testing technique than a feature of communication, I will not employ the distinction here.

Many test formats, such as spoken and written essays, and reading and listening tests, are relatively non-reciprocal. As we have seen, non-reciprocal tasks are quite common in non-test language use, and so appropriate non-reciprocal test tasks are a necessary part of LSP testing. There are, of course, inappropriate uses of non-reciprocal tasks, often owing to practical constraints on the testing situation (availability of resources, for instance), but when possible, test formats should reflect the target language use situation, as I discussed above with regard to the input format.

Scope

A second characteristic of the interaction between the input and the response is its **scope**, which pertains to the amount or variety of input that the participant must process before responding. This depends on the amount and/or variety of input the language user is required to process in order to complete the task, and this varies on a continuum between narrow and broad. Both the input and the response can vary in scope. For example, a person may be required to read a lengthy report and write a relatively brief summary for distribution to busy executives. Alternatively, a task may require listening to a short recorded phone message and jotting down a note. Or, several related pieces of input may be processed in producing a response, as when a physician must synthesize the results of a physical examination, lab reports, and consultants' reports when writing up a patient's case history. Even when the input is relatively lengthy, a given task may require a response of only a sentence or two, such as scanning a text for a specific piece of information; similarly, a small amount of input can trigger a very lengthy response, as when a supervisor says, 'By the way, John, get me a report on the Beasley negotiations by Tuesday.' In LSP tests, scope is typically limited by time constraints and by the necessity to provide a variety of tasks for assessment; nevertheless, there is a trend in the testing field generally toward longer, richer input and responses. In LSP testing there is certainly a need to provide rich contextualization cues to help ensure the engagement of appropriate discourse domains, and this argues in favor of broadening the scope of the input.

Directness

A final aspect of the interaction between the input and the expected response is that of the **directness** of the interaction: the degree to which the response depends on the input as opposed to the language user's own specific purpose background knowledge. As in the case of the other aspects of the interaction between input and response, this one takes the form of a continuum: the task of listening to a lecture and taking notes is a fairly direct one, although a certain amount of background knowledge is necessary for interpreting the relative importance of various points, for example. On the other hand, the request from the boss for a report on a series of business negotiations will require a rather greater degree of dependence on specific purpose background information and is thus more toward the indirect end of the continuum. In LSP tests, degree of directness will influence interpretations regarding specific purpose language ability. For example, a task in which the test taker is asked to read a passage about energy from various fuels and then list four sources of energy the author termed natural forces would be a fairly direct task, requiring little background knowledge. We might interpret performance on such a task as representing language knowledge, without engaging the test taker's specific purpose discourse domain to any great degree. However, a task which required the test taker to read the energy text and then summarize it, focussing on the most important points, would be somewhat less direct, since the test taker would have to call upon some specific purpose knowledge to assess the relative importance of the points made in the text. Finally, a task involving the test taker in writing a proposal for deriving usable energy from geothermal sources beneath the earth's crust would be highly indirect, requiring a great deal of specific purpose knowledge, both content knowledge about geothermal energy, and rhetorical knowledge about proposal writing.

In LSP tests, a major goal is to provide sufficient contextual cues in the input to engage an appropriate discourse domain in the test takers. This involves the engagement of specific purpose background knowledge. As I noted in the example above where the task was simply to list the four types of energy the author of the text called natural forces, the task is fairly mechanical, and it is possible that the test taker could carry it out without engaging his or her specific purpose background knowledge at all, since he or she could simply draw on language knowledge to do the matching task needed. It is not the case, however, that only relatively indirect tasks will do for LSP tests. The issue is not whether the interaction between input and response is more or less direct; rather, the critical point is whether the task provides sufficient contextualization cues in the form of specific purpose test task characteristics to engage the appropriate discourse domain. If the intended domain is engaged, and if the test task is reflective of the characteristics of a target language use task, the result will be a performance interpretable as evidence of specific purpose language ability.

Characteristics of assessment

This final set of characteristics is, like the others, derived from an analysis of the specific purpose TLU situation, this time focussing on the definition of the construct, the features of specific purpose language ability necessary for performing TLU tasks, and the procedures for carrying out the assessment. In Chapter 2, I discussed the analysis of specific purpose language ability in the target language use situation, and showed how this analysis leads to a definition of the construct in an LSP test. Recall that I distinguished between the construct of specific purpose language ability in the TLU situation, and the construct to be measured in the LSP test: language performance in real life requires a complex and wide range of characteristics of language ability and background knowledge; however, it is never possible to measure this complete range in an LSP test, constrained as it is by such aspects as money, time, personnel, and educational policies. An extremely important focus in the present chapter is the development of the actual criteria by which test performances will be judged, and the idea that these are derivable from the analysis of the target language use situation. An important feature of tasks, in both target situations and language tests, is the set of assessment criteria employed as well as the procedures for carrying out the assessment, and it is the function of the assessment component of the analytical framework to make these criteria and procedures explicit. Thus, the assessment component consists of a construct definition, a set of assessment criteria, to be called criteria for correctness, and a set of procedures for rating or scoring the performance.

In the same way that the construct definition is derived from an analysis of the characteristics of language in the TLU situation, using the framework developed in Chapter 2, the criteria for correctness are also derived from an analysis of the TLU situation, this time using a framework based on the concept of **indigenous assessment criteria** (Jacoby 1998). Jacoby defines indigenous assessment criteria as those used by subject specialists in assessing the communicative performances of apprentices in academic and vocational fields. Performance assessment practices are part of any professional culture, from formal, gatekeeping examination procedures, to informal, ongoing evaluation built into everyday interaction with novices, colleagues, and supervisors. Indeed, professional development is just a specialized form of socialization, a general process long recognized as the vehicle through which culturally specific language, discourse, cognition, and skills are transmitted and developed through social interaction (see Jacoby 1998 for a review of the literature). Competent professionals are able to articulate assessments, the criteria employed, and ways in which language performances might be improved to both colleagues and to the persons being assessed. The criteria are accessible to researchers primarily by means of an analysis of the discourse in which they are displayed, and, therefore, the researchers will need to engage in very careful study of the assessment interaction and discourse in the target language use situation, with help from discourse analysts and from specialists in the target field. For example, Jacoby has studied the indigenous assessment criteria employed in a physics research group preparing for conference presentations (1998); McNamara and colleagues are studying the indigenous assessment criteria articulated by medical practitioners (McNamara 1997a); Douglas and Myers studied the criteria used by veterinary professionals in assessing the communication skills of veterinary students (Douglas and Myers, in press). The investigation of indigenous assessment is still a very new, undeveloped possibility for specific purpose language testing, but the expectation is that by studying various types of assessment activities in professional and vocational settings, we may be able to establish criteria for the specific purpose testing enterprise. Jacoby and McNamara (in press) caution, however, that there are difficult problems associated with applying these indigenous criteria, derived from highly specific, dynamic contexts of use, to language tests, no matter how situationally authentic the tests may be. I discuss some of the potential problems below.

Examples of the types of indigenous assessment criteria that may emerge from an analysis of the TLU situation include the following: ability to communicate the significance of the topic in terms of the specific purpose field; appropriacy of the length or timing of the performance; perceptions of the completeness of the task; clarity, explicitness, economy of expression; appropriate procedures of argumentation and persuasion; technical elements of delivery and visual coherence; accuracy of specific purpose content; linguistic error; overall quality (Jacoby and McNamara, in press). It is important to note that such criteria as these will necessarily differ from target situation to target situation. The above list was derived from an analysis of the interaction among physicists critiquing each other's conference talk rehearsals (Jacoby 1998), and should not be interpreted as universal criteria for specific purpose assessment: they would be relevant only to the development of an LSP test designed to make inferences about candidates' ability to make oral presentations at academic conferences and meetings, and they would no doubt require adaptations to fit the practical constraints of a test situation. This observation leads to the next point, which concerns making the transition from the TLU indigenous criteria to the criteria that will be employed in the test.

A crucial consideration is the construct definition. The construct is key to understanding both TLU indigenous assessment and LSP test criteria for correctness: in the TLU situation, the construct is often, but not always, an implicit part of the professional or vocational culture; in tests, the construct must be carefully and explicitly stated, derived from an analysis of language use in the TLU situation, but also reflecting our best understanding of what it means to know and use a language in specific purpose contexts. As I discussed in Chapter 2, the analysis of the features of specific purpose language ability provides the input for the construct definition, for it must reflect the realities of language use in the target situation. The criteria for correctness and rating procedures must in turn reflect the construct to be measured, and this will often mean that some aspects of the indigenous assessment criteria may not be relevant to the assessment of performance on the test tasks. For example, in a recent study of indigenous assessment criteria in a veterinary college (Douglas and Myers, in press), it was found that one important criterion in the assessment of students' interaction with clients was their appearance – whether they were neatly and appropriately dressed during a performance assessment. Examples of comments on appearance by the assessors are shown below:

they all looked clean 'n well groomed
did Jason have a tie on?
looked nice 'n freshly prepped
immaculately clean
he used a clean glove
he paid I think particular attention to his appearance
I was quite impressed when he took out a little valet [bag] with
    clean boots

It may or may not be likely that in a specific purpose test of veterinary communication ability, appearance would be seen as a possible assessment criterion, but this example illustrates the necessity for an interaction between characteristics of the TLU situation and the definition of the construct to be measured, and for this reason, the construct definition is included as one of the characteristics of assessment. The construct definition can thus be seen as a theoretical statement of what aspect or aspects of a language user's communicative language ability will be required to carry out the communicative task; the criteria for correctness, derived from an analysis of indigenous assessment criteria, become in effect the operational definition of the construct. This is because the criteria for correctness, as McNamara (1996) has pointed out, are the proverbial bottom line in language tests: the most carefully constructed LSP test, the most technically correct statement of the construct definition, and the most ingeniously devised test tasks will all be rendered meaningless if the criteria used to judge performances on the tasks do not adequately reflect the construct. In determining the criteria for correctness, the test developers must make constant reference to the construct to be measured to ensure that the criteria faithfully represent it. Furthermore, an appeal to the construct to be measured may be seen as a way of tempering the transition from TLU assessment criteria to test criteria and offer a solution to the dilemma posed by Jacoby and McNamara (in press): 'the more assessment criteria are derived from task-specific and profession-specific real-word concerns, the more they run the risk of being less generally useful beyond their specific context.' By judging the indigenous criteria against the definition of the construct to be measured, it may be possible to achieve a more generalizable set of correctness criteria since the criteria for correctness will reflect both the characteristics of specific purpose language ability in the target situation and the constraints placed on what aspects of the ability will be measured.

It is important to remember that what we are interested in here are the criteria for correctness; how we will quantify those criteria in the test to derive an actual score for the performance is a matter of general language testing practice, and there are various approaches to be considered. In particular, the development of a rating scale for the assessment of extended production (e.g., essays, oral interviews) is an extremely important issue for communicative language testing, and test developers should consider carefully the use of global, analytic, and criterion-referenced scales. (For detailed discussion of the development of rating scales, see Alderson *et al.* 1995, Chapter 5; Bachman and Palmer 1996, Chapter 11; McNamara 1996, Chapter 7; and North 1994).

Finally, remember that in the framework for analyzing LSP tests, I have distinguished between assessment, characteristics derived from an analysis of the target language use situation, and evaluation in the rubric, which refers to the information the test taker is given with regard to criteria for correctness and procedures for rating. The assessment characteristics will normally be much more extensive than the characteristics of evaluation, and will include a technical discussion of the construct definition, as well as details of the criteria for correctness and rating procedures.

Conclusion

In this chapter I have discussed external features of context, using Hymes's SPEAKING mnemonic as a framework, with some changes in terminology. I noted that while external context can be described using such features as those above, an essential feature of context is that it is dynamic, continually changing, and that these changes are controlled and signaled by the participants in a communicative situation. Thus, the signals that participants use to indicate changes in context are of crucial importance to them as they assess the context and plan their response to it. I employed the notion of discourse domain to clearly distinguish the external features of context from the internal interpretation of them by language users, and noted the importance in specific purpose language tests of providing a sufficient number of contextualization cues in the form of test task characteristics, to enable test takers to engage the intended discourse domain. I adapted Bachman and Palmer's framework to describe task characteristics in both the specific purpose language use situation we wish to test and the LSP test we want to develop. The framework includes characteristics of the rubric, input, expected response, inter-action between the input and response, and assessment, and offers a useful way of ensuring that the test and the target situation share essential characteristics which make it possible to make inferences about specific purpose language ability on the basis of performance on the test tasks. I also discussed a number of ways that test devel-opers can enrich the contextual variables in their tests to exploit the richness of the authentic materials that characterize LSP tests. The essential message of Chapter 3 is that it is only by making use of the framework of characteristics to analyze the target language use situa-tion and incorporating relevant characteristics into test tasks that an authentic interaction between the test taker's language ability and the test tasks can be elicited.

The framework of characteristics I have developed in this chapter is intended to be used to analyze specific purpose target language use situations, providing a basis for test development, as well as for analyzing existing specific purpose language tests to determine their degree of specificity, and in Chapters 6 and 7, the framework will be used to do exactly that. To conclude, I will summarize the framework. At this point, the reader may wish to return to Table 3.1 above to review the framework of TLU and test task characteristics.

The characteristics of the rubric are intended to orient the language user to the nature of the communicative event apart from the specific purpose content. They include (1) the specification of the objective; (2) procedures for responding to the situation; (3) the structure of the communicative event, in terms of the number of tasks involved, their relative importance, and the distinction between them; (4) the amount of time allotted to the tasks; and (5) evaluation, in terms of criteria for correctness and procedures for rating the performance. Characteristics of the rubric are often implicit in non-test language use situations, being a part of the cultural norms of a professional, vocational, or academic milieu. In test situations, however, the characteristics of the rubric must more often be explicitly stated to ensure that all test takers are equally aware of them. Remember that the evaluation characteristics refer to what the language user is ex-plicitly told about the criteria upon which the language performance is to be judged and the procedure the judges will use in making the evaluation. In an LSP test, the evaluation criteria are derived from an analysis of the target language use situation, and the complete description of them will appear as characteristics of assessment, usually in more technical terms than can be used in the rubric.

The characteristics of the input refer to the specific information that language users must process in dealing with a communicative situation. These characteristics include the prompt and input data. The prompt provides information about the context: (1) the setting, (2) the participants, (3) the purpose of the event, (4) its form and content, (5) the tone being conveyed, (6) the language being used, (7) norms of interaction, and (8) the genre of the spoken or written communication. The prompt must also include information about the problem to be addressed during the communicative event. The input data is the material – visual, auditory, and/or physical objects – that participants in communicative events process and respond to. There are two primary considerations in analyzing the input data: its format and its level of authenticity. Data format is analyzed in terms of whether it is visual or auditory (or both), the means by which it is delivered (including live interaction, audio and video recording, print, or computer screen), and its length in terms of both time and number of words. Level of authenticity refers to both the degree to which the input data in a test reflects the characteristics of the TLU situation, and the degree to which the data engages the test taker's communicative language ability. Recall that the level of authenticity, unlike the other characteristics, applies to input data in the test, rather than to the data in the target language use situation, which is by definition authentic. Also remember that while the input data is often genuine or created to reflect most of the language characteristics of genuine input data, the prompt is most often written by the test developers specifically for the test and is intended to provide contextualization cues to help ensure that the test takers will engage an appropriate discourse domain in dealing with the input data.

The expected response characteristics are those relevant to the way in which the participant in the communicative event responds to it. Responses may be written, spoken, or physical, or some combination of these. The type of response may be (1) extended production, usually defined as longer than a sentence; (2) limited production, a word, phrase, or sentence; or (3) a selected response, making a choice among a number of alternatives. The response content characteristics embody those features of specific purpose language ability and background knowledge that are to be assessed. As was the case with input data, level of authenticity is a consideration with the expected response in the test, and both situational and interactional characteristics need to be taken into account.

The interaction between input and response has to do with the nature of the communicative event in terms of (1) reactivity, whether the input can be altered as a function of the response to it, as in a live conversation, for example; (2) scope, the amount and variety of material in the input or response; and (3) directness, the amount of background knowledge that must be called upon in order to respond to the input. Both the input and the response may vary along these dimensions. For example, an interviewer may change the way a question is posed after noting the response to it, and the interviewee may alter the response in light of newer information; a short piece of input data, such as a query from a student, can result in a rather extended response from an instructor; and input can vary in the amount of contextualization it supplies, just as responses might vary similarly.

Finally, the characteristics of assessment include (1) the construct definition, a statement of what aspects of specific purpose language ability are to be measured, usually derived from an analysis of the TLU situation, guided by our theoretical understanding of what it means to know a language, and limited by constraints on the testing situation; (2) the criteria for correctness, the operationalization of the construct, based on an analysis of indigenous assessment criteria in the TLU situation; and (3) a systematic set of procedures for carrying out the rating/scoring of the performance. These are extremely important characteristics of both target language use situations and test tasks, and a great deal of care must be taken by LSP test developers to ensure that the construct definition and the assessment criteria are clearly, completely, and precisely stated.

In Chapter 5 I will use the framework to develop rating instruments for the analysis of both the target language use situation and LSP tests that are produced on the basis of the analysis. In the next chapter, I will discuss the transition from theory to practice in LSP testing, focussing on the strategic component in specific purpose language ability as an interface between internal abilities and external context, and summarizing the theory of specific purpose language testing I have developed in the first three chapters.

....

CHAPTER FOUR

Strategic competence: between · knowledge and context

Introduction

In this chapter, I want to focus on strategic competence, which mediates between the LSP background knowledge and language knowledge components, on the one hand, and the external features of context which the language user / test taker responds to, on the other. Thus, strategic competence is really the interface between the internal and the external. I will begin by introducing a distinction between two types of strategies within strategic competence, metacognitive strategies and communication strategies. I will then develop a hypothetical example of a test taker's use of these strategies as he or she works through an LSP performance test, finally turning to a discussion of the main points of the theory of specific purpose testing that has been developed so far in the book, pointing the way toward the practice of testing language for specific purposes.

The interface between the external and the internal in specific purpose language use

In this section, I will discuss the processing of specific purpose language in which strategic competence takes a central role: it is important for LSP testers to understand how test takers deal with the information provided for them in the test prompts and input data. Unless testers take care to provide sufficient contextual cues for test takers to attend to, there will be little in the test performance that can be interpreted as evidence of specific purpose language ability. I will begin the discussion, therefore, with a look at the function of strategic competence, followed by a more detailed look at the processes that it comprises.

Strategic competence

As I argued in Chapter 2, strategic competence serves as a mediator or interface between the learner-internal traits of background knowledge and language knowledge and the external context, controlling the interaction between them. Language users, whether in a real-life language use situation, in a classroom, or in a language test, interpret context in much the same way: they assess the characteristics of the situation, engaging an appropriate discourse domain, or creating a temporary one; they establish goals for responding to the situation; they make a plan for meeting the goals, deciding what elements of knowledge will be required, and they control the execution of the plan by retrieving the required knowledge and organizing it into a coherent response. The difference between a language testing situation and a non-test language use situation is, of course, that a language test is generally a much more focussed, intense language use situation and all the information that the test taker requires in assessing the communicative situation must be provided in the test itself, particularly in the prompts and input data, but also in the rubric (and, indeed, the location of the test itself, although I have not discussed this aspect except in passing). Therefore, test developers have a major responsibility for providing sufficient contextual information to enable the test takers to establish the context, to know where they are, and engage an appropriate discourse domain. I discussed this important aspect of LSP tests in Chapter 3, and the main point of focus here is that language tests are in principle no different from so-called real-life situations with regard to the language user's interaction with the context in planning a communicative response.

Strategic competence consists of two primary types of cognitive processes or strategies, which I will call **metacognitive strategies** and **communication strategies**, following Chapelle and Douglas (1993). Metacognitive strategies direct the language user's interaction with the context, while communication strategies are called on by the metacognitive strategies to take over direction when the features of the context are specifically identified as communicative (i.e., when meanings must be negotiated or discourse created). This two-tiered system is hierarchically arranged so the higher-level metacognitive processes can engage communicative processes at a lower level. Both types of strategies involve assessment, goal setting, planning, and execution, the main difference being that the metacognitive strategies are more general and the communication strategies are focussed specifically on communicative language use. As LSP testers, we are primarily interested in communication strategies because of their obvious effect on language test performance; however, I will consider metacognitive strategies briefly, since sometimes test tasks may be such that the metacognitive strategies are all that is required for a response, and, as you will see, this is not a desirable state of affairs in an LSP test.

Note that Bachman and Palmer (1996) use the term metacognitive strategies to describe the components of strategic competence, and suggest that such strategies are involved in all cognitive activity, not just language use. I believe it is useful to distinguish at least the two types I have described here as metacognitive and communicative strategies since this allows us to more specifically account for differences in communicative and non-communicative language test tasks, and this distinction is important for LSP testing, as it is in all communicative language testing. It is also important, I think, to recognize a distinction between communicative and non-communicative language use as fundamental to the distinction between communicative and non-communicative language tests. It is certainly possible, and perhaps not uncommon, to devise test tasks which do not engage the test taker's communicative language ability in that they do not require the expression, interpretation, or negotiation of meaning in discourse. I will discuss these points in a bit more detail below.

Metacognitive strategies

Metacognitive strategies are directly responsible for performance in situations not requiring language, such as carrying out a laboratory procedure, or operating an overhead projector. For example, upon entering a chemistry laboratory, a student would employ metacognitive strategies to assess the context, noting the various pieces of equipment available, the types and quantities of chemicals, the location of various safety apparatus, down to the room temperature, lighting, and so on. The student might then decide upon a goal for the use of the lab equipment and materials, say carrying out an analysis of the acidity of a certain substance. Next, the student would organize a plan for achieving the goal, deciding upon necessary materials and equipment for the task. Finally, the student would carry out the plan by assembling the required apparatus and chemicals and using them appropriately to complete the analysis. Although these metacognitive strategies – assessment, goal setting, planning, and execution – are not primarily concerned with language use, they do have access to language knowledge, which they can use in rather mechanical, non-communicative tasks, such as reading measurements or chemical labels in the lab experiment above, or in other contexts, doing cross-word puzzles, certain language classroom drills, and even some language test tasks. Some test tasks may not be perceived as communicative by the test taker, and, consequently, performance on them will be mistakenly interpreted as evidence of communicative language ability. For example, in Chapter 3, I considered a test task in which the test taker was asked to read a passage about energy from various fuels and then list four sources of energy the author termed natural forces. Such a matching task requires little use of background knowledge, nor does it require much negotiation of meaning or the creation of discourse, the two defining features of communication (Chapelle 1998). We might interpret performance on such a task as informing us about language knowledge, but it does not tell us much about communicative language ability, not to mention specific purpose language ability. However, a task which required the test taker to read the energy text and then summarize it, focussing on the most important points, would be somewhat more communicative and related to specific purpose language knowledge, since the test taker would have to call upon some background knowledge to assess the relative importance of the points made in the text and would need to create some level of linguistic meaning. Finally, a task involving the test taker in writing a proposal for deriving usable energy from geothermal sources beneath the earth's crust would be highly communicative and specific purpose, requiring a great deal of specific purpose knowledge, both background knowledge about geothermal energy, and rhetorical knowledge about proposal writing, as well as the creation of complex meanings in coherent discourse. I will consider the engagement of communication strategies in the next section.

Communication strategies

This set of strategies works specifically with language by bringing relevant knowledge into use at the right time, and in the right relationship to the resources demanded by the task. It is important at this point to recognize differences in the way researchers have conceived of communication strategies. It has been perhaps most common that they are defined with reference to communication problems, often owing to deficiencies in language knowledge. Corder (1983), for example, defines a communication strategy as 'a systematic technique employed by a speaker to express his meaning when faced by some difficulty' (p. 16). By difficulty Corder means the speaker's inadequate command of the language used in the interaction. However, in this book, I will view communication strategies in a broader context of language processing, following Bialystok (1990), who points out in this regard that communication strategies are engaged even when there have been no obvious difficulties. Strategic competence, and specifically communication strategies, will thus not be viewed either as simply controlling options for working around breakdowns in communication or for enhancing language production, but rather as an essential part of the general language use process.

In describing communication strategies, I will review the four types of strategies which were introduced in Chapter 2: assessment, goal setting, planning, and control of execution. Communication strategies are engaged by the metacognitive component when the language user perceives the situation as communicative. The essential feature distinguishing communicative from non-communicative language use is the creation or interpretation of linguistic meanings in discourse (see Chapelle 1998, Chapter 2, and Bachman and Palmer 1996, Chapter 4, for detailed discussions of this point). I discussed in Chapter 3 how context is a dynamic, interactive phenomenon, and so it is with specific purpose communicative discourse: there must be an interaction between language knowledge and background knowledge, on the one hand, and contextual features as internalized by the language user, on the other. Now, let us look at each of the four types of communication strategies in an LSP testing context.

Assessing the discourse

The assessment strategies analyze features of the specific purpose communicative situation and attempt to engage an appropriate discourse domain. For example, upon entering a classroom at the beginning of a new term, a teacher no doubt engages in a rapid assessment process, scanning the room to see whether there is chalk in the tray, the location of the overhead projector (or whether there is one), the state of the lighting, ventilation, and temperature, and the students themselves in terms of such features as number, gender mix, age range, general appearance, and their relative state of quiescence or excitement. Should the teacher ascertain, for example, that the students were all about his or her own age, this assessment would probably result in the engagement of a different discourse domain than if the perception were that the class comprised students 15 or 20 years younger. This assessment and engagement of a discourse domain would influence the nature of the communication that the teacher would employ. In a language test, the assessment of the communicative situation works in very much the same way. Indeed, recall the *TEACH* test referred to in Chapter 1, a performance test for international teachers in an English-medium university. In much the same way as described above, the test candidate enters the classroom in which the test is to take place and assesses the communicative situation, noting the presence of a blackboard and chalk, a teacher's table, and a small group of students. However, in the case of the *TEACH* test, the test taker would also note the presence of a television camera and a technician, and be greeted by a test administrator. These features, and the discourse domain they engender, no doubt affect greatly the candidate's subsequent communicative goal, plan, and execution. More generally, the discourse domain a test taker engages in beginning to carry out a test task may or may not resemble the one the test developers intended, and this certainly affects subsequent strategies. It is important to remember that assessment of the discourse is an ongoing, recursive process, and that the language user's own responses become objects of assessment as the discourse proceeds, and the discourse can be adapted to accommodate perceived non-comprehension, communication breakdowns, and so on.

Setting communicative goals

The discourse domain is used by the goal-setting process, which determines the communicative goal, the test taker's communicative objective. In non-test language use, there are quite a few options for goal setting: the language user may decide which task of several to tackle first, and what order to attempt the rest, he or she may decide not to respond at all to the communicative situation, or to respond in a novel way for some personal reason. The teacher entering a class for the first time, for example, may decide, having observed that the students were fairly young and unruly, to establish a degree of authority and prepare to say in a loud, commanding tone, 'Everyone sit down and be quiet!' In a language test, since it is a focussed communicative situation, the choice of goals is typically much more restricted: the range of tasks is pretty narrow, and not much choice is given about which ones will be attempted or in what order. To return to the example of the *TEACH* test, the test candidate may have as a goal to get through the procedure in as efficient a manner as possible, providing as much information and leaving as little time for questions as can reasonably be contrived.

Linguistic planning

The communicative goal is the input for the planning procedure, which results in a communicative plan for accomplishing the goal. Planning strategies involve deciding what aspects of specific purpose background knowledge and language knowledge will be needed to reach the intended goal. In the situation I suggested above, in which the teacher had as a goal the early establishment of authority, planning would involve the retrieval of appropriate lexis and imperative verb forms, functional knowledge of how to manipulate and control one's interlocutors, and the decision to eschew norms of politeness. The communicative plan may also take account of the possibility that certain aspects of background knowledge or language knowledge necessary for completing the task are not available, and so a plan must deal with the deficiency, by means of such strategies as avoidance, paraphrase, translation, appeal for assistance, or the use of gestures (Tarone 1977). In the *TEACH* example, the candidate might plan to begin with a definition followed by an anecdote to place the topic into a real-life context, followed by a theoretical explanation of the phenomenon, and concluding with a number of examples of applications. Such a plan would entail the engagement of both technical and non-technical language, knowledge of heuristic and ideational functions, and the use of formal and informal registers and some idioms and cultural references. Whether the candidate could successfully carry out such a plan is the object of the next aspect of communication strategies.

Control of linguistic execution

The language user must finally execute the plan by making a communicative response: retrieving appropriate language and background knowledge, organizing it, and engaging in either production or comprehension by means of appropriate 'psychophysiological mechanisms' (Bachman 1990) – mouth or ear, eye or hand. As is proverbial, the best-laid plans often go awry. The teacher wishing to strike fear into the hearts of the class might spoil it all by nervously squeaking the command in a high-pitched voice; the *TEACH* candidate might produce a flawed performance by employing too technical a level of vocabulary and overly complex syntax in the opening definition.

With regard to the operation of strategic competence in assessing an unfamiliar context, language users attempt to make sense of a communicative situation by piecing together an interpretation as best they can. This can have disastrous consequences when these interpretations are erroneous from the point of view of a speaker or writer. It is quite common for a language user to get the wrong end of the stick, as we say, engage an inappropriate discourse domain, and rattle along for quite a while under a deviant set of assumptions about what the context is. Oller (1979: 41) cites examples of this sort of problem in dictation test data: a test taker having heard 'pertinent facts' wrote 'person in facts' and after hearing 'to find practical means of feeding people better and means of helping them avoid the terrible damage' wrote 'to find particle man living better and mean help man and boy tellable damage.' Another example of this sort of miscommunication in an LSP context can be found in Perdue (1984: 77). In a roleplayed interview between a prospective employer and an industrial trainee, the following exchange took place:

INTERVIEWER: Can you tell me about the welding that you learnt?
TRAINEE: Yes, there is a – acetylene welding, acetylene gas welding and electronic welding.
INTERVIEWER: Hm – sorry – and – what?

The interviewer was attempting to find out what the trainee himself had learned about welding and specifically what experience he had had. The trainee interpreted the request as a sort of examination question, an attempt to find out what he knew about welding in general. In other words, the interlocutors didn't agree on an interpretation of the context, and this led to a communication breakdown.

It is also possible that a learner can assess a situation adequately, but lack the language ability to deal with it. An example of this comes from the *SPEAK* test (Educational Testing Service 1986). A test taker, responding to the instruction to 'describe a bicycle in as much detail as you can,' produced the following answer:

A bicycle consist of a – two wheels – one by – and a one triangle –
and two pedals – a chain – and a seat – in in China – most of a –
bicycle – have a ring – on the bar

Fagundes (1989: 71)

In this case, the learner knew what was required in the situation but lacked the linguistic knowledge – lexis, for the most part – to carry it out. Thus, he offers 'one by (one)' for one in front of the other, 'a one triangle' for triangular frame, 'ring' for bell, and 'bar' for handlebar. The point of these two examples is that LSP test developers need to be aware that test takers are desperately seeking cues in the test instructions and input to help them make an assessment of the communicative situation, establish a discourse domain and plan a response. In the second example, it would appear that the test taker was aware of what was required of him in the task; what he lacked was the language knowledge necessary to bring it off. This allows the test user to interpret the test taker's performance in terms of level of language knowledge, which is the purpose of this particular language test.

The earlier welding example, in which the context was misunderstood by the test taker, is more problematic for the LSP tester. The specific purpose situation is that of a job interview in the trainee's field of expertise, welding. In this case, we don't know whether the problem lies in a failure of the interviewer to provide sufficient contextualization cues, or whether the deficiency was in the trainee's background knowledge about job interviews. The performance is thus difficult to interpret. This example highlights the necessity of providing plenty of cues in the form of test method characteristics in the test prompt and input data so that the test takers have a reasonable opportunity to assess the situation and figure out where they are in engaging an appropriate discourse domain and planning a communicative response. In cases where test takers vary greatly in their level of specific purpose background knowledge, it may be necessary to test for this in order to disambiguate results. (See the discussion of inferencing in Chapter 1 and below.)

This discussion of strategic competence is intended to help us understand and appreciate the complexity of the interpretive task that an LSP test presents to the test taker. But, how does this information help us understand what goes on when a test taker is confronted with an LSP test? Let's consider a hypothetical example.

The tale of Carol

Let us imagine that Carol, a prospective employee in the field of international commerce, has been told by an employer to take the *Oxford International Business English Certificate* examination (University of Oxford Delegacy of Local Examinations 1990), a specific purpose language test, to demonstrate her abilities to handle the language of international business. Three days before the test Carol went to register and was given a page of instructions (the rubric) and eight pages of a case study with technical information about a firm called *Kudos Tours* (input). The instructions were non-specific purpose and told her that she would have three days to prepare for the examination using the case study material, that she may write notes in the case study booklet while she is preparing for the examination, and that she must take the material into the examination with her.

The input, the case study text, is quite field specific, as the excerpt in Extract 4.1 will demonstrate.

Extract 4.1

The Annual Report includes the following accounts:

BALANCE SHEET FOR YEAR ENDING 31 DECEMBER 19--

		£000
Fixed assets		
Intangible assets	300[1]	
Tangible assets	600[2]	
Investments	800[3]	
		1 700
Current assets		
Debtors and prepayments	3 400	
Cash at bank	80	
		3 500
		5 200

.

.

.

continues

NOTES

[1] Goodwill

[2] Office equipment, cars, buses and mini-buses and a small commercial property.

[3] Shares in Global Air, an Air Carrier started and run by the younger members of the Kudos family.

University of Oxford Delegacy of Local Examinations (1990: 3)

Carol has been given three days to read this material, and she spends a lot of time digesting it, looking a number of terms up in her business dictionary, and writing copious notes in the margins. When she enters the examination room, Carol is confronted by a test administrator who greets her and directs her to a table, one of about 30 in the room. Carol employs her metacognitive strategies and assesses the characteristics of the situation: a rather nondescript examination room with yellow-painted walls, an examiner's table at the front, test takers' tables; other test takers sitting rather stiffly in their chairs. She establishes a cognitive goal with respect to the situation, in this case, probably something like 'get through this ordeal as painlessly as possible!' She now develops a plan for meeting the goal, which may be 'listen carefully to the administrator, and try to follow the instructions.'

The administrator passes out the examination booklets for the reading and writing tasks and tells the test takers that they may not open the booklets until they are told to do so, but that they will then be given five minutes to read them through. He tells the test takers that they should attempt all the questions and write all their answers in the spaces provided in the booklet, that they may use dictionaries, and that they will have one hour and thirty-five minutes to do the test. Carol opens her booklet and begins to read through it as instructed. She finds that there are six tasks, four fairly lengthy writing tasks, a short-answer reading task, and a proofreading task. She assesses this new situation, decides on a goal of doing the reading and proofreading tasks first, as a warm-up, plans the resources she will need for accomplishing the reading task, primarily involving her knowledge of specific purpose language and her ability to apply her specific purpose background knowledge in solving the problems posed by the questions. Her metacognitive strategies will be insufficient for this task, since it involves quite a bit of interaction between the text and her language and background knowledge. As a result of having spent three days reading the case study material, the input data for the reading task, a fax message, is highly contextualized in Carol's mind, and she engages her communication strategies to assess the new situation. Now, her assessment involves the engagement of an appropriate discourse domain, probably that of Finance Director, a role that has been assigned in some of the other test tasks, and she begins to read the input data. Her communicative goal is to understand the gist of the message. Her communicative plan is to draw upon specific purpose background knowledge to interpret the content of the fax, and upon language knowledge of syntactic structures, morphological and phonological units, the rhetorical form, and register, level of formality, and genre of business communication she requires to accomplish her goal. She executes the plan by skimming the fax and interpreting the gist: a company proposing a merger with Kudos is attempting to change the provisional agreement to its own advantage.

Carol now employs her communicative assessment strategies again, but this time to assess what information her audience – the examiners – want about this fax. Her plan is now to read the questions before going back to the text of the fax for a more detailed reading, and she begins to execute this new plan.

Carol's performance in the test situation is thus a dynamic process of assessment of the context, moment by moment, establishing communicative goals relevant to the current situation, and plans for meeting the goals. In interpreting her performance, the examiners must take into account the degree to which the test developers provided her with sufficient situational cues in the form of test method characteristics, reflecting the characteristics of the target language use situation, to allow them to make inferences about her specific purpose language knowledge in the context of international business. It is important for LSP test developers to bear in mind that the tests they produce will be approached by test takers in much the same way as they approach any communicative situation: they will bring assessment, goal setting, planning and execution strategies to bear in interpreting and responding to the test situation. All the information that is essential to making appropriate interpretations and engaging appropriate discourse domains must be provided by the test developers in the form of rubric and input, and, as LSP testers, we have a responsibility to ensure that we provide this information in as clear and authentic a manner as possible. I will conclude this chapter by reviewing the main points of the theory of specific purpose language testing before going on to a discussion of the practice of LSP test development in Chapter 5.

Summary of the theory of testing language for specific purposes

In this book so far I have discussed a number of theoretical issues and in this chapter I have tried to pull them together by focussing on strategic competence as a mediator between the internal and the external, the cognitive and the physical, in LSP testing. Here I want to summarize where I think we are now in the search for principles to guide the development of specific purpose language tests and to look ahead to the final chapters of the book in which I will discuss the practice of our LSP testing enterprise.

I have defined a specific purpose language test as one in which test content and methods are derived from an analysis of a specific purpose target language use situation, so that test tasks and content are authentically representative of tasks in the target situation, allowing for an interaction between the test taker's language ability and specific purpose content knowledge, on the one hand, and the test tasks on the other. Such a test, I suggested, allows us to make inferences about a test taker's level of language ability with reference to a specific purpose domain. The type of inferences we make on the basis of test performance is a crucial consideration in the LSP testing enterprise, and so the issue of inferencing is an important one in a theory of specific purpose testing. I argued also that LSP tests are necessary because (1) language performance varies with context, and therefore our interpretations of a test taker's language ability must vary from situation to situation, and (2) technical language has specific purpose characteristics that people who work in the field must control, so we need to make inferences about test takers' specific purpose language ability. Another key point was that authenticity does not lie only in the simulation of real-life texts or tasks, which I referred to as situational authenticity, but also in the interaction between the characteristics of such texts and tasks and the language ability of the test takers. In other words, authenticity is not a property of spoken and written texts themselves, or even of the tasks associated with various professions, vocations, and academic fields. Rather, authenticity is achieved only when the properties of the communicative situation established by the test rubric, prompts, and input data are sufficiently well-defined to engage the test takers' specific purpose language ability.

I discussed the construct of specific purpose language ability, defining it as the interaction between specific purpose background knowledge and language ability, by means of strategic competence engaged by specific purpose input in the form of test method characteristics. I thus argued that specific purpose background knowledge is a necessary feature of specific purpose language ability and must be taken into account in making inferences on the basis of LSP test performance. Since the construct contains, by definition, specific purpose background knowledge, we must consider whether it will be necessary to distinguish between the two types of knowledge – language knowledge and specific purpose content knowledge – in interpreting test performance: in some testing situations it may be, while in others it may not. Yet another decision that must be made with regard to the construct definition is precisely what components of specific purpose language ability we will attempt to measure:

whether the test situation calls for us to define communicative language ability in great detail, or whether a more general definition will do. If the purpose of the test is to determine whether candidates' English language ability is sufficient for them to be admitted to a medical residency program, for example, then a broadly defined construct of language ability, such as language ability for communicating in medical contexts, may be enough for test users to interpret the results; however, if the situation calls for a profile of component abilities as input to a remedial course of instruction, then a more detailed specification of the construct is necessary. I also noted that it is necessary to decide whether to include strategic competence in the construct definition or not: it may not be necessary for certain testing purposes to measure strategic competence.

In reviewing research on the relationship between language knowledge and specific purpose background knowledge, I discussed the following points: (1) the test input must be rich in specific purpose cues that will help insure that test takers will engage an appropriate discourse domain; (2) the more highly specialized test content becomes, the greater the influence of LSP background knowledge in its interaction with language knowledge in the communicative performance; (3) there does seem to be a threshold of language ability required before test takers can make effective use of their LSP background knowledge; and (4) since test developers themselves cannot easily assess the degree of specificity of input materials, they must turn to subject specialists for guidance.

I discussed the features of external context that are relevant to the development of LSP tests, including the setting, participants, purpose, message form and content, tone, language, norms of interaction, and genre. I suggested that context is a dynamic, continually changing concept that is constructed by the participants in a communicative situation, and that what really counts in thinking about context is the internal interpretation of it by the participants themselves. This aspect of context I called discourse domain, and suggested that it is a function of strategic competence to engage discourse domains in specific purpose language use. Increasing the likelihood that test takers will engage appropriate discourse domains in approaching specific purpose test tasks is an essential concern of test developers, and they must provide a rich array of specific purpose contextualization cues in the test input to insure that test takers know where they are and will engage in interactionally authentic language use.

Finally, I proposed a framework to describe tasks in both the specific purpose language use situation we wish to test and the LSP test we want to develop: characteristics of the rubric, input, expected response, interaction between input and response, and assessment. I argued that it is only by analyzing the target language use situation in terms of specific characteristics and then employing those characteristics in developing test tasks that an authentic interaction between the test taker's language ability and the test tasks can be produced.

I conclude this chapter by summarizing the main points for easy reference:

- Definition: a specific purpose language test is one in which test content and methods are derived from an analysis of a specific purpose target language use situation, so that test tasks allow for an interaction between the test taker's language ability and specific purpose content knowledge, on the one hand, and the test tasks on the other.
- LSP tests are necessary: language performance varies with context, and technical language has specific purpose characteristics that people who work in the field must control.
- Authenticity: the simulation of real-life texts or tasks and the interaction between the characteristics of such texts and tasks and the language ability of the test takers.
- The construct of field specific purpose language ability: the interaction between specific purpose background knowledge and language ability.
- The components of specific purpose language ability we will attempt to measure depend on what level of detail the test purpose calls for.
- Test input must be rich in specific purpose cues to help insure that test takers will engage an appropriate discourse domain.
- The more highly specialized test content becomes, the greater the influence of specific purpose background knowledge.
- There is a threshold of language ability required before test takers can make effective use of their background knowledge.
- LSP test developers must often turn to subject specialists for guidance.
- The features of external context relevant to the development of LSP tests are setting, participants, purpose, message form and content, tone, language, norms of interaction, and genre.

- Context: dynamic, continually changing, constructed by the participants in a communicative situation.
- Framework for describing TLU and test tasks: composed of the characteristics of the rubric, the input, the expected response, the interaction between input and response, and assessment.

We must continually link theory and practice by adhering to qualities of good LSP testing practice that I will propose in Chapter 5. These qualities, or principles, form an interface between the theoretical framework for specific purpose language testing and the down-to-earth realities of the test development enterprise. In Chapter 5, I will also discuss techniques for investigating the target language use situation, converting the task characteristics of the TLU situation into test tasks, and producing a set of specifications for the design and construction of specific purpose language tests.

....

CHAPTER FIVE

From target language use to test tasks

Introduction

In Chapter 2, I discussed a theory of language ability, and in particular the theoretical construct of specific purpose language ability that we attempt to measure with LSP tests. In Chapter 3, the topic was the nature of context and the theory of how context can be described in terms of task characteristics which can then be translated into test tasks. In this chapter, I will develop guidelines and techniques for constructing LSP tests, focussing particularly on techniques for investigating and describing the target language use situations that form the basis for identifying specific purpose test tasks. The same techniques will also provide a basis for evaluating LSP tests, in terms of test method characteristics, and for interpreting test performance, based on the understanding that test performances are the result of an interaction between test taker attributes (e.g., language ability and specific purpose background knowledge) and the context, as established by the characteristics of the test methods. I will begin the discussion of techniques for LSP test development by considering techniques for investigating target language use situations: grounded ethnography, context-based research, and subject specialist informant procedures. I will then outline a framework for analyzing specific purpose TLU situations, based on the discussion in Chapter 3, considering a concrete example along the way. I will end with a discussion and example of LSP test specifications, finally illustrating how to apply the analytical framework to the description of test task characteristics.

Techniques for investigating the target language use domain

We saw in Chapter 2 that input data vary greatly in their level of specificity and that this variation is not necessarily obvious to test developers. This is symptomatic of a general problem in LSP testing: the tester is seldom an expert in the field in which he or she is attempting to measure language ability and so must seek expert help in order to understand both the key features of the target language use situation and the characteristics of input data that will form the basis of the LSP test. I will briefly discuss three approaches to the investigation and description of the target language use situation: grounded ethnography, context-based research, and subject specialist informant procedures.

Grounded ethnography and context-based research

Grounded ethnography is an approach to describing and understanding a target language use situation from the perspective of language users in that situation. The technique has been defined as follows:

> a means for the researcher to understand an event by studying both its natural occurrence and the accounts and descriptions of it provided by its coparticipants.
>
> Frankel and Beckman (1982: 1)

Ethnography itself, of course, is an approach to the study of behavior from the differing viewpoints of the participants, and has been around since the late 1960s (see, for example, the collection of studies edited by Cazden *et al.* 1972). Ethnographic research is one of a number of approaches known as qualitative or process-oriented research techniques. Generally, ethnographic studies involve detailed descriptions of the research setting, in terms similar to those discussed in Chapter 3: setting, participants, purpose, etc. The goal is to produce an account of the principles which guide participants in cultural activities in behaving the way they do, interacting with each other, and interpreting each other's utterances and behaviors. Such studies may often involve the researchers themselves as participant observers, keeping notes or diaries for later analysis (see Denzin, 1996, for current discussion of ethnographic techniques).

What Frankel and Beckman bring to ethnographic research is the concept of grounding, in which the viewpoints of the participants are derived from their own observation of videotaped recordings of the actual events under analysis. This grounding, Frankel and Beckman claim, makes the participants' accounts much more immediate and direct than when they are asked, for example, to recall the events in question. They also find that videotaping of the events, using hidden or inconspicuous cameras, is less intrusive than studies in which the researcher is a participant observer. Frankel and Beckman's technique involves videotaping events in the TLU situation and then asking the participants to view the videotapes individually with them. The researchers instruct the participants to stop the tape when they see or hear something that they consider worthy of comment. This commentary, typically audio-recorded, is transcribed and inserted into the transcript of the original videotape, at the point where it had occurred in the review session, thus providing the researchers with the participants' own assessment of specific aspects of the performance. The videotapes are viewed and commented upon not only by the participants, but also by experts in the field being investigated, and by other researchers, who could bring, for example, discourse analysis skills or anthropological perspectives to the data. The outcome is a rich data base from which to draw insights into what in the performance was essential, problematic, or highly valued by participants and others in the field.

Although there is currently some controversy about the value of untrained participant commentary (see, for example, Jacoby 1998), I believe that the technique of grounded ethnography is an extremely useful one for LSP test development. Testers will find the commentary provided by the participants to be very helpful as they attempt to understand their language behavior in specific purpose contexts which are likely to be outside the experience of the test developers. As an example, let us say we are working to develop a test of medical English and are investigating physician/patient interviews. We could videotape some interviews, with the permission of the participants, of course, and ask the physician and patient to view the tape independently and provide commentary on significant aspects of their interaction. Hypothetically, the physician might comment that he or she had asked the patient about his or her home life in order to ascertain why the patient was not taking the prescribed medicine; the patient, on the other hand, might comment on the same segment of the interaction that the physician was prying into his or her private life and should stick to the problem of his or her health. This sort of commentary can provide important insights for the tester into aspects of language use in the target situation that would simply be inaccessible otherwise. As time, personnel, and/or financial considerations constrain the investigation of the TLU situation, the commentary may have to be limited to that provided by one or the other of the participants, or a representative sample of the participants, but if possible, all participants should be given the opportunity to provide commentary, since multiple viewpoints can provide rich insights into the target language use situation.

It is clear, too, that this technique will be useful in the analysis of indigenous assessment criteria discussed in Chapter 3. For example, should a patient comment that a physician seemed uncommunicative, this is a form of assessment, and the test developer would greatly benefit from an analysis of the criteria that the patient employed in making the evaluation. Alternatively, it is conceivable that another physician, on watching the taped interaction, might comment that a line of questioning by the physician being observed seemed not well motivated. This would offer another avenue for investigating criteria of assessment and should be followed up by the LSP tester. Of course, it is almost certainly true that participants often employ implicit assessment criteria, and may be unable to articulate them clearly, but such is the problem of the analysis of TLU situations: characteristics will seldom be obvious to the non-specialist test developer, and they may not be obvious to the participants themselves. It is thus no straightforward matter to investigate these indigenous criteria, not only because the participants may be largely unconscious of them, but also because they are likely to be highly contextualized and quite task specific (Jacoby and McNamara, in press) and therefore difficult to transfer to a language testing context. Nevertheless, this is one of the most exciting areas of investigation in language test development and deserves the attention of LSP practitioners and language testing researchers.

Douglas and Selinker (1994), building on earlier work in grounded ethnography and subject specialist informant techniques, which are discussed below, have provided a number of guidelines for what they call **context-based** research: the study of second language acquisition and use in important real-life contexts. In their empirical research, they were interested in understanding the ability of a non-native speaker to use English in talking about and writing about a technical field. In the research methodology they suggest, they first make a distinction between primary data and secondary data:

> **Primary data**: the interlanguage talk or writing we wish to study.
> **Secondary data**: commentary on the primary data.
> Douglas and Selinker (1994: 120)

Douglas and Selinker discuss two categories of secondary data: commentaries on the primary data by the participants themselves, and various types of expert commentaries upon the primary data. They have used other linguists, ethnographers and ethnomethodologists, and specialists in the target fields as sources of this type of secondary data; each brings various perspectives and methods to bear on the primary data. Douglas and Selinker argue that primary interlanguage data are always ambiguous and they make a case for the necessity of understanding the data from the perspectives of the participants who created them, and that of expert commentators. I will employ the categories of primary and secondary data in the analysis of a TLU situation below. Furthermore, in addition to studying the features of LSP interactions, it is necessary to study the relationship between those features as they unfold in real time, a point related to that I made in Chapter 3 that LSP contexts are dynamic and constantly changing as a result of negotiation among the participants as they construct the context turn by turn. It is this dynamic aspect of context that is perhaps the most vexing challenge to context-based research, as McNamara (in press) points out in discussing the need for a richer model of communicative competence than we have so far been able to develop. We will not be able to solve this problem in this book, but at least we must constantly keep in mind that in our efforts to describe the features of specific purpose language use situations, and, subsequently, those of LSP test methods, we test developers are largely dependent upon the participants in those situations for our understanding, and that the use of grounded ethnography, subject specialist informant procedures, and the principles of context-based research are necessary. I turn now to a brief consideration of a second approach to understanding target language use situations, subject specialist informant procedures.

Subject specialist informant procedures

Assuming that the persistent LSP test developer is able to obtain satisfactory recordings of interaction in the specific purpose TLU situation and samples of authentic input data, there still remains the difficulty of determining what in the data is worth focussing on; in other words, what aspects of the data are highly valued by professionals in the field (Bley-Vroman aand Selinker 1984). This inability to determine focus is caused in part by the fact that the test developer is usually someone who knows little about the specific purpose situation in which he or she is working. For example, Swales (1981), in discussing his analysis of article introductions in technical journals, admits that he found it difficult to establish any criteria for classifying reference to previous research along a scale from substantial to cosmetic: 'We suspect that it is only a specialized informant who can make such an assessment' (p. 12).

This is certainly the view of Selinker (1979), who, in an extremely important paper for LSP test developers, proposed utilizing specialist informants as a means of understanding input data in LSP disciplines with which the test developers have little or no expertise. In the article, Selinker restricts his discussion to written texts, but it seems clear that the procedures he establishes for working with subject specialist informants are applicable to understanding input data of all sorts. To paraphrase a key question Selinker grapples with: What does an LSP test developer who is not trained in a particular LSP discipline need to know in order to understand language use in that discipline? Selinker proposes nine areas that specialist informants can potentially help the LSP tester with:

- *Technical terminology:* e.g., pyrimidine, dimer, nucleotide.
- *Common language words used technically:* e.g., 'recognition' as used in biology to mean that there is some biological system present in an organism that becomes aware that some damage has occurred.
- *Relative strength of claims made by language users:* e.g., the use of hedging to reduce the degree of responsibility a participant wishes to take for a particular interpretation based on observed facts.
- *Contextual paraphrases:* the question of whether a particular word or phrase which occurs in one place in the discourse refers to the same concept as does a different word or phrase which occurred earlier; e.g., duplicate versus replicate with extraordinary fidelity.

- *Grammatical choice:* certain small grammatical changes make large conceptual differences; e.g., efficiencies of repair mechanisms versus efficiency of repair processes, where the switch from plural to singular makes a conceptual difference to the expert reader.
- *Modal words:* whether such usages as 'must exist' and 'must be subject to,' for example, refer to obligation or to possibility.
- *Rhetorical structure:* why, for example, a formal definition is embedded in a causal subordinate clause.
- *Punctuation structure:* the significance, for example, of the following punctuation pattern: . . . three ways in which an organism might respond . . . (1) repair the damage in situ; (2) replace the damaged portion, (3) bypass the damage. The use of a semicolon to separate (1) from (2) and a comma to separate (2) from (3) embodies a scientific conceptualization.
- *Connectives:* the degree to which such words as however, thus, furthermore, then, and yet are substitutable for each other and how each relates to the concepts being discussed in the discourse.

This list shows the range of potential difficulties the LSP test developer faces when confronted with the task of understanding language use in unfamiliar technical contexts. As Selinker points out, we don't even know what we don't know!

It is essential that the LSP tester make use of the specialist informant in a principled way in analyzing the TLU situation during the test development process. In Chapter 2 I claimed that the specific purpose target situation is not definable merely in terms of special content or of special language alone, but rather is a complex context created by the professionals who control the content and language in purposive interaction. This means that only through an analysis of interaction in conjunction with an analysis of content and language in the special purpose domain can the test developer arrive at an understanding of the target language use situation and the problems that need to be addressed in the test.

One additional aspect related to the use of subject specialists in the analysis of specific purpose target language use situations is that of their sensitivity to language as an object of study. Selinker points out the necessity, for example, of working with informants who 'have a feel for the technical language of [the] discipline and [are] open to linguistically-oriented questions' (p. 213). There is some preliminary research (Elder 1993a) which suggests that such naive judges are quite capable of playing a role not only in analysis of the situation, but in the actual assessment of specific purpose language ability. Elder suggests that subject specialist raters of communicative ability may take a strong view of communicative performance, judging communicative success rather than the quality of language *per se*. Elder's work also suggests that while there is a substantial relationship between their assessment of overall ability, subject specialist judges of specific purpose language performances do in fact assess specific purpose language differently from language specialists. This point is highlighted in some work in Australia with the *Occupational English Test*, where it was found that, in spite of having passed the *OET*, candidates for medical licensure were coming to the clinical assessment with English language skills inadequate for the task (Lumley 1998). A subsequent research study suggested that the criteria the medical professionals were using as a basis for complaining about the English skills of the candidates were somehow different from those being assessed by the *OET*. McNamara notes that some of the physicians had remarked that they were not certain the test tasks adequately represented the actual clinical situation in which the examinees would eventually work: 'whatever the doctors were complaining about was not being captured by the *OET*' (McNamara 1996: 241). Such a finding is at the heart of the concern I have expressed here for investigating indigenous assessment criteria, and reinforces the point that specific purpose language test developers do in fact have something to learn from subject specialist informants, and should involve them early in the analysis of the target language use situation.

As I suggested above, there are drawbacks and potential problems associated with the use of subject specialist informants. For example, I noted the necessity of working with informants who are sensitive to technical language and who are tolerant of linguistically oriented questions. It is also the case that working with informants can be a very time-consuming process – Selinker and his colleagues worked with their informant for three months to understand a five-page article on genetics! It is seldom that test developers have the luxury of spending so much time to understand a single text. Huckin and Olsen (1984) suggest that the optimal use of a subject specialist informant is first to help the researcher achieve a top-down understanding of the purpose of the LSP text or interaction and its main content; only then are the researcher and the informant, having arrived at mutual frames of reference, ready to explore lower level, bottom-up rhetorical and grammatical aspects of the primary data. This initial top-down approach will, in other words, help the researcher become more efficient in learning from the informant.

A framework for analyzing tasks in specific purpose TLU situations and LSP tests

In Chapter 2, I outlined the characteristics of specific purpose language ability, and in Chapter 3, I discussed the characteristics of tasks in the target language use situation: rubric, input, expected response, interaction between input and response, and assessment. These two sets of characteristics thus form an essential link between the target situation and the test, and I will employ these frameworks as a means of comparing the TLU situation and the test later in the chapter.

As an example, we will consider a TLU situation, that of a US university chemistry class, and see how the framework is used. The steps in the process of analyzing a TLU situation include (1) a problem definition, (2) preliminary investigation, (3) primary data collection, (4) secondary data collection, and, finally, (5) an analysis of language and tasks in the TLU situation using the relevant frameworks.

Example target language use situation

Step 1: problem definition

Let us imagine that we have been given the task of producing a specific purpose test for prospective university instructors from outside the US to measure their communicative English ability in the context of the university classroom. University administrators have had complaints from students (and from their parents) that international instructors are sometimes incomprehensible in the classroom, so the idea is to give new instructors an LSP test of their ability to teach in English, and to require those who do not pass the test to attend English classes. The Chemistry Department offers an introductory chemistry course, First Year Chemistry, that is required of all entering students, regardless of their field of study, and many of these classes are taught by international instructors. Thus, the largest single group of international instructors is in the Chemistry Department, and we decide to begin our investigation of the target language use situation there.

Step 2: preliminary investigation

We first consult the supervisor of First Year Chemistry to find out about the structure of the course and the duties of the instructors in it. We learn that there are two main instructor assignments: supervising laboratory classes and teaching recitation classes. The labs are very highly controlled and a great deal of support is given to the instructors in the form of lab manuals and other types of instructional material. The recitation classes are much less controlled: students come to these classes to get help from the instructors with homework problems assigned by a professor in the twice-weekly lectures. There is a high degree of interaction in these classes, with the students asking questions, and the instructor guiding them through problem-solving procedures. On the advice of our subject specialist informant, the First Year Chemistry supervisor, we decide to analyze the communicative situation in the recitation classes, and we decide to begin with a class taught by Julio, a second year teaching assistant from Mexico. We obtain permission from the supervisor, and from Julio and his students, to videotape a class.

Step 3: primary data collection

Julio's recitation class: Julio is from Mexico, and is an experienced instructor, a second year graduate student in Chemistry, hoping to receive a PhD in a couple more years. The class we videotape is one just before an examination, so the students are very concerned with getting advice about the exam and how to prepare for it. One of them asks about a particularly vexing equation describing a chemical reaction, and Julio begins his explanation. He writes the equation on the blackboard, and a transcript of the beginning of his explanation follows:

JULIO: I want to put some kind of numbers here [pointing to the equation] so that all these will be equal, all right? So what do I put here – what do I put for this one?
STUDENT: Three halves.

JULIO: What's it now? Three? Three halves? Are you sure? OK.
            Three halves, or two thirds. All right? I'll give you a
            choice again – multiple choice. How many of you think
            it's three halves? Good. How many of you think it's two
            thirds? Only one. Sometimes the majority doesn't win
            . . . OK, I'll tell you . . . in this case the majority is wrong
            . . . I don't think it's thr . . . ah three halves. What makes
            you think it's three halves?

STUDENT: For every two . . . there's three Y . . .

JULIO: Yeah, because you look at this – the three here it goes
            with the Y so you bring the two across, it becomes three
            halves, right? Just . . . now there are two ways of doing
            this. So your answer is this . . . you are saying this, OK?
            [writes another equation on the blackboard] If this is
            true, can you tell me which one is bigger? In terms of
            number, which one is bigger? Is this a bigger number, or
            this one is bigger number?

STUDENT: Second one.

JULIO: This one is bigger number? Are you sure? So you are
            saying maybe ten times three half equals to eight?

STUDENT: There's a negative there.

JULIO: Uh . . . that is also negative . . . the negative . . . now,
            don't confuse yourself with the negative . . . the negative
            only means it's disappearing . . . it really has nothing to
            . . . you know . . . don't confuse yourself with the math-
            ematics . . . with the negative. The negative is more a
            sign here telling you that this is being disappeared when
            the reaction goes, and the positive means that it
            appears. OK. There are two ways of solving this problem,
            OK? One way is asking yourself which one disappear
            faster, X or Y? Just tell me – which one disappear faster?

STUDENT: Y.

Step 4: secondary data collection

Having made the tape of the class, we next employ the grounded
ethnography and specialist informant techniques I discussed earlier
in this chapter. We play the tape separately for the instructor, some of
his students, the First Year Chemistry supervisor, and fellow applied
linguists and invite their comments on what they find interesting or
problematic in the class. We use this commentary to inform ourselves

about what is of significance in the interaction which may be translated into test tasks. The following discussion is a distillation of our informants' commentary.

Notice that Julio employs a very interactive style: he does not simply demonstrate the procedure for doing the problem, but rather seeks to involve the class in the process by asking wh-questions: 'what do I put here – what do I put for this one?' He also challenges the students to think about the problem and their own responses to it: 'Three halves? Are you sure?' Julio offers the students two approaches to the problem as a way of helping them see it from different perspectives: 'There are two ways of solving this problem, OK?' Later in his explanation, he points out to them the practicality of the second, rather more mechanical, way of approaching the problem: 'Now, that's one way of looking at it. Now that requires some logical thinking. But in exam, probably you got so so tense up, you know, you don't think clearly. So let me teach you another mathematical way, you know, it's just simple mathematics.' Two students ask Julio questions: 'How did you know that Y disappears faster than X?' and 'What about the concentration?' Julio also employs a lot of comprehension checks: all right?, OK?, and a number of discourse markers – So . . . , OK, Now . . . – to help the students follow his explanation. He also uses the imperative when he wants to especially emphasize a point: 'don't confuse yourself with the negative'. He uses a few cultural references: 'I'll give you a choice again – multiple choice' and 'Sometimes the majority doesn't win . . .' The students tell us that they don't have much trouble understanding Julio – his pronunciation is OK, he usually meets their expectations for how instructors 'ought to act,' and he 'knows his chemistry.'

Step 5: analysis of target language use and task characteristics

The above analysis gives us a lot of material with which to build a test task, but, of course, in an actual test development project, we would observe and record many more examples of the target language use situation. The data provided here are only a sample of the type of analysis we would want to employ. We will first describe the nature of language in the TLU situation, employing the framework of characteristics of language I developed in Chapter 2. Table 5.1 illustrates the results in the present example. Here we see that the construct

Table 5.1. *Language characteristics of target language use situation (chemistry class)*

Categories	Characteristics
Language knowledge	
Grammatical knowledge	
Vocabulary	Technical chemistry terminology, basic mathematical terminology, pan-technical terminology
Morphology/Syntax	Wh-questions, declaratives, tag questions, imperatives
Phonology/Graphology	Pronunciation of key terms; rhythm, intonation, stress; clear writing on blackboard
Textual knowledge	
Cohesion	Process markers: *now, so, one way, another way*
Organization	Process/Problem solving structure; conversational turn taking
Functional knowledge	Heuristic, ideational, and manipulative functions
Sociolinguistic knowledge	
Dialect/Variety	Spanish/English interlanguage; standard midwest US
Register	Chemistry, academic
Idiom	Tense(d) up
Cultural reference	Multiple choice; sometimes the majority doesn't win
Strategic competence	
Assessment	Undergraduate chemistry recitation class
Goal setting	Help students solve homework problems, prepare for upcoming exam
Planning	Use an interactive style: involve and challenge students by asking questions; help them think through the problems by giving advice about alternative ways to solve them, using comprehension checks and discourse markers, imperatives
Control of execution	Comprehend oral questions, written problems; produce oral explanations, written solutions on blackboard
Background knowledge	Chemistry, mathematics, pedagogy, US academic culture

underlying the TLU language performance of the international instructor is fairly complex, involving all the components of language knowledge in our framework. Textual knowledge and sociolinguistic knowledge seem particularly important to the work of the instructor. As I discussed in Chapter 2, the construct of specific purpose language ability must also include relevant types of background knowledge, most notably specific purpose background knowledge, but also other knowledge areas. For example, in the case of our chemistry instructor, he demonstrates knowledge not only about chemistry, but also about mathematics and US academic culture in his use of language in the chemistry classroom. Julio's strategic competence allows him to weave his language knowledge and his background knowledge in a complex performance, employing both spoken and written modalities to help his students solve homework problems and prepare for an exam.

Next, we can employ our framework of TLU task characteristics, as shown in Table 5.2. Note that some of the characteristics are implicit in the context of the TLU situation, most notably the objective, procedure for response, and evaluation in the rubric, and problem identification in the input. In our language test, we will probably need to make these explicit to insure that all test takers are aware of them. Notice also that the distinctions between tasks are sometimes blurred: it is not always clear when one problem ends and the next begins. Furthermore, the students' questions can come out of the blue. For example, in Julio's class, at one point, a student asked the question, as something of a non-sequitur, 'What about the concentration?' This took Julio rather by surprise, and he floundered for a short time: 'The con . . . uh, the concentration? . . .' In our tests, we usually try to make the tasks more clearly defined so the test takers can more easily work their way through them, and also for psychometric reasons since, for some statistical procedures, there is a need to make test tasks independent of each other so that certain types of statistical analyses can be carried out. Yet, as we know, language use is never quite so clear cut – contexts blend into one another, and language tasks share characteristics and are difficult to separate clearly. Therefore, in LSP testing, as in communicative testing in general, we will find it difficult to distinguish tasks as clearly as we might like, or as testing and measurement practice might demand.

Another point I should make in looking over the analysis of the TLU situation of the chemistry class is that evaluation in the rubric is

Table 5.2. *Characteristics of the target language use situation (chemistry class)*

Characteristics	TLU situation
Rubric	
Objective	Implicit in situation: to review homework problems prior to exam
Procedures for responding	Implicit: interact orally and on blackboard with students in explaining homework problems
Structure	
Number of tasks	Varies; problems raised by students
Relative importance	Varies; instructor advises students on what's important for exam
Task distinctions	Can be blurred – one problem may blend into another similar one; student questions can come at any time
Time allotment	50-minute class
Evaluation	Implicit
Input	
Prompt	
Features of context	
Setting	Typical chemistry classroom: instructor behind long teacher table, raised on platform, blackboard, OHP, textbook; students in desks, have lecture notes, text-book; class is in middle of term, just before an exam
Participants	25 undergraduate students, most not chemistry majors, widely varying educational preparation, majority from Iowa, ethnically homogeneous, roughly equal number males and females; they are familiar to instructor
Purpose	Review homework problems, answer questions in preparation for exam
Form/Content	Interactive question/answer format; chemistry problems assigned as homework: reaction equations
Tone	Friendly, but businesslike
Language	Instructor uses Spanish/English interlanguage; students use standard midwest US English; some technical register
Norms	Teacher/student interaction, elements of casual conversation
Genre	Question/answer session, 'recitation' class
Problem identification	Implicit overall, but explicit as students ask questions

Input data
   Format   Written material in textbook, lecture notes; oral questions from students
   Vehicle of delivery   Live and written
   Length   50-minute class – length of individual exchanges varies
   Level of authenticity
      Situational   By definition!
      Interactional   Teacher deeply engaged in interaction with students, material

Expected response

Format   Oral explanation of problem, accompanied by writing on blackboard

Type   Extended response

Response content
   Language   Vocabulary appropriate to the topic and audience
   Background knowledge   Chemistry, mathematics, N. American academic culture

Level of authenticity
   Situational   Instructor is building on past work students have done: highly contextualized
   Interactional   Deeply engaged

Interaction between input and response

Reactivity   Highly reciprocal: adaptation on both sides as necessary for mutual comprehension

Scope   Very broad: high degree of input must be processed

Directness   Fairly indirect: instructor must use own experience to help students prepare for exam

Assessment

Construct definition   Specific purpose language ability required in the TLU situation is quite complex: chemistry and mathematical terminology; pan-technical terminology; the use of Wh-questions, declaratives, tag questions, imperatives; the cohesive use of process markers; organization knowledge of process/problem solving structure and conversational turn taking; use of heuristic, ideational, and manipulative functions; idioms and cultural references; and the strategic use of an interactive style, involving and challenging students by asking questions; helping them think through the

Table 5.2 (*cont.*)

Characteristics	TLU situation
	problems by giving advice about alternative ways to solve them, using comprehension checks and discourse markers, imperatives. Background knowledge: ability to explain their topic in language first year undergraduates can understand, and some awareness of academic convention.
Criteria for correctness	Indigenous criteria: students are concerned with pronunciation, comprehensibility; cultural awareness; level of content knowledge; personality (friendly, helpful, responsive)
Rating procedures	Implicit: students assess the instructor informally by means of their questions, comments, classroom behavior, work habits, lateness, absences

implicit: students do evaluate their instructors, but there are no explicit guidelines for doing so (a formal evaluation of instructors by their students is conducted at the end of the semester at Julio's university, but does not figure in this particular data set); the LSP test developer must attempt to locate the criteria by which students (and others) judge the competence of their instructors. In our analysis here, we learned during the collection of secondary data that students value what they term 'good pronunciation,' a 'friendly, helpful' personality, and 'knowing his chemistry,' as outlined under assessment in Table 5.2. We will try to employ these implicit criteria in the development of explicit criteria for correctness in the test that will reflect real-world values so that we can make valid inferences about test taker language ability, as outlined in our construct definition.

Finally, we should note that, with regard to the characteristic of authenticity in the input data and expected response, the TLU situation is by definition authentic. It is not degree of authenticity that we are interested in here, but rather the significant features of the instructor's interaction with the context that make for authenticity, and which we want to incorporate into our test as far as possible. When we consider the characteristic of authenticity in our analysis of test methods, however, we will be interested in the degree to which the tasks are situationally and interactionally authentic.

Now that we have analyzed the characteristics of the TLU situation in our test development operation, we are ready to take a crucial step in the test development procedure, one that we have not yet discussed in this book: the development of test specifications.

Test specifications

The term **test specifications**, or specs for short, usually refers to a document that serves as a kind of blueprint for test developers and item writers, a reference point for validation researchers, and sometimes a source of information for score users. This document contains precise information about such topics as the purpose of the test, the ability to be measured, characteristics of the test takers, a description of the content of the test, scoring criteria, and sample test items or tasks. Specs are dynamic, changing due to feedback from members of the test development team, from teachers who may be consulted at various points, from subject specialist informants, and from experience gained in trialing, or piloting the test tasks (Lynch and Davidson 1994). The document results from an iterative process that ideally involves many people: test developers, teachers, specific purpose informants, learners, language users, and score users.

In Chapter 1, I said I would take a criterion-referenced approach to specific purpose test design, and that involves using principles of test specification developed in the context of criterion-referenced testing, particularly as suggested by Davidson and Lynch (1993). They propose a procedure, which they call a Criterion-referenced Language Test Development (CRLTD) Workshop, for developing criterion-referenced tests. CRLTD involves first identifying those persons who are concerned not only with the development of the test, but also with language instruction, instruction in the specific professional or academic field, and the use of the test results, who then meet as a planning group to discuss the testing situation, or **mandate**. Then this large group divides into smaller working groups of 3 to 5 persons, and each group produces a draft specifications document, or specs, in particular outlining the principles for developing test items or tasks. Next, the working groups exchange draft specs and attempt to write a test item or task to each other's specifications. The whole group then reconvenes to discuss how well each set of draft specs generated sample items or tasks and what revisions might be needed. Finally, the entire process is repeated. The result is a set of specs that should serve as a useful guide for item writers and test assemblers.

The procedure outlined above embodies a number of important aspects of good test development practice: (1) test development is best done in groups; (2) a wide variety of expertise is essential for the development of LSP tests; (3) specification writing is an iterative process; and (4) specs themselves evolve and change as more information, experience, and expertise are brought to bear on them.

Components of specifications

Below is a list of components for test specifications. There are many other possibilities for what specs should contain (see, for example, Bachman and Palmer,1996; Alderson *et al.* 1995; Lynch and Davidson 1994; Hughes 1989; B. J. Carroll 1980), but this list embodies the essentials for good LSP specifications.

1 *Describe the purpose(s) of the test:* These may include explicit decisions we want to make based upon our inferences about language ability or capacity for language use. These might include the certification of air traffic control trainees for service, medical practitioners for licensure, or prospective international teaching assistants for the classroom. This section should also outline any constraints on the test situation, such as limitations on equipment, personnel, time, etc., and any special considerations, such as the speed with which results must be reported, the type of information score users require, etc.

2 *Describe the TLU situation and list the TLU tasks:* This makes explicit the domain within which we want to make inferences about language ability or capacity for language use, as well as the language tasks to be carried out in that domain. This is an important part of the specs and involves a description of the place(s) the target communicative events take place in, the materials and equipment involved, the time and physical conditions, the participants, and the types of communicative tasks being carried out. This information is based on the characteristics of the rubric, input, expected response, relationship between input and response, and assessment, which I discussed in Chapter 3, and have illustrated in Table 5.2 above.

3 *Describe the characteristics of the language users / test takers:* Here the specs make explicit the nature of the population for which the test is being designed. We specify such information about the target population as age, nationality(ies), native language(s), other languages, and level and type of educational background. The purpose of this section of the specs is to describe both the kinds of people the test takers are expected to interact with linguistically and the test takers themselves.

4 *Define the construct to be measured:* This section makes explicit the nature of the ability we want to measure, including grammatical, textual, functional, and sociolinguistic knowledge, strategic competence, and background knowledge. This section of the specs should thus provide a description of the precise aspects of specific purpose language ability we are interested in making inferences about as a result of test performance, based on a detailed analysis, as illustrated in Table 5.1 above. As I discussed in Chapter 2, the construct definition is based on an analysis of specific purpose language ability in the TLU situation, and, more specifically, the construct to be measured takes into account constraints on the testing situation brought about by such factors as time, money, personnel, and the interests of the sponsors of the test.

5 *Describe the content of the test:* Here we specify the types of test tasks to be included, based on the analyses of the target language use situation and the construct definition. Features to be covered should include the following: organization of the test, including the number of tasks and a brief description of each, the time allocation for tasks, the length of text included in the task, and the specification of the test tasks (referring to the description of TLU situation and test task characteristics and construct definition as illustrated in Tables 5.1 and 5.2 above).

6 *Describe criteria for correctness:* This provides a description of how responses will be judged correct, or how they will be assigned to levels on a rating scale, and how a total score will be calculated. These criteria are derived from the analysis of assessment criteria in the TLU situation and with reference to the definition of the construct to be measured. They may be quite simple, in the case of multiple-choice or true/false tasks, for example, or more complex, as in the case of cloze or gap-filling tasks, where any acceptable response might be considered correct, or written essays and open-ended speaking tasks, where quite extensive

scoring guidelines might be required. In calculating a total score, decisions need to be made on whether each item/task will count equally or whether some will be given more weight than others, or, in the case of essays and speaking tasks, whether a single holistic score will be given, or whether task scores will be given and averaged.

7 *Provide samples of tasks/items the specs are intended to generate:* Each type of item or task that is specified should be demonstrated.

8 *Develop a plan for evaluating the qualities of good testing practice:* These include validity, reliability, situational and interactional authenticity, impact, and practicality. These qualities are ones that are common to all well-designed and well-executed tests, not just LSP tests, and they amount to a set of principles for ensuring that the tests we produce are as good as we can make them in terms of (1) the interpretations we make of test performance (validity), (2) the consistency and accuracy of the measurements (reliability), (3) the relationship between the target situation and the test tasks (situational authenticity), (4) the engagement of the test taker's communicative language ability (interactional authenticity), (5) the influence the test has on learners, teachers, and educational systems (impact), and (6) the constraints imposed by such factors as money, time, personnel, and educational policies (practicality). This section of the specs thus includes details of what evidence the test developers intend to provide to justify the validity of interpretations of test performance (i.e., that such interpretations are appropriate in terms of the construct, the relevance and coverage of test content, the relationship between performance on this test and performance on other measures, and the ability of performance on this test to predict useful aspects of performance on non-test tasks in the target domain); how they plan to demonstrate test reliability (i.e., that the scores are accurate, consistent measures of the intended construct); how the test input and expected response share task characteristics of the target language use situation, resulting in the situational authenticity of the task; how the authentic characteristics of the test task will engage an appropriate discourse domain in the test takers, bringing about the quality of interactional authenticity, or involvement with the test task; what impact, washback, or consequences, the test will likely have on test takers, educational programs, and society in general; and what human, technological and financial resources will be required to produce,

administer, score and report results of the test, all considerations leading to its practicality, or, where resources needed are greater than those available, to its impracticality.

In summary, the production of the test specifications document is an indispensable part of the test development process. It not only helps the test development team to focus on important considerations in test development, but also the process of producing the document requires the developers to be very precise about why they are producing the test and what it is they wish to measure. The finished document will serve as a guide for the construction of the test: it provides item writers with parameters for the production of items and tasks, and it provides scorers and raters with guidelines for their work. The specifications document is also a source of information for test users on the objective of the test and the limitations on what it measures and interpretations of test performance that may appropriately be made.

An essential and yet the most difficult aspect of producing test specifications is making the leap from the analysis of the target language use tasks to the specification of test tasks. Translating the TLU task characteristics into LSP test tasks requires a large amount of judgement and the weighing of alternatives, often making compromises based on practical considerations related to budgetary and time constraints. It is not too much to say that this is the essence of the art of LSP testing, and this book cannot hope to provide great insights into the intricacies of the language tester's art. Such insights come only with experience and the thoughtful evaluation of existing tests, and, in Chapters 6 and 7, we will consider a number of examples of LSP test tasks and hope to gain some understanding of the craft of good LSP task development.

As Bachman and Palmer (1996) point out, 'not all tasks will be appropriate for use as a basis for development of test tasks' (p. 106), because they may not meet all the criteria for good testing practice, as I described above. For example, with regard to reliability, it may be that a TLU task allows for too many sources of inconsistency to be rated reliably in a testing situation. Some tasks may be so highly field specific that raters cannot be trained to assess language ability reliably in such context-embedded performances. In the case of *validity* considerations, some TLU tasks may be inappropriate sources of information for the types of inferences we wish to make about the test takers' language ability. For example, one TLU task for tour operators may involve talking with airline representatives about flight schedules, but such a narrowly focussed task might tell us very little about the sociolinguistic knowledge of prospective tour guides. In assessing the impact of a TLU task, it may be that the task is so overly specific or insignificant as to have a disproportionate impact on pedagogy or social values. For example, medical personnel might occasionally find themselves giving directions for locating a particular pharmacy, but to include such a task on a test of medical English ability might give disproportionate importance to this aspect of language use. As a last example, in terms of practicality, a TLU task may require more equipment, personnel or time than is reasonably available in the test situation. In the case of air traffic control training, simulating the computer equipment involved in the TLU situation in a test situation would probably make the cost of the test prohibitive.

I should point out that in my discussion of the qualities of good language testing practice, I have drawn heavily on the concept of the qualities of test usefulness in Bachman and Palmer (1996). They elaborate this concept as the basis for the whole process of test development and use and suggest that the qualities function as a metric by which tests and the test development process can be evaluated. In this book, I have referred to the qualities of good language testing practice to distinguish my list from that of Bachman and Palmer since I have focussed the qualities a bit differently so as to make them more relevant to LSP testing. Specifically, Bachman and Palmer consider authenticity and interactiveness to be separate qualities of usefulness, while I have proposed a single quality of authenticity, with two aspects, situational and interactional authenticity. I think that in LSP testing, it makes sense to think of authenticity as a dichotomous concept (as outlined in Bachman 1991, in fact) because, following Widdowson, I discussed authenticity in Chapter 1 not as a property of LSP texts or tasks, but as residing in language users as they interact with texts and tasks. In LSP testing there is no authenticity without both the TLU situational features and the interaction of the language user's knowledge with the LSP task. In their book, Bachman and Palmer maintain that both authenticity and interactiveness are necessary qualities of test usefulness, and I wish in this book to emphasize even more clearly the two interrelated faces of this central concept in specific purpose language testing.

Thus, in making the transition from the analysis of the target language use tasks to test tasks, we must bear in mind the qualities of test usefulness and often either adapt TLU tasks to the test situation, or eliminate some of them altogether. Below is an illustration of a specifications document for a measure of specific purpose language ability for prospective chemistry teaching assistants based on the example in the previous section.

1 *The purpose(s) of the test*

The test will be part of an assessment and training program for international candidates who have been offered instructional positions at a large US university. The test will be used to determine whether candidates have an adequate level of English ability to handle classroom teaching and/or laboratory supervision assignments in their own field of study. The test should also provide some diagnostic information for the training program for those candidates whose English ability is not considered adequate for classroom or laboratory responsibilities.

Constraints on the testing situation: The entire test should not last more than 10 minutes. Candidates' performance must be rated quickly, so that departments will know whether they can employ the candidates immediately in their programs, or whether they will require remedial English classes. The test situation will be limited to classroom teaching, as it is considered too difficult to simulate laboratory settings in a number of disciplines. Each performance will be videotaped both to provide a record and so the candidate can review the performance.

2 *The TLU situation and TLU tasks*

Candidates will be instructors in a number of disciplines in the university, including mathematics, veterinary physiology, computer science, architecture, statistics, electrical and mechanical engineering, biochemistry, economics, physics, geology, chemistry, and English. They will interact with US undergraduates, typically first year students, in both lecture/recitation classes of 15–30, and one-on-one in tutorials and office hour visits. They also supervise students in various laboratory sessions, but a decision was made early on not to include this context in the test.

Characteristics of the TLU situation:

Instructor and students meet in a typical university class-room, containing a blackboard, an overhead projector and screen, instructor's table, student desks. Room is comfortable, well-lit, quiet. Classes meet in the daytime and evenings, for 50 minutes, and currently are well into the term. Most of these students are not majoring in chemistry and so have varying degrees of knowledge and motivation.

Characteristics of TLU tasks:

Varied: reviewing reading and problems assigned to students by their professor, giving instructions, offering advice about the best way to carry out an assignment, defining and explaining concepts, summarizing, providing concrete examples, eliciting discussion from students, eliciting and answering questions. In terms of assessment, the undergraduate students are concerned with their instructors' pronunciation, comprehensibility, cultural awareness, level of content knowledge, and personality (friendly, helpful, responsive).

3 *Characteristics of the test takers*

Both men and women, typically aged from mid-twenties to mid-thirties. Come from a variety of national, linguistic, and ethnic backgrounds in Europe, Asia, Africa, and Latin America. Usually well qualified in their respective fields of study, the reason they were offered instructorships. Varying levels of communicative English ability, teaching experience, and experience with US academic and social culture, though the majority are newly arrived in the US.

4 *Definition of the construct to be measured*

Grammatical knowledge:

Phonology: pronunciation must be 'comprehensible' to US undergraduates not used to interacting with non-native speakers; rate of speech and length pauses should be 'fluent'; key terms, rhythm, intonation, and stress.

Morphology/syntax: production and comprehension of Wh- and yes/no questions, statements; use of relative clauses, conditionals, imperatives, negatives; tense and aspect markers, tag questions.

Vocabulary: field specific chemistry, mathematics, and pan-technical terminology.

Textual knowledge:

Rhetorical organization: descriptions of processes, relationships, mechanisms; instructions, definitions, summaries, problem solving; cohesive markers of processes.

Functional knowledge:

Heuristic, manipulative, and ideational functions.

Sociolinguistic knowledge:

Dialect: Spanish/English Interlanguage production; standard midwest US comprehension.

Register: chemistry, general academic, social.

US classroom idioms, cultural references, figures of speech: some receptive knowledge of US classroom idiom (e.g., *pop quiz, office hours, grading on 'the curve'*).

Background knowledge:

Although no separate score will be given for specific purpose background knowledge, raters will be aware that it is part of the construct of specific purpose language knowledge. In performing the test tasks, the test takers should display some ability to explain their topic in language first year undergraduates can understand, and some awareness of academic convention.

5 *Content of the test*

Organization of the test:

Number of tasks: two.
Description of tasks: task 1 will be brief explanation of a topic in a textbook in the test taker's major field; task 2 will be a brief question/answer session with students on points raised in the explanation.

Time allocation:

Five minutes for task 1; 3 minutes for task 2.

Length of input data:

Varies, 2–6 pages.

6   *Scoring criteria*

   1 Criteria for correctness: language ability will be rated on a
     scale of 0–3 on grammar, pronunciation, fluency, and
     comprehensibility; cultural ability will be rated on a 0–3
     scale for familiarity with cultural code, appropriate non-
     verbal behavior, and rapport with class; communication
     skills will be rated on a 0–3 scale for development of ex-
     planation, clarity, use of supporting evidence, eye contact,
     use of blackboard, and teacher presence; interaction with
     students will be rated on a 0–3 scale for basic listening
     ability and question handling and responding; and overall
     impression will be rated on a 0–9 scale.

   2 Scoring procedures: each task will be scored indepen-
     dently by two raters, using the appropriate scales and the
     two ratings averaged. If the two raters' scores are more
     than 1 point apart, the tape will be scored by a third rater,
     and the two closest total scores averaged for the final test
     score.

7   *Samples of topics*

   Mathematics: even and odd functions in Fleming, pp. 27–28.
   Physiology: events of the cardiac cycle in Lab Manual,
   pp. 103–109.
   Architecture: visual properties of form in Ching, pp. 50–55.
   Economics: supply, demand, and market equilibrium in
   Fleishner, pp. 80–83.

8   *Plan for evaluating the qualities of good testing practice: re-*
    liability, validity, authenticity, impact, and practicality

   1 Reliability: intra-rater and interrater reliability studies;
     periodic rater 'refresher' training sessions.

   2 Validity: test takers' self-assessment of language ability
     both before and after training program and before and
     after teaching assignment; students' and supervisors' as-
     sessment of instructors' language abilities, by means of
     questionnaire; test takers rate their degree of involvement
     in terms of field specific knowledge and language knowl-
     edge required in the test.

   3 Situational authenticity: evaluate the situational authen-
     ticity of the test by means of a questionnaire given to test
     takers and supervisory personnel, covering the rubric,
     input, and expected response, asking their views on how

well the test tasks reflect what teaching assistants have to do in actual classrooms.

4 Interactional authenticity: give test takers a questionnaire asking them to judge the extent to which they felt as if they were actually engaged in real teaching as they carried out the test tasks.

5 Impact/Consequences: interview supervisory personnel and training program instructors about how test results affect the selection and training processes.

6 Practicality: human resources: Director, employed by Graduate College, raters paid by English Department and Graduate College; material resources: office space and classrooms available, video recording equipment available from Media Resources. Time is main constraint: candidates must be tested within a few days of their arrival on campus and scores sent to their departments very soon after testing.

In producing this specifications document, I have drawn on many elements of the analysis of the TLU situation as recorded in Tables 5.1 and 5.2 above. Note that the proposed test will have a dual purpose of evaluating the candidates' level of English ability for teaching in their major field and also of offering some diagnostic information for the training program. Constraints on the test include a rather short testing time, quick score turnaround time, an emphasis on classroom teaching, and videotaping of the performance. Each of these constraints affects in some way the link between the characteristics of tasks in the TLU situation and those in the test. Although lab supervision was eliminated as a possible test context, mainly for logistical reasons, many of the characteristics of TLU tasks, including giving instructions, offering advice, and answering questions, are relevant to the lab situation. This highlights a benefit of using the framework of task characteristics to analyze TLU tasks and translate them into test tasks: performance on the test may be generalizable to the lab supervision context as well as to the recitation class context. Reference to the task characteristics will help in making the link between the two teaching situations.

The construct includes a variety of types of language knowledge, particularly the ability to explain technical information in language that first year students will be able to follow, and field specific background knowledge in the candidate's major field, as well as some knowledge of US academic convention. The test has been designed to consist of two parts, a short explanation of a topic in the candidate's major field and a brief question and answer session with students. The scoring criteria include scales for language ability, cultural ability, communication skills, and interaction with students. These criteria have been derived from the analysis of the TLU situation, which was itself conducted by means of a questionnaire. It was found that first year undergraduate students were concerned with their instructor's pronunciation and comprehensibility, awareness of US academic cultural conventions, their level of content knowledge, and their personality (friendly, helpful, responsive to questions). Finally, the plan for evaluating the qualities of good testing practice includes methods for investigating all six of the qualities of reliability, validity, situational and interactional authenticity, impact, and practicality. Other features of the analysis will influence the operationalization phase of the LSP test development process, which I will discuss in Chapter 8.

Analysis of test task characteristics

As a way of summarizing the discussion, and for purposes of comparison, let us now look at the framework for analyzing the TLU situation alongside the test task characteristics that the specifications outline, in Table 5.3.

The middle column shows the characteristics of tasks in the target language use situation from Tables 5.1 and 5.2, while the right-hand column contains the test task characteristics that we might propose as a result of our analysis of the target situation, as outlined in the specifications document. We can see that the TLU situation is quite complex, and that the test method characteristics are less so, but fairly complicated nevertheless. With regard to several of the characteristics, there is a high degree of similarity between the TLU situation and test methods; note, for example, the procedure for response, setting, participants, language, norms of interaction, input data format, expected response format and type, scope, and degree of directness. On the other hand, there are a number of characteristics where the correspondence between the TLU situation and the test methods is less close, often reflecting the more focussed nature of the testing procedure: distinctions between tasks are quite sharp in the test, and much less so in the TLU situation; the test takes about 10

Table 5.3. *Comparison of task characteristics of the TLU situation and test (chemistry class)*

Characteristics	TLU situation	Test tasks
Rubric		
Objective	Implicit in situation: to review homework problems prior to exam	Explicit: to assess English oral ability in context of chemistry instruction
Procedures for responding	Implicit: interact orally and on blackboard with students in explaining homework problems	Explicit: explain a procedure for solving an equation, answer questions from students
Structure		
Number of tasks	Varies; problems raised by students	Two: explain procedure, answer questions (number of questions varies somewhat)
Relative importance	Varies; instructor advises students on what's important for exam	Question handling is given slightly more importance by raters
Task distinctions	Can be blurred – one problem may blend into another similar one; student questions can come at any time	Quite distinct – a timer bell rings when the question/ answer session is to begin
Time allotment	50-minute class	2-minute preparation, 5-minute explanation, 3-minute question session
Evaluation		
Criteria	Implicit	Explicit: overall comprehensibility; cultural ability; communication skills (organization and presentation); interaction with students; overall impression
Procedures	Informal	Two raters use a standard form to score performance independently; third rater in cases of disagreement; all categories scored on a scale of 0–3, except the last, scored on a scale of 0–9

Table 5.3 (*cont.*)

Characteristics	TLU situation	Test tasks
Input		
Prompt		
Features of context		
Setting	Typical chemistry classroom: instructor behind long teacher table, raised on platform, blackboard, OHP, textbook; students in desks, have lecture notes, textbook; class is in middle of term, just before an exam	Typical classroom: teacher table, blackboard, OHP; student desks; test taker told to imagine class is in middle of term, not beginning
Participants	25 undergraduate students, most not chemistry majors, widely varying educational preparation, majority from Iowa, ethnically homogeneous, roughly equal number males and females; they are familiar to instructor	3–4 undergraduate students unfamiliar to test taker, may not be taking chemistry, same educational and ethnic make up as those in TLU situation; as noted above, room also has testing personnel, video technician
Purpose	Review homework problems, answer questions in preparation for exam	Assessment of English ability for teaching chemistry
Form/Content	Interactive question/answer format; chemistry problems assigned as homework; reaction equations	Lecture format; reaction equations; question/answer format at end of lecture
Tone	Friendly, but businesslike	Serious, formal
Language	Instructor uses Spanish/English interlanguage; students use standard midwest US English; some technical register	Same as TLU situation
Norms	Teacher/student interaction, elements of casual conversation	Same as TLU situation, though less casual
Genre	Question/answer session	Lecture, question/answer session
Problem identification	Implicit overall but explicit as students ask questions	Explicit: explain topic clearly in language students can understand; answer questions

Input data		
Format	Written material in textbook, lecture notes; oral questions from students	Written materia textbook; oral q from students
Vehicle of delivery	Live and written	Live and written
Length	50-minute class – length of individual exchanges varies	Written material: 2–5 pages; oral questions: 3 minutes
Level of authenticity		
Situational	By definition!	Shares many features of TLU situation: high situational authenticity
Interactional	Teacher deeply engaged in interaction with students, material	Test taker somewhat engaged in interaction with students, material: moderate interactional authenticity
Expected response		
Format	Oral explanation of problem, accompanied by writing on blackboard	Oral explanation, some writing on blackboard
Type	Extended response	Extended response
Response content		
Language	Vocabulary appropriate to the topic and audience	As in TLU situation
Background knowledge	Chemistry, mathematics, N. American academic culture	As in TLU situation
Level of authenticity		
Situational	Instructor is building on past work students have done: highly contextualized	Expected response shares many features of TLU situation
Interactional	Deeply engaged	Test taker moderately engaged in interaction with situation and students, but not building on past work
Interaction between input and response		
Reactivity	Highly reciprocal: adaptation on both sides as necessary for mutual comprehension	Moderately reciprocal: test taker can adapt message as necessary, student questioners might not
Scope	Very broad: high degree of input must be processed	Same as TLU situation

Table 5.3 (*cont.*)

Characteristics	TLU situation	Test tasks
Directness	Fairly indirect: instructor must use own experience to help students prepare for exam	Fairly indirect: test taker must employ background knowledge to prepare explanation, answer questions

Assessment

Construct definition	Specific purpose language ability required in the TLU situation is quite complex: chemistry and mathematical terminology; pan-technical terminology; the use of Wh-questions, declaratives, tag questions, imperatives; the cohesive use of process markers; organization knowledge of process/problem solving structure and conversational turn taking; use of heuristic, ideational, manipulative functions; idioms and cultural references; and the strategic use of an interactive style, involving and challenging students by asking questions; helping them think through the problems by giving advice about alternative ways to solve them, using comprehension checks and discourse markers, imperatives. Background knowledge: ability to explain their topic in language first year undergraduates can understand, and some awareness of academic convention.	Overall language comprehensibility: pronunciation, grammar, fluency; cultural ability: familiarity with cultural code, appropriate non-verbal behavior, rapport with class; communication skills: development of explanation, clarity of expression, use of supporting evidence, eye contact, use of chalkboard, teacher presence; interaction with students: basic listening ability, question handling and responding; overall impression.

Criteria for correctness	Indigenous criteria: students are concerned with pronunciation, comprehensibility; cultural awareness; level of content knowledge; personality (friendly, helpful, responsive)	Language: 0 = unintelligible 1 = errors interfere 2 = errors do not interfere 3 = completely comprehensible Cultural ability: 3 = aware of norms of interaction, politeness, gesture, formality Communication skills: 3 = organization, behavior displays qualities of 'good' teacher Interaction with students: 3 = comprehends questions easily, responds appropriately
Rating procedures	Implicit: students assess the instructor informally by means of their questions, comments, classroom behavior, work habits, lateness, absences	Two raters rate the performance 'live'; if raters disagree, third rater views videotape; ratings averaged

minutes, while the class is 50 minutes; the objective of the two communicative events is clearly different – instruction versus assessment; the tone of the interaction is more serious in the test situation; and the genre elicited by the test method is a prepared lecture, rather than an on-line question/answer session as in the TLU situation. Some of these characteristics are implicit in the target situation and explicit in the test, particularly those of the rubric and the statement of the problem.

Perhaps the most serious differences, though, are in characteristics relating to situational and interactional authenticity: while the input data in the test is very similar (and in fact may be identical) to that of the TLU situation, the level of interaction both with it and with the students is likely to be quite different, thus affecting our interpretation of the authenticity of the test performance. It is almost certainly the case that the instructor in the actual classroom is much more engaged in the communicative event, in the dynamic construction of a context in interaction with the students and the material than is the test taker in the test situation. The test method characteristics can probably never entirely match those of the TLU situation, since, as we have noted on a number of occasions in this book, an LSP test is a very focussed language use situation, designed to elicit language performances under controlled conditions from which inferences can be made about the test takers' specific purpose language ability. Thus, we must remind ourselves that authenticity and interactiveness are matters of degree in LSP testing, and that any given task may be relatively more or less authentic and interactive than another. All we can reasonably attempt is to make the correspondences between the TLU situation and the test tasks as close as we can by systematically analyzing the characteristics of tasks in the TLU situation and incorporating them into our test. It is my belief that this procedure will allow for more valid interpretations of performance than would otherwise be the case, and make it easier for us to demonstrate that validity more clearly.

Summary and conclusion

In this chapter I have considered techniques for analyzing target language use situations in terms of task characteristics and for translating these into test tasks. I attempted to demonstrate how the principles of grounded ethnography, context-based research, and subject specialist informant procedures can be used to identify relevant target situation tasks. I then used language and task characteristics frameworks to relate the target situation characteristics to the test task characteristics in an example case. It is clear from this discussion that the frameworks do not provide us with an automatic, idiot proof procedure for translating target characteristics into test tasks. The procedures I have outlined in this chapter still require the experienced judgement of the test developer, the artful, creative mind of the applied linguist, for successful development of a specific purpose language test. What the techniques and frameworks do provide is a means of controlling the test development process, of keeping track of the characteristics of target situations that are relevant to test task development. The techniques will be useful only to the extent that those employing them have a clear understanding of the nature of communicative language ability and of the principles of good testing practice.

Looking back at the topics and tests I have considered so far in this book, we can outline a number of practical principles for the development of field specific tests.

- It is essential that field specific test developers understand the target language use situation from the perspective of language users in that domain. To this end, I discussed grounded ethnography as a general approach to describing and understanding the TLU situation. It involves obtaining commentary from participants in the language use situation on recorded – usually videotapes, but also audiotapes and written documents – examples of their language use. This commentary forms the basis for understanding what in the performance was interesting, noteworthy, unusual, or problematic from the point of view of the participants; in other words, how they themselves interpreted the communicative event.
- I also discussed the use of subject specialist informant techniques as a way of obtaining more information about the TLU situation, this time from the perspective of experts in the field who were not participants in the communicative event being studied but who can provide insights into understanding and interpreting it that are perhaps not available to the participants themselves. For example, in seeking to understand classroom interaction between an international teaching assistant and his or her students, experienced instructors, serving as subject specialist informants, can offer commentary on the quality of the teaching performance not necessarily obvious to either the teaching assistant or his or her students.
- I developed a framework for analyzing field specific TLU and test situations and used it to examine a number of examples of test tasks. We saw that tasks vary in specificity in terms of the rubric, providing information about how to proceed with the task, its structure and duration, and what it is measuring; the input, including the prompt, which provides information about the problem to be addressed and the context in which the task takes place, and the input data, authentic aural and/or visual material which is to be processed in performing the test task; the expected response, which may vary in field specific characteristics in much the same ways as the input can; the interaction between the input and the expected response, which may vary in reactivity, directness, and scope; and assessment, in which indigenous assessment criteria in the TLU

situation are used to guide the development of scoring criteria in the testing situation.

- A key stage in making the transition from the TLU situation to test tasks is the production of test specifications, a document that serves as a blueprint for the test. The specifications, or specs, describe the general design features of the test, the construct, the types of tasks that it will include, scoring criteria, sample items or tasks, and a plan for evaluating the qualities of good testing practice. In fact, it is these qualities that often constrain the smooth transfer from TLU situation to test task: more often than not, TLU tasks will require some modification for use in a field specific language test.

In the next two chapters, I will use the language and task frameworks to analyze a number of existing LSP tests in order to see how the principles and procedures I have outlined so far in this book have been carried out in practice by test developers.

....

CHAPTER SIX

Specific purpose tests of listening and speaking

Introduction

In this and the next chapter, we will take a close look at a number of LSP tests to see both how they reflect the qualities of LSP tests that I have outlined in the book, and how they exemplify various approaches to the art of LSP testing. In this chapter, we will examine tests of listening and speaking, while in Chapter 7, we will turn our attention to tests of reading and writing. We will begin with an analysis of one prominent LSP test, the *Occupational English Test*, employing the framework for analyzing task characteristics developed in earlier chapters. The purpose of this analysis is to demonstrate how the framework can be used in a detailed and systematic analysis of an LSP test to closely examine its specific purpose characteristics. We will then take a slightly less detailed look at a number of other tests of listening and speaking in a variety of LSP contexts: language for academic and vocational purposes, teaching, international business, international tourism, and air traffic control. In the discussion I will use the framework characteristics as a guide, but will not conduct a complete and thorough analysis. The purpose is to survey a number of approaches to LSP testing to see how they exemplify various features of LSP testing practice that I have outlined in this book. These particular tests were selected for inclusion here because they illustrate a variety of LSP assessment techniques and illustrate the qualities of good testing practice. It is not my intent to critique the exemplar tests, since we generally will not be looking at entire tests or even entire sub-tests. In addition, we will be looking only at specimen or practice materials, not actual test tasks. However, in considering the ways in which various teams of testers have tackled the problems of LSP test development, I hope to bring us to an appreciation of the art of LSP testing in all its variety and creativity.

Sample analysis of test task characteristics

The framework for analyzing tasks in specific purpose target language use situations and LSP tests, which I developed in Chapters 2 and 3, contains the features of the construct of specific purpose language ability, as I discussed in Chapter 2 (Table 2.2), including language knowledge, strategic competence, and background knowledge, and the task characteristics of the rubric, input, expected response, relationship between input and response, and assessment. However, when using the framework to analyze an already existing LSP test, since we do not have access to the actual target language use situation, some of the aspects of the analysis, including those of specific purpose language and indigenous assessment criteria, cannot be determined in any detail. We have to depend on published accounts of the analysis of the TLU situation, and may be able to fill in some of the characteristics of language and tasks, but this information will remain sketchy at best. We can, for example, try to provide an analysis of specific purpose language ability or of indigenous assessment criteria by referring to published information about the test development process, but because this process was of course not based on the framework proposed in this book, the account here will necessarily be hypothetical. Nevertheless, it is important to undertake such an analysis since it will allow us to see how the framework can assist in determining the relevance of the construct to be measured to the TLU situation and the degree of authenticity of tasks in a specific purpose test.

The Occupational English Test (OET)

To demonstrate the use of the framework to carry out a detailed analysis of an LSP test, I will consider a well-known specific purpose test, the *Occupational English Test* (*OET*), originally administered by the National Office for Overseas Skills Recognition of the Australian government Department of Employment, Education and Training. In 1991 administrative responsibility for the *OET* was transferred to the Language Testing Research Centre of the National Language and Literacy Institute of Australia (NLLIA), at the University of Melbourne (McNamara 1990a, 1996). The *OET* was developed to assess the English language ability of immigrant health professionals seeking admission to Australian training and licensure examinations, and is available throughout Australia and at some 50 Australian embassies and consulates overseas. Eleven medical professions are represented in the various forms of the test: dentists, dieticians, nurses, occupational therapists, pharmacists, physicians, physiotherapists, podiatrists, radiographers, speech pathologists, and veterinarians. In 1994, of approximately 1200 candidates, about one-third were physicians, the largest single group. The test consists of four components: profession specific writing and speaking sub-tests, and reading and listening sub-tests, both of which are non-profession specific. In the speaking component, which is of particular interest to us in this chapter, test takers are first interviewed informally for about a minute, during which time the interlocutor asks about the candidate's professional background and future plans. This warm-up interview is not assessed; its purpose is 'to allow the test taker to get used to the interlocutor and to establish him/herself as a person with professional competence in the eyes of the interlocutor' (McNamara 1990a: 175–176). Next, the test taker participates in two roleplays, each lasting about five minutes, with the interlocutor, who takes the role of a patient or client, or the relative of a patient or client, while the test taker assumes his or her professional role (physiotherapist in the example below). During the administration of the speaking sub-test, the test taker (candidate) and the interlocutor (roleplayer) are each given a card containing a prompt for the roleplay, as shown in Extract 6.1.

The test taker's performance is assessed by means of a rating scale, as shown in Figure 6.1. The assessment is made by the interlocutor during the roleplay, if the interlocutor is a trained assessor (as is the case in most administrations in Australia). In cases where the interlocutor is not trained to assess the performance (often overseas), the assessment is made after the test from audio cassette recordings. The raters are instructed to consider the middle of the scales as

Extract 6.1

CANDIDATE'S CARD

SETTING: Hospital clinic.

PATIENT: An elderly person who is recovering from a stroke (CVA). The patient is making slow progress in learning to walk again.

TASK: Talk to the patient about the following pieces of equipment
- a wheelchair
- a walking frame
- a walking stick

Explain the advantages and disadvantages of each one. You would like the patient to be as independent in his or her movements as possible. You feel the frame is not suitable. You want the patient to have a stick. You do not want the patient to have a wheelchair at this stage.

ROLEPLAYER'S CARD

SETTING: Hospital clinic.

PATIENT: You are an elderly person who is recovering from a stroke. You feel you are making painfully slow progress, and don't really expect to be able to walk again.
You feel you should be allowed to have a wheelchair.

TASK: Ask the physiotherapist when you will be given a wheelchair. Insist on your need for this equipment. Explain that you feel that the painful exercises you are doing at the moment are pointless, and that you are pessimistic about your chances of making real progress.
Be difficult!

McNamara (1996: 108)

representing the minimum proficiency required to communicate in the professional domain. The scale ranges from 1, representing the lowest level of proficiency, to 6, representing native or near-native proficiency. The total score on the test task consists of the score given for overall communicative effectiveness plus the average score for the other categories combined. So, if a candidate is given a 5 for overall

Figure 6.1 *OET* speaking sub-test rating scale

```
OVERALL COMMUNICATIVE EFFECTIVENESS

    Near-native flexibility and range  _|_|_| |_|_|_  Limited

INTELLIGIBILITY

                      Intelligible  _|_|_| |_|_|_  Unintelligible

FLUENCY

                             Even  _|_|_| |_|_|_  Uneven

COMPREHENSION

                         Complete  _|_|_| |_|_|_  Incomplete

APPROPRIATENESS OF LANGUAGE

                      Appropriate  _|_|_| |_|_|_  Inappropriate

RESOURCES OF GRAMMAR AND EXPRESSION

                    Rich, flexible  _|_|_| |_|_|_  Limited
```

McNamara (1996: 113)

communicative effectiveness, and an average of 4.8 for the other categories (e.g., $4 + 6 + 5 + 5 + 4 = 24/5 = 4.8$), he or she would receive a total score of 9.8.

Now let us use the frameworks I developed in Chapters 2 and 3 for specific purpose language ability and LSP test task characteristics to examine the LSP properties of the *OET*. I will begin with a discussion of the specific purpose language ability that is assessed in the *OET*, based on an analysis of the test input and scoring scale described above.

Characteristics of specific purpose language ability in the OET

If we examine the input prompt in Extract 6.1 and the scoring grid in Figure 6.1 using the framework of specific purpose language ability, we can get an idea of the features of language knowledge, strategic competence, and background knowledge required for performance on the *OET*. Table 6.1 shows the results of such an analysis.

We can see that this test has the potential for eliciting quite a rich language performance in terms of specific purpose language ability.

Table 6.1. *Characteristics of specific purpose language ability* (OET)

Categories	Characteristics
Language knowledge	
Grammatical knowledge	
Vocabulary	Knowledge of lexis: resources of expression
Morphology/Syntax	Knowledge of forms: resources of grammar
Phonology	Accent: intelligibility
Textual knowledge	
Rhetorical organization	Not specified
Cohesion	Not specified
Functional knowledge	Explicit: ideational and heuristic (explain advantages and disadvantages); implicit: manipulative (recommend, advise, argue)
Sociolinguistic knowledge	
Dialect/Variety	Implicit: understand Australian English
Register	Language a layperson can understand: appropriateness of language
Idioms, Cultural references, figures of speech	Interlocutor may employ such features: appropriateness of language
Strategic competence	Must engage a physical therapy discourse domain, employing oral production and comprehension skills in interacting with client
Background knowledge	Must be familiar with ambulatory equipment and its uses, therapeutic exercises and their functions

Only textual knowledge is not included in either the input or the scoring criteria. Grammatical knowledge is fairly traditionally represented in the scoring grid, with intelligibility referring to accent or pronunciation, and resources of grammar and expression referring to knowledge of morphology, syntax, and vocabulary forms (McNamara 1996). Functional knowledge is explicitly called for in the prompt card, where the test taker is instructed to talk to the patient about the advantages and disadvantages of the three pieces of equipment: this task thus combines ideational and heuristic functions. Moreover, there is implicit in the interaction a requirement for the manipulative function in that the test taker must recommend a particular piece of equipment and persuade the patient to accept it. It is also implicit in the task that standard Australian English is the dialect that must be comprehended by the test taker, including cultural references, idioms, and figures of speech, and that the candidate should produce language that a person unfamiliar with medical terminology could understand. For example, it was felt by the informants consulted by the test developers that a problem for overseas trained medical professionals was a lack of 'ordinary colloquial language to refer for example to bowel movements or of not recognizing that for the patient "stomach" might mean a quite different and far more extensive anatomical area than an anatomy textbook might suggest' (McNamara 1996: 192). This notion is intended to be captured in the evaluation category appropriateness of language.

The construct of specific purpose language ability also includes appropriate background knowledge to accomplish the test task, although this knowledge is not assessed directly in the *OET*. It is clear that the test takers will have to know something about wheelchairs, walking frames, and sticks in order to talk to the patient about their relative advantages and disadvantages in the particular case at hand. Furthermore, the candidates will need to communicate information about various forms of therapeutic physical exercises in order to convince the patient that they are not as pointless as he or she apparently thinks. Finally, the test taker must use strategic competence to engage an appropriate physical therapy discourse domain to mediate between his or her language knowledge and background knowledge in executing a complex performance, interacting with the interlocutor on-line to achieve a communicative goal, or recommending a particular line of treatment and convincing the client to follow it.

The reader will have noticed a mismatch between the characteristics of specific purpose language ability that may be elicited during the performance of the test task and the *OET* scoring grid shown in Figure 6.1, above. This has been something of a problem with the *OET*, and I will discuss it in more detail under the heading of assessment in the next section.

Task characteristics of the OET

We will begin the analysis of tasks in the *OET* with the characteristics of the rubric as shown in Table 6.2.

Table 6.2. *Characteristics of the rubric (OET)*

Characteristics	
Objective	To demonstrate ability to speak in context of professional interaction
Procedures for responding	Speak to interlocutor, interaction will be audiotaped
Structure	
Number of tasks	Three: short 'warm-up' interview, two roleplays
Relative importance	Warm-up not assessed, roleplays of equal importance
Distinction between tasks	Quite clearly distinct
Time allotment	1-minute warm-up, 4–5 minutes for each roleplay
Evaluation	
Criteria	Unclear how much information test takers are given
Procedures	Test takers see the interlocutor/assessor filling in the rating grid after each roleplay but are not otherwise given information about the procedure

Rubric

The rubric of the *OET* speaking sub-test is provided both in sample materials given to the candidates before the test and in oral instructions given by the interlocutor at the time of the test. The interlocutors and raters are most often trained and experienced ESL teachers. Medical professionals are not used at any stage of test administration, and candidates are told explicitly that the *OET* is a test of speaking, not a test of professional knowledge. The interlocutor is instructed to make every effort to see that the test taker understands everything on the prompt card. Note that the time allotted for each roleplay is four or five minutes, so a fairly substantial speech sample can be collected. The two roleplays are quite distinct and unrelated. For example, in addition to the roleplay described above, a test taker might participate in one set in a community health center, talking to the parent of a nine-year-old asthmatic boy. Therefore, the test taker must shift contexts fairly rapidly – the candidate is given about a minute to study the second roleplay, during which time the assessor is making a preliminary judgement about the performance on the first. It is unclear from the discussion of the testing procedure discussed by McNamara (1990a, 1996) how much information the candidates are given about the evaluation criteria, but almost certainly they are aware that they will be evaluated on overall communicative effectiveness, intelligibility, fluency, comprehension, appropriateness of language, and resources of grammar and expression. The evaluation criteria are quite linguistically oriented, and, as we will see in the discussion of assessment below, this has in fact led to some dissatisfaction.

The field specific test task characteristics of the input, expected response, interaction between input and response, and assessment are shown in Table 6.3.

Input

In this example, we can see that the specific purpose characteristics are fairly well defined: the characteristics of the LSP context in the prompt and input data provide a number of contextualization cues, both on the test taker's prompt card and in the oral input from the interlocutor. As for the LSP context, a clinical setting is specified and the participants are identified. The purpose, form, and content of the interaction are fairly explicit, although the fact that the test taker will have to persuade the difficult patient to use a walking stick instead of the wheelchair he or she wants becomes clear to the test taker only as the interaction progresses: the patient asks when (not if!) a wheelchair will be given to him or her, insists on the need for a wheelchair, and explains his or her pessimism about the exercise program and ever being able to walk again. Although the tone is not specified for the test taker, it certainly is for the roleplayer, and the test taker should soon realize that the patient is being difficult. The identification of the problem in the interaction is fairly well specified: Talk to the patient about . . . Explain the advantages and disadvantages . . . You want . . . You do not want . . . However, the key problem, requiring the test taker to argue for the use of the stick rather than the wheelchair, is developed implicitly in the interaction itself.

The input data is in the form of the oral input from the roleplayer, since the test taker has access only to his or her own prompt card. As indicated in Table 6.3, the interactional authenticity of this input is only moderately high, since the roleplayer is not a trained **simulated**

Table 6.3. *Specific purpose test task characteristics (OET)*

	Candidate's card	Roleplayer's card
Characteristics of the input		
Prompt		
LSP context		
Setting	Hospital clinic	Hospital clinic
Participants	Physiotherapist	Elderly stroke patient
Purposes	Explicit: explain advantages and disadvantages of equipment; implicit: persuade patient to use stick	Explicit: insist on need for wheelchair, express pessimism about making progress
Form/Content	Explain advantages and disadvantages of various ambulatory equipment; explain reasons for recommending stick	Ask when wheelchair will be given; insist on need; express pessimism about walking again
Tone	Implicit: professional manner	Be difficult!
Language	Face to face oral interaction, English interlanguage	Face to face, standard Australian English
Norms	Professional/patient relationship in Australian context	Same as for candidate
Genres	Professional consultation	Same as for candidate
Identification of problem	Explain advantages and disadvantages of three types of equipment; argue for use of walking stick	Insist on need for wheelchair, express pessimism about ever walking again
Input data		
Format	Live	
Vehicle	Oral input from roleplayer	
Length	Prompt: 15 lines	
	Oral input: 4–5 minutes	
Level of authenticity		
Situational	Setting, participants, purpose not unusual in physiotherapy	
Interactional	High to moderate: roleplayer is not highly trained in his or her role	
Characteristics of the expected response		
Format	Oral	
Type	Extended	

Response content
| Language | Vocabulary understandable by patient; persuasive functional knowledge |
| Background knowledge | Knowledge of equipment |

Level of authenticity
| Situational | Fairly high: this is a common type of situation |
| Interactional | Moderate level of interaction between test taker and interlocutor |

Characteristics of the interaction between input and response

Reactivity	Reciprocal
Scope	Moderately broad: must process information on card
Directness	Fairly indirect: must use background knowledge

Characteristics of assessment

Construct to be measured	Overall communicative effectiveness (flexibility and range); intelligibility; fluency (evenness); comprehension (completeness); appropriateness of language; resources of grammar and expression (richness, flexibility)
Criteria for correctness	Middle of scale represents minimum competence; scores at the left end of the scale represent native/near-native competence
Rating procedures	Assessor first gives a provisional rating after the first roleplay, then another provisional rating after the second, and finally a 'definitive' assessment based on his or her overall judgement of both roleplays

patient in the sense the term is used in highly specific purpose medical assessment. For example, at the University of New Mexico School of Medicine, simulated, or standardized, patients are actors 'trained to accurately and consistently portray a patient encounter for teaching or assessment purposes' (University of New Mexico 1992: 80). It takes about three hours to fully train a simulated patient for a single roleplay: the actor is given a real case history to study, and specific responses to expected questions are rehearsed, as are posture, affect, reaction to pain, and so on. In such assessment procedures, highly authentic interactions can take place. In the case of the *OET*, however, the level of authenticity of the input must be said to be only moderate. In this regard, McNamara and Lumley (1993) conducted an investigation of the effect of interlocutor competence on subsequent ratings of the *OET* speaking sub-test. One of the variables they looked at was raters' perception of the interlocutor's competence in adopting the role of a patient or client. They report that although the *OET* raters are given extensive training as raters, they receive little training as interlocutors, and it is thus likely that there is quite a bit of variation in the performance of interlocutors, both within and between individuals. McNamara and Lumley found that if the raters believed the interlocutor to be less than very competent, they gave higher ratings to the test taker, perhaps compensating for what they saw as an unfair hindrance.

Expected response

Both the situational and the interactional authenticity of the input have the potential to be fairly high. The task of advising a patient on the most suitable alternative among a range of treatments and equipment is a common one in physiotherapy, and the interaction between the test candidate and interlocutor is full of potential for the engagement of both language knowledge and background knowledge as the candidate attempts to convince the patient to accept the walking stick. However, as I discussed above, a great deal of the interactional authenticity will depend upon the skill of the examiner/interlocutor at playing the role of a difficult patient. Thus, it is likely that the authenticity of this task varies quite a bit from administration to administration.

Interaction between input and response

The relationship between input and response is fairly reciprocal since it is likely that the interlocutors do provide a certain amount of performance feedback, perhaps unconsciously, to the test takers in the form of facial expression and backchanneling cues, as well as by modifying their input in response to the candidate's own discourse. The scope of the input that the test taker has to process is moderately broad: not only is the information on the prompt card fairly complex, but, in addition, the test taker must process information from the interlocutor about his or her expectations and state of mind in assessing the communicative situation and responding to it. And finally, the scope of the response in the five-minute roleplay is fairly extended and provides a good amount of assessment data. In terms of directness, the test taker must employ quite a bit of background knowledge to perform the test task: knowledge about ambulatory equipment and the advantages and disadvantages of each type must be brought to bear in responding to the prompt. In addition, some knowledge of therapeutic exercises and their efficacy for stroke patients is necessary.

Assessment

In the analysis of the TLU situation with regard to the *OET*, observations of medical practitioners at work in clinical settings and discussions with specialist informants were undertaken (McNamara 1990a). In addition, a questionnaire was given to a group of overseas trained medical practitioners to get some indication of the types of communication tasks they engaged in and their perceptions of the relative difficulty of the various tasks. It was found that understanding colloquial language and cultural references from patients, taking case histories from patients and presenting them to colleagues, and explaining medical ideas in language easy for patients to understand were among the most difficult of the oral tasks the practitioners faced. Thus, the ability to understand the language of patients and the ability to express medical information to them were seen as key areas to be assessed. In addition, as we saw in the analysis of specific purpose language ability, there are a number of characteristics, including functional knowledge (ideational, heuristic, and manipulative functions), sociolinguistic knowledge (e.g., Australian variety of

English, a non-technical register easily understood by patients, and some cultural references and figures of speech), strategic competence (the engagement of a physical therapy discourse domain), and specific purpose background knowledge (e.g., ambulatory equipment and therapeutic exercises) that appear to be elicited by this task in the *OET*.

However, the rating scale actually employed in the *OET* was not derived from this research into assessment criteria and does not reflect many of the characteristics of specific purpose language ability or indigenous assessment that I have discussed. In fact, McNamara (1996) reports that a decision was made to adapt the existing scale of the Foreign Service Institute (FSI) for use in the *OET*. The FSI scale had been developed for use by the US government in non-specific purpose testing of the language skills of foreign service officers (see Wilds 1975 for a discussion of this scale). With regard to this decision, McNamara (1996) indicates, as I mentioned in Chapter 5, that candidates who passed the *OET* and who subsequently engaged in professional practice were often criticized by their peers and supervisors as being deficient in communication skills. It appears that the primarily linguistic orientation of the *OET* rating scale – overall communicative effectiveness, intelligibility, fluency, comprehension, appropriateness of language, and resources of grammar and expression – is not tapping at least some of the things the professionals care about in real-life LSP communicative situations. This experience provides further justification for the approach I advocated in Chapter 3 for analyzing indigenous assessment criteria as part of the investigation of the target language use situation.

Summary

In this rather detailed analysis of one task in the *OET* speaking sub-test, we have seen that it is fairly complex in terms of specific purpose test method characteristics. In the characteristics of the rubric, I noted that candidates are told explicitly that the *OET* is a test of speaking ability in English, not a test of professional knowledge, so that the rating of their performance would be fairly linguistically oriented. We also saw that there was a marked distinction between the two roleplay tasks, which were typically unrelated to each other, and that therefore the test taker must shift contexts fairly rapidly. This no doubt contributes to a somewhat reduced authenticity in the sub-test overall. The evaluation criteria are indeed quite linguistically oriented, and I discussed how this has led to some dissatisfaction among the professional peers and supervisors of test takers. Thus, our analysis of the rubric has brought a clearer understanding of some of the strengths and weakness of the *OET*, and has suggested ways in which interpretations of performance on the speaking sub-test might need to be tempered, particularly with reference to the evaluation criteria.

In the analysis of the characteristics of the input, I noted first that setting, participants, purpose, and form and content are all fairly explicitly identified in the prompt. Although the tone is not specified for the test taker, it certainly is for the roleplayer, who is instructed to 'be difficult!' The ability of the test taker to deal with the tone of the interaction will need to be taken into account in interpreting test scores. The identification of the problem in the interaction is fairly well specified – explain the characteristics of three types of ambu-latory aids – however, the key problem, requiring the test taker to argue for the use of a walking stick rather than a wheelchair, is developed implicitly in the interaction itself. The input data are in the form of oral input from the roleplayer, and I asserted that this results in only moderate authenticity since the interlocutor is not a trained simu-lated patient. The relationship between input and response is fairly reciprocal, since the interlocutor no doubt provides some communi-cative feedback and adapts the form of the message during the inter-action. Further, we found that there is a relatively indirect relationship between input and response in that the test taker must employ a fair amount of background knowledge to perform the test task, and the scope of the input that the test taker has to process is moderately broad since there is a good deal of information on the prompt card to process.

Finally, I noted how the assessment criteria for the *OET* were derived from observations of medical practitioners at work in clinical settings and from discussions with specialist informants, and there was an attempt to cover most of the characteristics of language knowledge: only textual knowledge is not specified in either the input or the evaluation criteria. Grammatical knowledge is fairly tradition-ally represented in the scoring grid, while ideational and heuristic functional knowledge are explicitly called for in explaining and in-structing, and there is an implicit requirement in the interaction for manipulative functions, arguing, persuading, or recommending, although these are not actually scored. That the language that must be comprehended by the test taker includes cultural references, idioms, and figures of speech, and that the candidate should be able to produce language that a client can understand, are implicit in the category appropriateness of language, though, again, since these are not explicitly scored, they cannot be considered part of the construct to be measured. Finally, though the construct of specific purpose language knowledge includes appropriate background knowledge in the form of information about ambulatory equipment and therapeutic exercise, such knowledge is not scored in the *OET*.

In conclusion, our analysis suggests that the *OET* speaking sub-test embodies most of the characteristics of LSP test development and design that I outlined in the first four chapters of this book. The test was based on an analysis of target language use situations involving both observation and the use of specialist informants. The test tasks involve interaction between the test takers' language knowledge and background knowledge on one hand, and characteristics of an LSP context on the other. The test takers are given information in the rubric about the objective of the test and how performance will be evaluated, and there is a rich assortment of contextualization cues in the test input to help the test taker orient him- or herself in an appropriate discourse domain. A major flaw in the *OET* speaking sub-test, as we saw, seems to be in making the link between the assess-ment criteria derived from the analysis of the target language use situation and the evaluation criteria employed in the scoring grid, a problem faced by all LSP test developers. Nevertheless, the *OET* pro-vides a fine model for both good LSP test development practice, and the pitfalls faced by us all as we attempt to provide a controlled environment for the assessment of specific purpose language ability.

I will now discuss a number of other LSP tests of listening and speaking ability, in rather less detail than I have in the case of the *OET*, but employing the same framework as a broad outline to guide the discussion. We will consider a range of approaches to the art of LSP testing: some fall toward the general end of the specificity con-tinuum, and one or two very close to the narrowly field specific end. We will look at tests for admission to academic and training pro-grams, tests for certification as teachers, and tests for other vocational purposes. I will begin with tests used as criteria for admission to academic and training programs.

Tests for admission to academic and training programs

International English Language Testing System (IELTS)

The *IELTS*, originally called the *ELTS* (*English Language Testing* Service), was introduced in 1980 by the British Council as a test for international applicants to British universities (see B. J. Carroll 1980 for a discussion of the *ELTS* development framework). The test is now administered jointly by the British Council, the University of Cambridge Local Examinations Syndicate, and the International Development Programme of Australian Universities and Colleges. It is taken annually by about 35,000 candidates at some 200 testing centers. The test comprises four modules – listening, speaking, reading, and writing. The *IELTS* listening and speaking sub-tests are taken by all candidates, whether applying for university degree programs or for vocational training, although the reading and writing sub-tests distinguish between academic and general training modules. The speaking component consists of an 11–15-minute interview on general topics. Here, I will examine one listening task briefly, and take a look at the reading and writing tasks in Chapter 7.

IELTS *listening task*

Rubric

Test takers are told that the test is in four sections, that they will hear a number of different recordings and will answer questions on what they hear, that they should write their answers in the question booklet, and that they will be given 10 minutes at the end of the test to transfer their answers to an answer sheet. The test lasts 30 minutes and contains about 40 questions. All the recordings are played once only.

Input

Some of the audio passages used in the *IELTS* listening test are scripted, but they do contain many elements of natural production, including false starts, self-correction, backchanneling cues, and fillers and other hesitation phenomena. Other passages are recordings from, for example, radio and television programs. A number of different dialects are represented as well, including standard Australian and some regional British accents. The passages range in length from about a minute to five minutes, and the shorter ones tend to be linked topically. The topics of the earlier sections of the test are survival-oriented, e.g., accommodation, the location of restaurants, changes in a schedule, and food and drink available at a university, and are conversational in genre; the later passages are more academic in nature, e.g., a lecture about air and water pollution. For example, Extract 6.2 is a transcript of an audio passage extracted from a BBC television program on acid rain.

This *IELTS* passage may be of interest to many of the test takers, and thus engage their communicative language ability interactively, but is probably not situationally relevant to most of them. As we can see below, the expected response based on this passage is a kind of multiple-choice task, requiring the test takers to listen carefully for specific information, but for no explicit purpose beyond the test itself.

Extract 6.2

Acid rain is a problem facing many countries at the moment and a global solution is required. One of the most concerning elements of the problem is that it disturbs the natural balance of lakes and rivers, poisoning fish and wildlife, and it even corrodes metal and stonework. In parts of Scandinavia, thousands of lakes are so polluted that they can no longer sustain fish life. Acid rain isn't an entirely new phenomenon – its effects started around the time of the industrial revolution of the 19th century – but it's getting worse. Britain contributes to the pollution problems in Denmark, Holland, Sweden and Germany, and at present we produce as much sulphur dioxide in the UK as France, Germany, Sweden, Norway, Denmark, Austria, Switzerland, Luxembourg and the Netherlands, all put together. Most of this pollution is caused by power stations, which have emerged as a result of Britain's rich coal deposits. But France, on the other hand, derives three-quarters of its electricity from nuclear power. But there are things we can do to help the situation, by reducing the amount of chemical pollutant we release into the atmosphere. And in Japan, Germany and the United States, power stations use a lime filtering process which removes around 90% of sulphur emissions.

University of Cambridge Local Examinations Syndicate (1995d)

Expected response

The test takers are told to listen carefully and answer questions 33 to 35 by ticking the relevant boxes in each column in the grid shown in Extract 6.3.

Extract 6.3

COUNTRY	33. Which countries are affected by Britain's pollution?	34. Which country relies heavily on nuclear power?	35. Which countries use lime filtering to reduce the amount of chemical pollutant released into the atmosphere?
Australia			
Belgium			
Denmark			
France			
Germany			
Holland			
Japan			
Sweden			
USA			

University of Cambridge Local Examinations Syndicate (1995d: 8)

This is an example of a fairly complex selected response task: the test taker must attend carefully to hear specific information and respond on-line while listening to the aural text. The four countries that must be ticked in question 33 are presented in a slightly different order aurally than they appear on the grid; this is also true of the three countries required for question 35. Once again, we see a task which is probably not very high in situational authenticity, since it is not one that shares many characteristics of a TLU situation. We might wonder about the interactional authenticity of such a task, as well, since, by listening for specific information in a fairly mechanical way, it may be that the test takers will not need to engage communicative strategies to any great degree: their general metacognitive strategies, accessing language knowledge directly, may be sufficient to carry out this task. In LSP testing, it is important always to provide sufficient cues in the input, in terms of the identification of setting, participants, purpose, and so on, to help ensure the engagement of communication strategies and a discourse domain appropriate to the target language use situation.

Interaction between input and response

There is a non-reciprocal relationship between input and response since there is no mechanism for feedback or modification of the message. The scope of the input in this task is moderately broad, while that of the response is extremely narrow – ticking appropriate boxes on the grid. Furthermore, the task requires a very direct, specific use of the input and almost no background knowledge in responding.

Assessment

The *IELTS* assessment criteria were derived from a survey of previous research into the language needs of tertiary level students, most notably that of Weir (1983), and thus reflect to some extent the concerns of those responsible for admitting applicants to various academic and training programs. *IELTS* scores are reported in terms of descriptive bands, in this case nine, as shown below.

> **Band 9** Expert User. Has fully operational command of the language: appropriate, accurate and fluent with complete understanding.
>
> **Band 8** Very Good User. Has fully operational command of the language with only occasional unsystematic inaccuracies and inappropriacies. Misunderstandings may occur in unfamiliar situations. Handles complex detailed argumentation well.
>
> **Band 7** Good User. Has operational command of the language, though with occasional inaccuracies, inappropriacies and misun-

derstandings in some situations. Generally handles complex language well and understands detailed reasoning.

Band 6 Competent User. Has generally effective command of the language despite some inaccuracies, inappropriacies and misunderstandings. Can use and understand fairly complex language, particularly in familiar situations.

Band 5 Modest User. Has partial command of the language, coping with overall meaning in most situations, though is likely to make many mistakes. Should be able to handle basic communication in own field.

Band 4 Limited User. Basic competence is limited to familiar situations. Has frequent problems in understanding and expression. Is not able to use complex language.

Band 3 Extremely Limited User. Conveys and understands only general meaning in very familiar situations. Frequent breakdowns in communication occur.

Band 2 Intermittent User. No real communication is possible except for the most basic information using isolated words or short formulae in familiar situations and to meet immediate needs. Has great difficulty understanding spoken and written English.

Band 1 Non User. Essentially has no ability to use the language beyond possibly a few isolated words.

Band 0 Did not attempt the test. No assessable information.

University of Cambridge Local Examinations Syndicate (1994: 6)

Each *IELTS* sub-test is scored separately, and the sub-test scores are then averaged to obtain the overall band score.

Summary

The *IELTS* listening task, as exemplified here, appears to be fairly close to the general end of the specificity continuum. The task requires a sophisticated ability to listen for specific information in a text, but may not engage communicative language ability to a very high degree, in light of the possibility that a test taker could successfully complete the task by engaging his or her language knowledge more or less directly from his or her cognitive strategic component, bypassing his or her communicative strategies. This is always a danger with tightly controlled matching tasks, as I hypothesized in the discussion of language processing in Chapter 4. The engagement of communicative strategies and appropriate discourse domains is an essential feature of LSP testing theory, and care should be taken to develop test tasks that will encourage the negotiation of meaning or the creation of discourse.

University Entrance Test in English for Speakers of Other Languages (UETESOL)

The Northern Examinations and Assessment Board, a consortium of British universities in the north of England, introduced the *UETESOL* in 1990 as a revised version of the Joint Matriculation Board's *University Entrance Test in English (Overseas)*, which had been introduced in 1966. The objective of the *UETESOL* is to assess the English language skills (listening, reading, writing, and speaking) of candidates for admission to British universities whose first language is not English. The test is intended to measure language skills considered to be common to the fields of science, engineering, social sciences, and business studies. The *UETESOL* contains five sections: writing, editing, reading, speaking, and listening. We will take a look at a listening task.

UETESOL *listening task*

The *UETESOL* listening skills test is in two parts, each consisting of thematically related conversations or extracts from radio and television programs, for example, and the test takers must refer to material in an examination booklet and respond to the input data by writing words or phrases, completing tables, graphs, or flow charts, or identifying diagrams or other visual material. We will look at an example of a task based on a conversation about heart rate in athletes, beginning with the rubric.

Rubric

The test takers are told that this is a test of their understanding of spoken English, and that they will hear a conversation, once only, between two people, one identified as Tim, who has enrolled as a member at a sports center, and Russell, his personal trainer. Candidates are told that they may take notes as they listen, and that they will have to enter the missing numbers in the boxes shown in Diagram 2 on page 10 of the test booklet. The entire conversation goes on for about six-and-a-half minutes, and involves two diagram labeling tasks; we will look at just the first of these. The evaluation criterion for the listening comprehension section of the *UETESOL* is simply accuracy in content, not of language.

Input

The transcript of the first minute or so of the conversation is shown in Extract 6.4.

Extract 6.4

RUSSELL: Ready for action?

TIM: I think so, but I'm a little nervous. For example, how do I know if I'm doing too much, or too little?

RUSSELL: That's a good point. I was going to deal with it later, but as you've brought it up, we may as well talk about it now. In order to judge whether you're doing too much or too little, you need to know your heart rate.

TIM: Heart rate?

RUSSELL: Yes – your heart's pumping ability. Remember, your heart is there to pump blood around your body. The more you exert yourself, the harder it has to work. So we have to be careful that you don't ask too much too quickly.

TIM: How can we make sure we don't do that?

RUSSELL: Quite easily. Look at the Target Heart Rate Chart here. Research has shown that it's safe – indeed, wise – to increase the heart rate to between 65 and 85 percent of the fastest speed at which your heart can pump for at least 20 minutes during a workout.

Northern Examinations and Assessment Board (1996a)

The aural input is accompanied by visual input – the diagram Russell and Tim are referring to, reproduced in Extract 6.5.

Extract 6.5

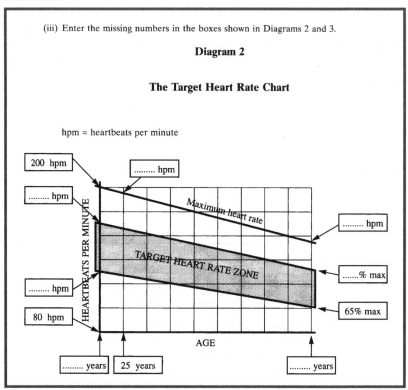

(iii) Enter the missing numbers in the boxes shown in Diagrams 2 and 3.

Diagram 2

The Target Heart Rate Chart

hpm = heartbeats per minute

Northern Examinations and Assessment Board (1996b: 10)

The aural input in this particular task is spoken fairly deliberately, with careful articulation. There are few features of natural conversation, such as false starts, hesitations, and fillers, and the text appears to have been scripted, not naturally occurring, although the script may have been based on a tape-recorded live conversation. The diagram is pretty clear, and could easily be a genuine one from a physical training manual. Situational authenticity, given the stated objective of the test – to assess listening skills 'in a context as close as possible to that likely to be encountered in an undergraduate course' (Northern Examinations and Assessment Board 1996c: 1) –

must be said to be moderately low in this task: one wonders how many international undergraduates would become members of a fitness club while studying at a university. However, it is no doubt true that the skill of listening carefully for specific information and writing it down is of great importance to undergraduate students, and the interactional authenticity of this task is likely to be moderately high.

Expected response

As we can see from the diagram in Extract 6.5, the test takers are expected to write numbers on the dotted lines in seven of the label boxes. They obviously can look at the diagram as they listen, and write any numbers they wish during the conversation, although they are told at the end of the input that they now have three minutes to label that and one other diagram (the subject of the remaining four minutes or so of the conversation, which I have not transcribed here). There is some question about the communicativeness of this task, since it is possible, as we saw in the *IELTS* task above, that the candidates could operate without much recourse to their communication strategies as they listen for specific items of information. They may not be interpreting much of the intended meaning in the discourse, processing only enough to catch the required elements of information.

Interaction between input and response

Once again, we see that reactivity is non-reciprocal, that the scope of the input is quite broad, while that of the response is pretty narrow, requiring only the writing of a number for each blank, and that the response is directly dependent upon the input, with little need for background information.

Assessment

The abilities being assessed include classifying information according to some criterion such as shape, size, or stage of development, ordering events, instructions, or steps in development, comparing and contrasting characteristics of two or more objects, for example, assimilating information, taking notes, and applying the information to specific tasks, and interpreting the attitudes or views of speakers (Northern Examinations and Assessment Board 1996c: 3).

Scores are reported on a four-point scale, as below:

A – a command of formal English with some appreciation of idiom

B – functional English but clearly not that of a native speaker

C – minimally competent English which will require support from strengths in other areas

D – too weak to be compensated by strengths in other areas

Ibid. (4)

Summary

This is an example of a test task that is, in terms of context, fairly far removed from anything in which most test takers would be likely to be engaged during their studies at a British university. However, in terms of the skills required to accomplish the task – listening for specific information and labeling a diagram – perhaps not unrealistic. The danger in such a task, as I have noted before, is that the test takers' communication strategies, and thus an appropriate discourse domain, may not be much used in such a mechanical, narrowly focussed listening task.

Let us turn now to two examples of tests used for certification of teachers, beginning with the *Proficiency Test for Language Teachers: Italian.*

Tests for certification as teachers

Proficiency Test for Language Teachers: Italian

The *Proficiency Test for Language Teachers* was introduced in 1993, having been developed by staff at the National Language and Literacy Institute of Australia, Language Testing Research Centre, at the University of Melbourne. The test has two main functions: (1) to serve

as a benchmark for teacher education by making the language requirements of the foreign language teacher explicit, and (2) to certify
language teachers by helping determine whether those applying for
employment in primary schools are proficient enough in the language
to perform their duties as language teachers. As is the case with other
test development projects carried out by the team at the University of
Melbourne, this one can serve as a model of LSP test development
practice. The researchers observed Italian language teachers in action
in three primary schools and one junior secondary school, and compiled an inventory of language functions performed by the teachers.
These included medium-oriented interactions (e.g., modeling the
target language and providing information about the target language),
message-oriented interactions (e.g., explaining processes, presenting
information about Italian culture, and telling and reading stories
aloud), activity-oriented interactions (e.g., giving instructions for a
game), interactions setting up the organizational framework for the
class (e.g., issuing directives about routine classroom business, disci-
plining students, responding to student questions), and language
used outside the classroom (e.g., preparing lessons, interacting with
members of the school community, and participating in professional
development activities). The test developers also used the language
teachers as specialist informants, consulting them about curriculum
and textbooks to establish the range of topics that teachers were likely
to cover. Test specifications were drafted, and the team began producing test tasks. The draft test was trialed on candidates enrolled in
undergraduate foreign language courses, postgraduate students in
foreign language education, and native speakers of Italian (see Elder
1993b for a full account of the development process). The *Proficiency
Test for Language Teachers: Italian* consists of five sub-tests: listening,
text editing, reading, writing, and speaking. We will take a look here at
the speaking test.

Italian teachers' speaking task

The Italian speaking test takes about 30 minutes to administer and is
an interview, entirely in Italian, between the test taker and an interlocutor. Two assessors may be present during the interview, or may
base their assessments on a tape recording of the interaction. There
are six phases to the interview:

1 *Warm-up conversation:* Interlocutor asks general questions about candidate's language background, interests, and experience. 2–3 minutes.

2 *Story-telling and retelling:* Test taker reads a story (approximately 300 words) aloud, as if to a group of students, then retells the story in his or her own words, using a series of picture prompts. 2 minutes preparation, 2 minutes performance.

3 *Giving instructions:* Test taker gives two sets of instructions (e.g., how to make something, how to play a game) as if to a group of students, using a set of picture prompts. 1 minute preparation, 3 minutes performance.

4 *Assigning and modeling a roleplay:* Using a pair of written roleplay cards, test taker assigns a role to the interlocutor, the other to him- or herself, then they act out the roleplay. 1 minute preparation, 2 minutes performance.

5 *Culture-related presentation:* Test taker chooses a topic from a set of alternatives and gives a short presentation about an aspect of Italian culture as if to students, using prompt materials provided immediately prior to the interview. 3 minutes.

6 *Explaining learner errors:* Using the results of the text editing sub-test, the interviewer chooses four of the errors identified and asks the test taker to explain the source and nature of them as if to a class of students. 3 minutes.

We will look in more detail at Phase 3, Giving instructions.

Rubric

The instructions given to the test takers prior to the interview are in English to help ensure that they know what will be required, but during the interview itself the instructions are given entirely in Italian. The English instructions are shown in Extract 6.6.

The test takers are thus given information about the objective of the task, procedures, and how they will be evaluated. In an introduction to the speaking section in the *Handbook for candidates*, test takers are told that they will be allowed one minute to prepare and three to four minutes speaking time and are given more information about the rating procedure, so this appears to be a fairly comprehensive rubric.

Extract 6.6

> The interviewer will hand you a sheet of paper with a set of pictures
> indicating the various stages involved in a simple construction activity
> or a children's game. Basic vocabulary is written on the sheet. You will
> be asked to explain, <u>as if to a group of learners</u>, how to go about the task.
>
> You will again be assessed on the range of language resources you bring
> to the task, on your level of accuracy and on the clarity of your
> instructions. Don't rush! Make sure you are clear about the various steps
> in the process before you begin. Use the pictures below to practise this
> task.

National Languages and Literary Institute of Australia (1993: 15)

Input

A sample of the input data is shown in Extract 6.7. This visual input
appears to be an authentic piece of instructional material for a
primary school language class.

Expected response

The test taker has to imagine him- or herself talking to his or her
class of school children in a monologue, with no feedback or true
interaction, and the test developers admit that this detracts from the
interactional authenticity of the task (Elder 1993b). However, they
decided to limit the interactiveness on the very reasonable grounds
that the adult interlocutor could in no way simulate the actual target
audience.

Interaction between input and response

The task is fairly non-reciprocal as I mentioned above, although the
interlocutor may offer explanation of the procedure if necessary: his
or her role in this task is that of a facilitator, not an interactant. The
scope of the input is moderately broad, the activity being designed for
a primary school audience, and that of the response is also fairly

Extract 6.7

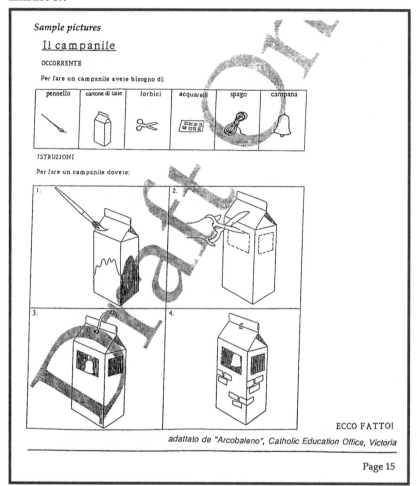

Sample pictures

Il campanile

OCCORRENTE

Per fare un campanile avete bisogno di:

pennello	cartone di latte	forbici	acquarelli	spago	campana

ISTRUZIONI

Per fare un campanile dovete:

1.

2.

3.

4.

ECCO FATTO!

adattato de "Arcobaleno", Catholic Education Office, Victoria

Page 15

Ibid.

broad – three minutes are allotted for the performance of the task. The task is somewhat indirect, in that the test taker might bring considerable background knowledge to bear about how to give instructions to primary school children, particularly an appropriate level of the target language and an awareness of what aspects of the procedure the children might have trouble with.

Assessment

The job analysis phase of the development process helped determine the assessment criteria: linguistic criteria, including pronunciation, grammatical accuracy, resources of expression (i.e., vocabulary), fluency, and comprehension, and classroom communicative competence criteria, including 'teacherliness,' the quality of language production in terms of its suitability for the classroom, and 'metalanguage,' the quality of the test taker's explanations of learner error. Thus, the assessment criteria are grounded in the context of the foreign language classroom, the target language use situation.

The results of the speaking assessment are reported as descriptive profiles in one of four levels: Level 4, Advanced professional competence; Level 3, Full professional competence; Level 2, Minimal professional competence; and Level 1, Limited professional competence. The profile for Level 2 is shown below.

Level 2, Minimal professional competence

This level is characterized by the speaker's ability to converse in a clearly participatory fashion, to initiate, sustain and bring to closure a wide variety of communicative tasks.

Candidates can handle with confidence but not with facility complicated tasks and social situations, such as elaborating, complaining and apologizing. Can communicate facts and talk casually about topics and current public and personal interest using general vocabulary. Can issue simple instructions, narrate and describe with some details, linking sentences together smoothly and utilizing such cohesive devices as conjunctions, pronouns, ellipses and repetitions. Can discuss concrete topics relating to particular interests and special fields of competence. There is emerging evidence of ability to support opinions, explain in detail and hypothesize. Shortcomings can often be smoothed over by a range of communicative strategies, such as pause fillers, stalling devices and different rates of speech, paraphrasing, or circumlocution, though some groping for words may still be evident. Fluency is rarely disrupted by hesitations. There is minimal groping for words except in specialized fields. Control of grammar is good: errors rarely interfere with understanding. There is some control of stylistic registers. The speaker is generally understandable without difficulty.

> *Speakers at this level would be able to effectively undertake teaching duties in second language instructional programmes where the target language was not the only vehicle of communication. They would tend to be more comfortable with beginning and intermediate school learners than with advanced level classes and would be best placed in a team teacher situation with support from more linguistically proficient colleagues.*
>
> Elder (1993c: 13)

This very detailed description of a 'minimum language proficiency threshold for effective teacher performance' (Elder 1993b: 12) is made possible by the extensive job analysis carried out prior to test development and the careful construction of scoring criteria related to the analysis.

Summary

In the speaking component of this proficiency test for Italian teachers, we see an example of performance criteria based on norms derived from the analysis of the TLU situation. The quality of the language produced is judged in terms of its appropriateness in the context of a primary school language classroom, and the criteria for this judgement are incorporated into the scoring guidelines. We will see another example of this sort of qualitative judgement in a Japanese language test for prospective tour guides later in the chapter.

Taped Evaluation of Assistants' Classroom Handling (TEACH)

The second LSP test of the language of teaching that we will examine is the *TEACH*, which I have referred to a number of times already in this book. The *TEACH* is a performance test developed in 1985 at Iowa State University, in the United States, to provide evidence of the oral English proficiency of prospective **teaching assistants** in a classroom in their own field of study. The term teaching assistant, in the US university context, refers to postgraduate students who have been offered employment as instructors in undergraduate classes as a way of financing their studies. In many scientific and technical disciplines in US universities, a significant proportion of teaching assistants are international students whose first language is other than English. The *TEACH* is used in addition to the *Speaking Proficiency English Assessment Kit (SPEAK)*, a general purpose test of oral ability (Educational Testing Service 1986), and attempts to identify what specific communication problems the new international teaching assistant (ITA) may have so that appropriate remedial instruction can be offered if needed. Test takers register for the *TEACH* a day before taking the test. At registration each candidate is given a topic from a list suggested by the department in which he or she expects to teach, a textbook in which the assigned topic appears, and instructions on how to prepare for the test.

Testing takes place in a university classroom containing 25–30 movable student desks, a teacher's table with a lectern, a blackboard, and an overhead projector and pull-down screen. The entire test lasts 10 minutes and consists of three parts: (1) a minute or two to allow the examinee to become familiar with the physical surroundings, meet the class (three student questioners, two or three raters, test proctor, and camera technician), and write a few key terms, formulae, etc., on the blackboard; (2) five minutes to explain some aspect of the assigned topic clearly and in words that an undergraduate class could understand; and (3) three minutes of questions about the topic asked by the student questioners.

TEACH *speaking and listening tasks*

Rubric

Extract 6.8 is the instructional material that the test taker is given the day before the test. This is an extremely complete rubric, giving the test taker a great amount of information about the objective, procedures for responding, the structure of the test, the time allotted, and criteria for correctness and the scoring procedures.

Extract 6.8

TEACH is a test designed to supplement *SPEAK* and to provide evidence of prospective teaching assistants' oral English skill in a classroom in their own field of study. *TEACH* attempts to identify what specific communication problems the new international teaching assistant (ITA) may have.

TESTING PROCEDURES

The test lasts 10 minutes. *TEACH* consists of three parts: (1) A minute or two to allow the examinee to become familiar with the physical surroundings, meet your 'class' (5 or 6 people who will listen to your presentation), and write a few terms, formulae, etc., on the chalkboard before you begin your presentation. (2) You will then have five minutes to explain some aspect of your assigned topic clearly and in words that an undergraduate class could understand. Then a timer will sound. (3) The 'class' will ask you questions about the topic for three minutes.

The topic assigned to you has been suggested by a professor in the department in which you hope to teach. I will lend you a copy of the pages from the textbook or laboratory manual in which the assigned topic appears. These pages must be returned to one of the test supervisors immediately after your videotaping session.

When you prepare for your presentation, you must assume several things:

1 You are giving an explanation or mini-lecture to an ordinary class of undergraduates.
2 Your lesson is happening sometime in the middle of the semester rather than at the beginning. You should *not* begin your presentation by saying, 'Welcome to this course. My name is . . .'
3 Since this lesson is part of an imaginary course, the students in your audience may ask you questions about quizzes, tests, etc. related to the topic you will explain to them. They will be familiar with the textbook and will know what your topic is beforehand, and have been told to ask questions about it and about classroom procedure.

A typical university classroom will be used for *TEACH* videotaping. The room will have a chalkboard. You are encouraged to use it to help in the explanation of your topic. (But remember: Talk to your audience, not to the board; write high on the board and in large enough letters and numbers so that students in the back of the room can see what you have written.) You may use notes for your presentation, as well as a copy of the textbook. However, <u>reading</u> from notecards or the textbook is not a good way to present material to a class and will lower your score. Although overhead transparencies and computer printouts can be excellent teaching aids, they may <u>not</u> be used for this test because (1) they may not be seen on videotape and (2) *TEACH* focuses on your ability to communicate in the spoken language.

A table microphone will record the audio portion of your presentation. It is important to speak loudly enough for students in the back of the room to hear you. Remember to speak clearly, and do not rush through your topic. It takes time for students to absorb new material. It would be better to cover only part of your topic thoroughly than to go quickly through the entire topic and confuse your audience.

RATING YOUR PERFORMANCE

Although several students will be used as questioners at the videotape session, the evaluators of your performance will be a team of professionals in the field of teaching English as a second language. They also rate *SPEAK* test tapes. Two or three of these evaluators will rate each *TEACH* performance; if they cannot agree, another evaluator will view the videotape and make a decision.

Evaluators will rate your performance in five categories:

1 overall comprehensibility of your spoken English
2 your ability to understand and answer students' questions
3 your ability to explain a topic clearly, using supporting evidence and/ or examples
4 your skill as a teacher addressing a class, using the chalkboard, showing interest in the subject and in the students as learners
5 indications of your awareness of the appropriate teacher–student relationship in a US university classroom setting

Iowa State University (no date (a): 1–2)

Input

The input data for the *TEACH* is in two forms, the written material from a textbook or other text in the test taker's field, and the live questions from the simulated students in the third part of the test. The written data consists of genuine texts, specifically recommended by experienced instructors in the various fields being tested. An extract from one such source is shown in Extract 6.9.

Extract 6.9

> A cardiac cycle follows from the fact that while all parts of the heart are inherently rhythmic, the structure with the greatest inherent rhythmicity determines the order of events by initiating an impulse which is propagated sequentially throughout the heart . . . The order of events in mammals begins with activity of the S-A node followed by artrial muscle, AV node, bundle of His, purkinje fibers, and ventricular muscle.

Iowa State University (no date (b): 1)

The text from which this extract comes, a physiology laboratory exercise, is seven pages long, approximately 1500 words, with several figures. The test taker has about 24 hours to process the material and prepare a five-minute lecture covering some aspect of the information, since there is too much material to cover completely in the allotted time. The live oral input data come from two or three student questioners during the test session. They have three minutes to ask questions about the content of the lecture and about classroom culture. The latter is intended to simulate the kinds of questions US undergraduates typically ask of their instructors about procedures, as in the examples in Extract 6.10.

Extract 6.10

> How much of this material will be on the next quiz?
>
> Do you grade on the curve or by straight percentage?
>
> Is this course a prerequisite for higher level courses in this department?
>
> Do you ever give open book tests?
>
> What's your policy about cutting class?

Iowa State University (no date (d): 3)

The purpose of such questions is to assess not only the candidate's familiarity with US classroom jargon, but also whether he or she can respond appropriately when he or she does not understand the gist of the question, e.g., by saying something like, 'I'm sorry, I don't know the answer to that question, but I'll check and let you know at the next class.' Clearly, this type of questioning can elicit responses interpretable as evidence of communication strategy use.

Expected response

The test taker is told to assume that the simulated class is taking place sometime in the middle of the term, not at the very beginning, and so should not start the lecture by introducing him- or herself. Apart from that, the candidate is left pretty much on his or her own to select and organize the information appropriately for the lecture. The responses to the student questions are expected to indicate an interest in interacting with the students and the ability to use strategies for coping with unclear or garbled questions. There is a high degree of situational and interactional authenticity, in other words.

Interaction between input and response

The interaction is fairly reciprocal, and the student questioners are told that they can interrupt the test taker appropriately during the lecture when they want something repeated, or to ask the test taker to speak louder. The candidate also receives a certain amount of visual feedback during the lecture, and quite a bit of oral and visual feedback during the question and answer section of the test. The scope of both the input and the response is fairly broad, requiring the processing and production of quite a bit of language and information. A good deal of specific purpose background information is required to process the input and make decisions about what information to include and how to organize it.

Assessment

The assessment criteria for the *TEACH* reflect, in a similar way to those for the Italian language teachers' test, both linguistic and classroom performance characteristics, as can be seen in the rating form shown in Figure 6.2. Raters score each performance using four categories: (1) overall comprehensibility of spoken English, (2) cultural awareness of appropriate teacher–student relationships in a US university classroom setting, (3) communication skills (explaining a topic clearly, using supporting evidence and/or examples, addressing a class, using the blackboard, and showing interest in the students as learners), and (4) ability to understand and answer students' questions. The raters are ESL instructors, not representatives of the ITAs' content areas, and this has consequences for the interpretation of the scores in terms of specific purpose language knowledge.

The standard rating form for the *TEACH* is reproduced in Figure 6.2. The performance is scored by two raters, independently, either live or after the test from the videotape. Their scores are averaged to obtain a final rating; if their scores diverge by more than one level, a third rater scores the performance from the videotape, and the two closest ratings are averaged. Since the raters are unlikely to be familiar with the test takers' fields of study, there is no attempt to judge the content of the presentations, although content must surely influence the raters' perceptions of such criteria as development of explanation, clarity of expression, and use of supporting evidence. As is the case with the *Occupational English Test*, the *TEACH* is meant to be a test solely of language ability and not field specific or professional knowledge; however, as we saw with the *OET*, background knowledge must play a role in the test takers' performance, and therefore needs to be taken into account in interpreting the performances. I will discuss this problematic aspect of scoring LSP test performances further in Chapter 8.

The criteria derive from previous work on spoken interaction, from observations of teachers at work in the classroom and consultations with experienced instructors in various disciplines, and from information from US undergraduates about what they find difficult about international teaching assistants' communication (Abraham and Plakans 1988). I have already mentioned that the raters are not specialists in the academic fields of the test takers, and that criteria that such specialists might apply in assessing the communicative performances of teaching assistants in their fields are not a part of the evaluation in the *TEACH* test.

Summary

The *TEACH* is a fairly complex performance test that likely involves a high degree of situational and interactional authenticity. Since the raters are ESL instructors and not content specialists, it is likely that their ratings are based largely on linguistic criteria, though influenced to some degree, and perhaps unsystematically, by the content of the test takers' presentations. The student questions can elicit

Figure 6.2 TEACH rating sheet

```
┌─────────────────────────────────────────────────────────────────┐
│                                                                   │
│                     TEACH rating sheet                            │
│                                                                   │
│                              (Low)              (High)            │
│  1 OVERALL LANGUAGE COMPREHENSIBILITY   0....●....1....●....2....●....3 │
│                                                                   │
│     A.  Pronunciation                   0  .  1  .  2  .  3       │
│                                                                   │
│     B.  Grammar                         0  .  1  .  2  .  3       │
│                                                                   │
│     C.  Fluency                         0  .  1  .  2  .  3       │
│                                                                   │
│  2 CULTURAL ABILITY                     0....●....1....●....2....●....3 │
│                                                                   │
│     A.  Familiarity with cultural code                            │
│                                                                   │
│     B.  Appropriate nonverbal behavior                            │
│                                                                   │
│     C.  Rapport with class                                        │
│                                                                   │
│  3 COMMUNICATION SKILLS                 0....●....1....●....2....●....3 │
│                                                                   │
│     A.  Development of explanation                                │
│                                                                   │
│     B.  Clarity of expression           0....●....1....●....2....●....3 │
│                                                                   │
│     C.  Use of supporting evidence                                │
│  ──────────────────────────────────────────────                  │
│     D.  Eye contact                                               │
│                                                                   │
│     E.  Use of chalkboard               0....●....1....●....2....●....3 │
│                                                                   │
│     F.  Teacher presence                                          │
│                                                                   │
│  4 INTERACTION WITH STUDENTS            0....●....1....●....2....●....3 │
│                                                                   │
│     A.  Basic listening ability                                   │
│                                                                   │
│     B.  Question handling and responding                          │
│                                                                   │
│  5 OVERALL IMPRESSION        0  1  2  3  /  4  5  6  /  7  8  9    │
│                                                                   │
│                              (poor)     (average)   (excellent)   │
│                                                                   │
│  Recommendation: Subject's overall English and classroom ability is │
│  good enough to be:                                               │
│                                                                   │
│  6 Instructor with minimal supervision         YES       NO       │
│                                                                   │
│  7 Leading a recitation section of a course                       │
│                                                                   │
│     taught by a faculty member                 YES       NO       │
│                                                                   │
│  8 Conducting a laboratory section             YES       NO       │
│                                                                   │
└─────────────────────────────────────────────────────────────────┘
```

Iowa State University (no date (c))

information interpretable as evidence of communication strategy use.

Tests for other vocational purposes

Certificate in English for International Business and Trade (CEIBT)

The *CEIBT* was introduced in 1990 by the University of Cambridge Local Examinations Syndicate and is intended to allow candidates whose first language is not English to demonstrate an ability to function efficiently in an office or business where English is used. There are three sub-tests: listening, oral interaction, and reading and writing. The tests are all set in the context of one international company, and the prompts and input data are all thematically related to that company. The speaking sub-test takes 10 to 15 minutes, and 15 minutes are given for preparation. The test is a roleplay, with the test taker playing the role of a company employee and the examiner that of a client. The test is in three parts, each lasting 3–5 minutes: greetings and a request from the client, questions from the test taker regarding the request, and conversation of a more general nature, accompanied by a specific request from the client. The listening sub-test lasts 45 minutes, with 5 minutes of reading time. Candidates hear tape-recorded input and have to carry out such tasks as taking a phone message and passing it on in writing to a third person; taking notes based on aural input; composing a fax or telex in response to a phone message; writing a short memo to a specific person requesting action; and amending or completing a message, chart, table, map, diagram, or graph. We will look at one speaking task and one listening task.

CEIBT *speaking task*

Rubric

Test takers are told in the information booklet (University of Cambridge Local Examinations Syndicate, no date) that the task will last three to five minutes, and that they will be assessed on their pronunciation, grammatical and lexical accuracy, appropriateness of language to function, clarity of intention, range of language use, ability to take the initiative in conversation and adapt to new topics or changes in direction, and ability to expand and develop ideas.

Input

The test takers are told that they are to imagine that they work for the Thomas Cook Travel Agency and have been sent to their Business Center in Hong Kong, and that the examiner will be a client. The prompt for the first speaking task is reproduced in Extract 6.11.

Extract 6.11

TASK FOR PART 1

In Part 1 you must speak to a prospective client who works for an organisation called 'Global Concern'.

The client has come to talk to you about arranging a conference in Hong Kong, and to find out which services you can provide.

The client arrived ten minutes early. Unfortunately you were not able to see him/her immediately. Apologise for this and then introduce yourself.

The client will then ask you some questions.

The client will ask you about:
- office hours
- hotels in Hong Kong
- payment of international tickets
- welcoming travellers at the airport and transferring them to the hotel

All the information you need is on the opposite page.

University of Cambridge Local Examinations Syndicate (no date: 20)

The input referred to in the prompt is reproduced in Extract 6.12. Thomas Cook is, of course, a well-known international travel company, and the input data in this task seems quite genuine, making for a fairly high level of situational authenticity. The level of interactional authenticity depends, as in all roleplays, to some degree on the ability of the interlocutor to play his or her part and engage the test taker in a communicative interaction.

Extract 6.12

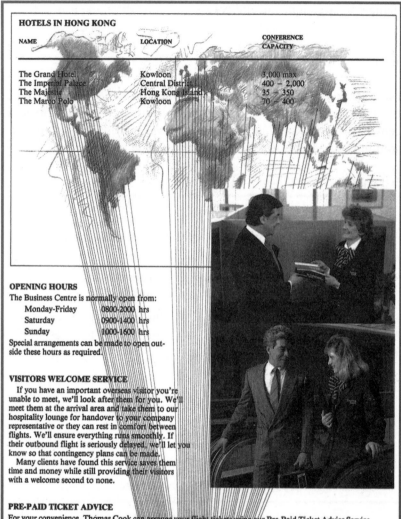

HOTELS IN HONG KONG

NAME	LOCATION	CONFERENCE CAPACITY
The Grand Hotel	Kowloon	3,000 max
The Imperial Palace	Central District	400 – 2,000
The Majestic	Hong Kong Island	35 – 350
The Marco Polo	Kowloon	70 – 400

OPENING HOURS

The Business Centre is normally open from:

Monday-Friday	0800-2000 hrs
Saturday	0900-1400 hrs
Sunday	1000-1600 hrs

Special arrangements can be made to open outside these hours as required.

VISITORS WELCOME SERVICE

If you have an important overseas visitor you're unable to meet, we'll look after them for you. We'll meet them at the arrival area and take them to our hospitality lounge for handover to your company representative or they can rest in comfort between flights. We'll ensure everything runs smoothly. If their outbound flight is seriously delayed, we'll let you know so that contingency plans can be made.

Many clients have found this service saves them time and money while still providing their visitors with a welcome second to none.

PRE-PAID TICKET ADVICE

For your convenience, Thomas Cook can arrange your flight tickets using our Pre-Paid Ticket Advice Service.

- Ticket Advice may be booked at your local Thomas Cook Agency
- Discounts with major airlines
- Ticket Advice is collected from your departure airport prior to checking in.

Ibid. (21)

Expected response

The test taker must interact with the simulated client in an appropriate manner, providing the requested information.

Interaction between input and response

The task is fairly reciprocal, a face to face live interaction, and involves a moderately broad amount of input and production. A great deal of the information required for the task comes from the input, but some degree of background knowledge about international conferences, travel, and hotels seems necessary to carry out this task, and would thus engage specific purpose language knowledge.

Assessment

The assessment criteria are linguistically based, and cover a wide range of the characteristics of language ability, including grammatical, textual, functional, and sociolinguistic knowledge.

Summary

This *CEIBT* speaking task is a well-specified, authentic, and engaging task. The written input data is attractively designed to simulate genuine texts and the task seems to have high interactive authenticity. Much hinges, though, on the ability of the interlocutor to play the part of the client with realism and flexibility.

CEIBT *listening task*

Rubric

The test takers are told that they will have to listen to a phone message and then compose a fax confirmation. They will need to refer to information in a previous task to complete this one. They are also told, in the information booklet, that they will be assessed on their ability to comprehend factual information, differentiate between general and specific information, interpret input delivered at normal speed spoken with a variety of native and non-native accents, and interpret tone and register, in a wide variety of material and topics. The specific instructions for this task are given in Extract 6.13.

Extract 6.13

Listen to the following message and send a FAX to confirm the reservation. (Refer to the Price List in Task 1 opposite for current prices.)

You will hear the message twice and space is provided for you to make rough notes.

University of Cambridge Local Examinations Syndicate (no date: 14)

Input

The taped input is in the form of a phone message, presumably left on an answering machine, though this is not made explicit. A transcript of the message is shown in Extract 6.14.

Extract 6.14

Hello. I'm phoning from B.B.A. International, in Switzerland. We'd like to reserve one of your Executive Offices on Friday 26th August for the whole afternoon from 2 o'clock to 6 o'clock, that's on Friday 26th August. Could you please send me a FAX to confirm the reservation. My name's Ali Baradar. That's spelled A L I   B A R A D A R and the company's name is B.B.A. International. Our fax number is 010 41 148 258934. I'll repeat that for you 010 41 148 258934. Could you also confirm current prices. We used your facilities last year but we're not members yet.

Ibid.

The aural input seems realistic enough (the fax number has the actual country code for Switzerland), although it appears to have been scripted rather than being a genuine message. It contains a fair amount of redundancy: the company name, date, and fax number are all repeated, but the country, time, and the actual requests for reserving an office and confirming the price are not.

The other piece of input, a price list for Thomas Cook's Heathrow Business Centre facilities, is visual and will already be familiar to the test taker, since it was the input for the previous task. The test taker must look down the list for the Executive Office rental, and note that there is a difference in hourly rates for members and non-members. Again, this visual input has the look of a genuine document.

Expected response

The candidate is given space to write notes and the actual fax message, as shown in the specimen answer in Extract 6.15. From the examiner's comment, it is clear that a key requirement is that all necessary information be included in the response. It is not clear how much good fax form is required in the response, but the specimen example certainly displays some knowledge of the genre. The level of situational and interactional authenticity is no doubt quite high in this task.

Interaction between input and response

This is a non-reciprocal task, as it would be in the target language use situation – answering machine messages are one-way – although, as I noted, some redundancy is built in, and the message is played twice. The length of the input is of medium scope – the message is a bit under a minute – as is that of the response. Finally, the test taker is fairly directly dependent on the input for completing the task, but some background information about business communication is required as well.

Assessment

The assessment criteria are, as we saw in the speaking task, fairly linguistically oriented, covering a wide range of communicative language abilities. These are no doubt important in the international business community, and reflect input from specialist informants.

Extract 6.15

SPECIMEN ANSWER

Listen to the following message and send a FAX to confirm the reservation (Refer to the Price List in Task 1 opposite for current prices.)

You will hear the message twice and space is provided for you to make rough notes.

ROUGH NOTES   BBA Int Swit   conc. offices

Fri 26 August   2-6pm

Ao   Barr   Aly Baradar

010 41 148258934

Current prices   Not members

Fax No   010 41 148 75 8934

FAX   To: Aly Bardar, BBA International
                                  Switzerland
          From: Pia Carlson, Heathrow Business Centre
          Date: 11th June 1970

I fax to confirm your reservation of an executive office for Friday 26 August from 2pm until 6pm.

The current price for the service requested is £30 per hour for non-members.

If you have any further queries do not hesitate to contact me.

Kind regards

Pia Carlson

Examiner's Comments

Fax well written, accurately conveying all necessary information.   CLEAR PASS

University of Cambridge Local Examinations Syndicate (1995d: 15)

Summary

This is an example of the use of highly authentic, perhaps even genuine, input data in a well-contextualized task. A fair amount of background knowledge seems necessary, particularly concerning business genre in the format of international facsimiles.

Japanese Language Test for Tour Guides

This is another of the tests produced by the NLLIA Language Testing Research Centre at the University of Melbourne, and has a dual purpose: to indicate to employers the language proficiency of applicants for positions as Japanese-speaking tour guides, and to provide a selection criterion for applicants to tour guide training courses. Thus, prospective test takers are of two types: those with some experience and/or training as tour guides, and those with no training or experience (Brown 1995). The test was produced in consultation with experienced tour guides, and the assessment criteria were based on their judgements about the necessary features of quality tour guide communication (Brown 1993), as well as more linguistically oriented features. The test is a 30-minute face to face interview, comprising six parts, all but the first of which are roleplays:

- *Warm-up:* Introductory questions about test taker's life, home, work, study, and interests. 2–3 minutes.
- *Optional tours:* Helping a client (the interviewer) choose an optional tour. 3–4 minutes.
- *Troubleshooting:* Dealing with an upset or worried client. 3–4 minutes.
- *Cultural presentation:* Describing aspects of Australian culture in a way relevant and interesting to a group of Japanese tourists. 3–4 minutes.
- *Giving instructions/information:* Explaining detailed instructions and/or describing facilities to a group of tourists. 3–4 minutes.
- *Itinerary and tourist attraction:* Explaining a day-tour itinerary and giving information about a tourist attraction. 5–6 minutes.

As I mentioned above, the assessment criteria encompass both linguistic and task fulfillment features. The linguistic criteria include resources of grammar and expression, fluency, pronunciation, vocabulary, use of polite forms, and comprehension, assessed across the whole interview. Some criteria are more salient in specific tasks; for example, use of polite language is given more emphasis in the more interactive tasks (e.g., helping the client choose an option, and troubleshooting). Task fulfillment is assessed for each of the five role-plays, and criteria include such factors as enthusiasm, empathy, making something sound interesting, persuasiveness, and awareness of interlocutors' needs or desires. Raters are drawn as far as possible from within the tour guide industry – experienced tour guides, tour coordinators, and tour guide trainers – but teachers of Japanese language are also trained as raters. Moreover, both native speakers and non-native speakers of Japanese are used as raters. A study of the effect of rater background (Brown 1995) found no significant differences in ratings produced by tour guide versus non-tour guide raters or between native versus non-native speakers of Japanese, given that the raters were adequately trained. Ratings are made on a six-point scale. We will look at the third task type, Troubleshooting.

Japanese Language Test for Tour Guides *speaking task*

Rubric

In a *Handbook for candidates* (National Languages and Literacy Institute of Australia 1992), the test takers are told the objective of the test – to find out how well their Japanese proficiency will enable them to function as tour guides – the time allocation, the structure of the test, and the scoring procedure – two assessors, one being the interviewer, the other an observer present during the interview. With regard to the Troubleshooting roleplay, candidates are told that their performance will not depend on prior experience of such problems, but that they may need to use general knowledge or common sense to solve the problem. They are also told that the manner in which they interact is important: 'it is not simply a matter of explaining, but of reassuring someone who is worried, or pacifying someone who is angry, while at the same time encouraging them to comply with your proposed solution' (*ibid.*: 6). To reinforce this point, candidates are given two extracts from tour guide training manuals emphasizing the importance of remaining calm and in control, never displaying irritation, anger, anxiety, or discontent, and answering the client with a smile.

Finally, the test takers are told that they will have one minute to read the roleplay task card before beginning the roleplay.

Input

A sample task card is shown in Extract 6.16.

Extract 6.16

Role: You are a guide sending off a group of Japanese tourists at the airport. The flight leaves at 5 p.m.
Issue: You arrive at the airport to find that the flight has been postponed until the next day because of technical problems. Your office has informed you that the group should return to the same hotel, dinner has been arranged and a half-day tour will be organised for tomorrow morning. One member of the group is rather upset at the change. Reassure him/her.

National Languages and Literary Institute of Australia (1992: 6)

In addition to this prompt, there will be aural input from the interviewer playing the role of the disgruntled tourist, and much of the authenticity depends on the skill with which the role is played by the interlocutor, as I have noted before. Certainly, this task has the potential for a high degree of interactional authenticity, with negotiation of meaning being of paramount importance as the test taker attempts to sympathize with and pacify the client, and enlist his or her cooperation, while explaining the details of the alternate arrangements.

Expected response

As we have seen, the test taker must not only display competence in communicative language ability, but fulfill the task in a manner consistent with qualities experienced tour guides believe to be characteristic of effective communication in the target language use situation. This will no doubt require a high level of communication strategy use.

Interaction between input and response

The task is highly reciprocal, moderately broad in scope, particularly in terms of the response, and requires some general background knowledge and common sense. It has the potential for engaging communicative language ability, and, to some degree, specific purpose language ability, with respect to the manner in which the test taker negotiates with the simulated client.

Assessment

A group of specialists were consulted to inform the test developers about criteria for assessing task fulfillment, and their input is reflected in the guidelines for raters that I discussed above. It would appear that the tour guides are looking for certain qualities of personality and interpersonal skills when assessing the communicative ability of prospective colleagues or trainees (Brown 1993).

Summary

This is another example of a roleplay in which the skill of the interlocutor is important in establishing the authenticity of the interaction. This highlights, as I have discussed in connection with the *OET*, the importance of interlocutor training in addition to rater training. Also, the assessment criterion of task fulfillment is an interesting attempt to incorporate TLU norms of interpretation into the test evaluation criteria, as we also saw in the test for Italian language teachers. The use of native- and non-native speakers of the target language, and of specialists and non-specialists in the target field as raters, are also aspects of this test that deserve careful study (Brown 1995).

Proficiency Test in English Language for Air Traffic Controllers (PELA)

The last vocational LSP test we will examine is from an early prototype of the *PELA*, a test designed to measure the English language proficiency of trainee air traffic controllers in Europe. The *PELA* was developed through the European Organisation for the Safety of Air

Navigation (EUROCONTROL) Institute of Air Navigation Services (IANS) in Luxembourg, between January 1992 and December 1993, and has the potential of being used to measure the specific purpose English language abilities of student air traffic controllers in the 38 countries of the European Civil Aviation Conference (Institute of Air Navigation Services 1994). The impetus for the development of the *PELA* was a 'requirement for the harmonisation of Air Traffic Services in Europe, and . . . the knowledge that nowhere is communication more critical and misunderstanding potentially so disastrous than in air traffic control' (*ibid.*: 4). This is, in other words, a high stakes test in more ways than one! The purpose of this prototype test, then, is to define and assess a 'criterial level in ATC English for newly qualifying ATC trainees' (Teasdale 1993: 143).

The language of air traffic control is an extremely well defined field specific domain, owing to the fact that there are established conventions for communication, published by the International Civil Aviation Organisation (ICAO), *Rules of the air and air traffic services* (International Civil Aviation Organisation 1985). This document 'defines the content, form, and ordering of elements of utterances, as well as specifying the circumstances in which specific phrases are to be used' (Teasdale 1996: 2). Even in the case of unusual circumstances not covered specifically by the ICAO recommendations, appropriate subsidiary phraseology is to be used, meaning, according to McCann, a member of the *PELA* development team, the use of the conventional style. McCann points out that 'In practice, phraseology, like other areas of language use, is subject to systematic and unsystematic local variation, personal language processing preferences, and a host of other performance and processing characteristics which disturb the generally orderly and predictable nature of the domain' (quoted in Teasdale 1996: 2-3). Therefore, even in this highly restricted field specific domain, analysis of the target language use situation must take into account variation from the prescribed forms.

The design and content of the *PELA* were based on a needs analysis that consisted of a 20-page questionnaire sent to air traffic controllers in 15 countries, requesting information on what should be tested and the minimum level of proficiency required, and recordings of over 12 hours of air traffic control transmissions from seven European cities. Both aspects of the needs analysis guided the drafting of overall test specifications and the test design. As I also noted in Chapter 5, one of the most difficult aspects of field specific test development is making the transition from test specifications to test tasks, often owing to practical considerations in the testing situation. The development of this prototype offers a number of excellent examples.

Teasdale (1996) points out that a key issue in air traffic control is that any movement by one aircraft, whether on the ground or in the air, has potential implications for any other aircraft in the vicinity. Air traffic control officers (ATCOs) have, therefore, to keep in mind the relative locations of those aircraft for which they are responsible. 'This dynamic aspect of ATCOs' work is perhaps the most difficult to take account of in the language testing context' (p. 141). In the *PELA*, the problems of only a single aircraft at a time are considered in the test tasks, a situation somewhat problematic for candidates in pre-testing, according to Teasdale. Nevertheless, because of practical considerations, this constraint remains a part of the test and simply has to be taken into account when performances are interpreted.

The *PELA* consists of a listening sub-test with a number of written limited production tasks, and a speaking sub-test with two production tasks. We will look at an example task from each sub-test, beginning with a listening sub-test on ground clearance and delivery.

PELA *listening task*

Rubric

Test takers are told that they will hear communications between two air traffic control officers (ATCOs) and five pilots, and that they will answer questions by writing the necessary information in the space provided. They are also informed that they will hear the recording once only, that the first speaker on the tape is a pilot, and that they will have one minute to read the questions before the tape starts.

Input

The tapes used in the *PELA* listening test are genuine recordings of ATCO/pilot radio transmissions where possible, or, when the quality of a genuine recording is unacceptable, re-recordings of these with appropriate background noises. The majority of ATC communication occurs through the use of headphones and microphones, so the use of this equipment in the test is entirely appropriate. Visual contact with aircraft in the target language use situation is by means of radar screens, and although radar simulators exist in the ATC training institutions, the differences in hardware and systems from center to center ruled out their use for the test (Teasdale 1996). An example of the type of input test takers hear is shown in Extract 6.17.

Extract 6.17

ATCO: DLH 1899 turn right heading 270 to intercept and follow the localiser

PILOT: roger, right turn 270 intercept follow the localiser cleared for the ILS approach DLH 1899

Teasdale (1996: 8)

Expected response

The questions in this task require limited production responses, as shown in the examples in Extract 6.18, referring to different input texts.

Extract 6.18

1 What does the pilot of DLH 1915 want to know?

_____

2 What does the pilot of BAW 459 say about his slot time when he contacts control the first time?

_____

3 What does the pilot of AZA 363 ask the ATCO?

_____

4 What two questions does the pilot of BAW 461C ask the ATCO?

(i) _____

(ii) _____

Institute of Air Navigation Services (1994: 23)

As the test developers are aware, this is not a particularly authentic response task, but it does provide an efficient means for assessing aspects of listening ability. Since the specimen materials for the *PELA* also include sample answers, we can see clearly the nature of the expected response, as shown in Extract 6.19 for question 1.

Extract 6.19

---

1 – if/whether the controller has any slot for him
- any slot
- if slot
- slot?

- **NOT** 'slot' only

- NB   *Pilot wants to know* <u>*whether*</u> *control has a slot for him –*
  answer must reflect this.

Ibid. (24)

This sample response illustrates the intention of the test developers to assess two distinct abilities: the ability to understand communications between ATCOs and pilots, and the ability to recognize the communicative function of messages with and without explicit indicators.

Interaction between input and response

There is a non-reciprocal relationship, and the scope of both the input and the response is only moderately broad. The candidate must listen for specific information in the input, as indicated by the questions, so the response is very directly related to the input. However, it is also likely that specific purpose background information is required merely to interpret the input and listen for the required information, so the level of interactional authenticity is likely to be fairly high.

Assessment

The assessment criteria are derived from the needs analysis, which involved consultation with experienced ATCOs. Very detailed specifications of desirable abilities were outlined, as the summary in Extract 6.20 indicates.

Extract 6.20

> **4 . . . THE CANDIDATE SHOULD BE ABLE TO UNDERSTAND**
> **COMMUNICATIONS**
>> **BETWEEN PILOTS AND ATCOS**
>> **BETWEEN ATCOS AND ATCOS**
>> **IN WHICH THE PILOT OR ATCO:**
>
>> 4.1 READS BACK/ACKNOWLEDGES ATCO'S MESSAGE
>> 4.2 REQUESTS APPROVAL OR CLEARANCE
>> 4.3 GIVES INFORMATION
>> 4.4 REQUESTS INFORMATION
>> 4.5 GIVES/REQUESTS REASONS
>> 4.6 REQUESTS OF THE ATCO TO DO SOMETHING
>> 4.7 CHECKS, CONFIRMS AND CLARIFIES
>> 4.8 GIVES/DENIES APPROVAL AND CLEARANCE (ATCOS ONLY)
>
> **5 . . . SHOULD BE ABLE TO RECOGNISE THE COMMUNICATIVE FUNCTION**
> **OF MESSAGES WITH AND WITHOUT EXPLICIT INDICATORS**

Ibid. (22)

Summary

This listening task reflects the detail in construct definition made possible by a thorough analysis of the TLU situation. It also illustrates some of the practical constraints involved in making the transition from TLU tasks to test tasks. Some degree of situational and interactive authenticity will inevitably be lost.

PELA *speaking task*

Rubric

This is a roleplay in which the test taker takes the part of an ATCO, and responds orally on a tape recorder to five different pilots. The rubric for this task contains elements of a specific purpose prompt as well as information about the test procedure, as shown in Extract 6.21.

Extract 6.21

Interactive Test Part 1

Candidate Information

Look at the first page of the booklet of Birmingham Ground Charts and the information given on this page.

You will hear 5 messages from different pilots.

Reply to the pilot messages in an appropriate way, using the information given below and referring to the chart booklet numbered 1–5.

Avoid responses such as 'affirm' or 'roger'.

Do not say 'say again' as the pilot messages will only be played once.

After each response, turn the page to the next numbered chart.

Your responses will be recorded onto cassette tape.

The following callsigns are used:

SPP = Sunwing
OAL = Olympic
RAM = Royal Air Maroc
DLH = Lufthansa
G-BMVE

You have the following information:

Runway in use	33
Displaced threshold	100m from threshold runway 33
The time is now	10:05
Latest met. report	10:00

EGGB 3501KT 4000 3CUSC018 3ACAS070 06/04 1001 NOSIG

Institute of Air Navigation Services (1994: 29)

This rubric gives the test taker important procedural and specific purpose contextual information he or she will need to complete the task. It appears to require a high degree of field specific background knowledge to interpret and process the information, so this rubric incorporates features of the input as well as of the rubric.

Input

The input data is in two forms, audio and visual. The audio data is simulated, but quite realistic, tape-recorded pilot–ATCO communication. The visual data is in the form of a ground chart for Birmingham International Airport. The chart is realistic – so much so that it contains a warning: 'Incomplete chart – not to be used for navigational purposes.' The Birmingham Ground Chart is reproduced in Extract 6.22. One problem for situational authenticity with regard to this chart is that, in the target language use situation, the ATCO would be familiar with his or her own local airport, but could not be expected to be familiar with airports and airspace elsewhere (Teasdale 1996). However, in order to incorporate the characteristics of the TLU situation into the test, in terms of authentic configurations of taxiways, runways, reporting points, and so on, the test developers chose to use a neutral airport ground chart that none of the potential test takers would be familiar with, giving them all an equal opportunity to familiarize themselves with relevant information before taking the test. It should be noted that the *PELA* no longer uses Birmingham airport as a basis for this type of task. New charts have been constructed and are available through the latest sample test material for students to study and become familiar with. The *PELA* developers aim to test proficiency in ATC English and not distract students with unfamiliar charts and test items.

Expected response

The test takers are expected, in this task, to use the conventional International Civil Aviation Organisation (ICAO) phraseology in responding to pilot queries. Owing to the somewhat decontextualized nature of the input – there is not actually an airplane! – the interactional authenticity is a bit problematic in this response task, as the test developers acknowledge:

> Although the phraseology for these type of instructions is straight-
> forward – for example, 'Air France 594, climb Flight Level 180,

Extract 6.22

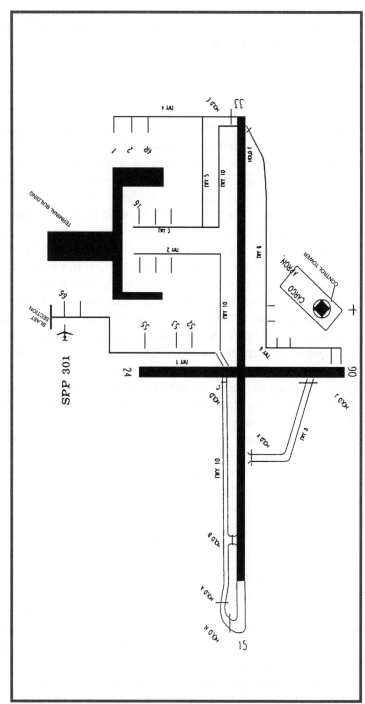

SPP 301

Ibid. (30)

turn left heading 010' – the minimal necessary conditions to elicit this type of regular, routine communication in a testing context [are] complex. Without an aircraft to control, the language ceases to have any referential meaning and becomes no more than another decontextualized token of phraseology.

Teasdale (1996: 141)

This is a central problem in any specific purpose testing enterprise, and it is related to an uncertainty about the amount and type of background knowledge the test taker must bring to bear in assessing the context and calling up relevant language knowledge to respond to the target situation. In the end, the problem is a matter of the validity of interpretations we make of test performance – what does the performance tell us about specific purpose language ability? Perhaps the best we can do, given our current state of knowledge about the nature of language ability and processing, is simply to acknowledge, as Teasdale does, that 'judgement is an intrinsic part of test design, development, and validation' (1996: 143). I will return to a discussion of the art of LSP testing in Chapter 8.

Interaction between input and response

Again, the input and the response are non-reciprocal. The scope of the input and the response are moderately broad, since longer pieces of language are being processed and produced than was the case in the listening component. As I discussed above, it is difficult to know with any certainty how much background knowledge is required in carrying out the task, but it is likely that some degree of specific purpose knowledge is necessary to comprehend the input and to provide a meaningful response.

Assessment

As was the case with the listening assessment criteria, those for the speaking component were derived from the needs analysis. They include the test taker demonstrating ability to give instructions, give and request information, give or deny approval and clearance, give and request reasons, and check, confirm, and clarify.

Summary

The *PELA* is a prototypical example of a classic narrowly focussed specific purpose language test, dealing with a highly restricted linguistic register and situational context. It illustrates both the best qualities of LSP test development – the use of specialist informants and observations of the TLU domain – and one of the most fundamental problems of LSP testing – the inability to simulate the dynamic nature of target language use in the test domain.

Summary and conclusion

In this analysis of a number of LSP test tasks, what have we learned about the art of testing speaking and listening for specific purposes? We have looked at a variety of tasks, ranging from very close to the general end of the specificity continuum, such as those used in *IELTS* listening, to the opposite extreme, narrowly field specific tasks, as in the case of the *PELA*. We have seen a variety of input types, ranging from roleplay prompts that specify setting, participants, and problem, to quite lengthy authentic listening texts, to elaborate, seemingly genuine, corporate documents. Response types have ranged from the very minimal selected response to complex extended performance tasks. The relationship between input and response has varied in our examples from quite narrowly focussed tasks requiring little background knowledge to ones in which a great deal of background knowledge was needed for successful performance. Finally, we have seen examples of assessment criteria based entirely on linguistic characteristics and some in which target language use norms of interpretation were incorporated into the rating of performance.

We will continue our discussion of examples of LSP tests in Chapter 7 by looking at a number of tasks involving reading and writing.

....

CHAPTER SEVEN

Specific purpose tests of reading and writing

Introduction

In this chapter we will examine a number of specific purpose tests of reading and/or writing. As in Chapter 6, the purpose here is to explore the various approaches LSP test developers have taken to test language for specific purposes. We will consider the same three categories of tests as we looked at in Chapter 6: those for purposes of admission to academic or training programs, those for certification as teachers, and those for other vocational and professional purposes. The first test we will consider, the *Oxford International Business English Certificate (OIBEC)*, will be analyzed at the same level of detail as the *OET* in Chapter 6. The *OIBEC* displays a high level of situational and interactional authenticity and is an example of good LSP testing practice.

Sample analysis of test task characteristics: *Oxford International Business English Certificate*: writing task

The *OIBEC*, developed by the University of Oxford Delegacy of Local Examinations, is aimed at business men and women working in international commerce who wish to obtain a certificate of competence in English language skills for purposes of promotion or changing employment (University of Oxford Delegacy of Local Examinations 1990). The test is given at two levels: First Level, a basic qualification, and Executive Level, an advanced qualification. Available in some 44 countries world-wide, the test takes about two and a quarter hours, comprising a 20-minute listening component, a 20-minute speaking component, and a one hour and 35-minute reading and writing component. A significant feature of the *OIBEC* is a case study booklet, which provides extensive information about a problem that forms the context of the test. The candidates are given three days to study this information, which consists of narrative, tables, letters, memos, and other printed input, and may take it and any notes they might make about it into the examination room, along with a dictionary. A sample from the Executive Level case study input data is given in Extract 7.1.

Extract 7.1

Kudos Tours is the best known of the European travel companies which specialize in exotic, long distance holidays. Its reputation is based on providing a first-class service to people who want up-market holidays in far away places.

Four years ago the Board attempted to accelerate the company's rate of growth and broaden its trading base by offering a de luxe, long distance conference service to the corporate market. Although the initiative was a success and added to the company's excellent reputation, the impact on profits was disappointing.

As the Managing Director points out in the current Annual Report:

The fact that the long haul tour business has been growing at an annual rate of fifty percent, has not led to a corresponding increase in profits for this company. The growth in demand has attracted competitors into the market and margins have been squeezed, particularly in the corporate tour and conference sector. Traditionally Kudos Tours has specialized in de luxe, individual packages. Although competition at this end of the range is less fierce and pressure on margins less intense, growth rates are correspondingly low. The low growth rates in this sector have adversely affected our profitability. The Board is actively considering alternative ways of increasing turnover. At the same time, we are concerned that mass trading might have a negative effect on the Company's exclusive position in the market.

University of Oxford Delegacy of Local Examinations (1990: 2)

The case study material goes on to paint a picture of a company in trouble: younger members of the Board insisted on entering on a risky venture to increase profits, which resulted in a huge loss of working capital and put the company in dire straits. The financial situation is outlined in the narrative and in tables such as a Cost and Savings table and a Cost of Seat Replacements table, which are shown in Extract 7.2 (below and next page).

Extract 7.2

COST AND SAVINGS TABLE: MEM AIRWAYS v GLOBAL AIR (figures in sterling)			
Weekly flights to	MEM Airways	Global Air	Weekly Savings
Orlando Florida by Boeing 767 (273 seats)			
per seat	250	205	
per week	68 250	55 965	12 285
Hong Kong by Boeing 747 (part charter, 100 seats)			
per seat	390	315	
per week	39 000	31 500	7 500
Nairobi, Kenya by Airbus (part charter, 50 seats)			
per seat	310	270	
per week	15 500	13 500	2 000
Colombo, Sri Lanka by 747 (part charter, 40 seats)			
per seat	360	300	
per week	14 400	12 000	2 400
Total weekly savings			£24 185
Savings over season (26 weeks)			£628 810

Ibid. (4)

Rubric

In the rubric for the reading and writing sub-test, candidates are told that (1) they will have a total of an hour and 35 minutes to complete the tasks, (2) the questions in the question paper relate to the Case Study of Kudos Tours, (3) they should attempt all the questions, and (4) they should write all of their answers in the spaces provided. They are reminded that the Case Study preparation material must be used and that a dictionary may be used.

Extract 7.2 *(cont.)*

COST OF SEAT REPLACEMENTS
(figures in sterling)

Weekly flights to	Taurus Transport	Global Air
Orlando Florida by Boeing 767 (273 seats)		
per seat	300	205
per week	81 900	55 965
Hong Kong by Boeing 747 (part charter, 100 seats)		
per seat	430	315
per week	43 000	31 500
Nairobi, Kenya by Airbus (part charter, 50 seats)		
per seat	400	270
per week	20 000	13 500
Colombo, Sri Lanka by 747 (part charter, 40 seats)		
per seat	430	300
per week	17 200	12 000
Total weekly cost	£162 100	£112 965
Cost for 12 weeks	£1 945 200	£1 355 580

Ibid. (8)

Input

The instructions and prompt for the first task are given in Extract 7.3.

Extract 7.3

1. Study the table headed 'COST AND SAVINGS TABLE: MEM AIRWAYS v GLOBAL AIR' on page 4 and the table headed 'COST OF SEAT REPLACEMENTS' on page 8 of the Case-Study.

Use the information in these tables to complete the following note from the Finance Director to the Managing Director.

[20 marks]

Ibid. (2)

The response is to be written on the page provided, shown in Extract 7.4.

Extract 7.4

I have now investigated the cost of replacing seats for the remaining 12 weeks of the season. MEM Airways no longer has seats available, so I have approached Taurus Transport. They are able to meet our needs, but at a price.

. . . .

. . . .

.

.

.   [50 lines]

.

.

. . . .

We therefore need to find £1,945,200 urgently, so I am meeting with the Bank Manager, Mr. Smithson, tomorrow morning.

Ibid. (2–3)

We can now use the framework for analyzing specific purpose language ability and test task characteristics to look at this *OIBEC* writing task in more detail.

Characteristics of specific purpose language ability in the OIBEC

Characteristics of specific purpose language ability in the *OIBEC* are outlined in Table 7.1. The features of the construct to be measured must be gleaned from the syllabus document and from the input data itself. Clearly, the task requires a wide range of vocabulary and syntactic forms, both to comprehend the input data and to complete the writing task. It seems clear from the syllabus material that cohesion and organization are important parts of the construct, since the syllabus material makes reference to setting out a letter correctly, and to abstracting required information and re-presenting it. Not much is said about ability to use language functions, but this

Table 7.1. *Characteristics of specific purpose language ability (OIBEC)*

Language knowledge	
Grammatical knowledge	
Vocabulary	Wide range, advanced level, business and financial terminology
Morphology/Syntax	Wide range, advanced level
Phonology/Graphology	Standard written forms
Textual knowledge	
Cohesion	Implicit: must synthesize information from Case Study documents
Organization	Implicit: correct business letter format
Functional knowledge	Ideational: presenting information from Case Study documents; manipulative: arguing the need for more money
Sociolinguistic knowledge	
Dialect/variety	Standard English
Register	Business/Commercial
Idiom	Some: 'at a price'
Cultural reference	Some implicit cultural knowledge necessary: commercial 'goodwill,' younger members of Kudos family 'not interested' in running the business
Strategic competence	Relate knowledge from reading input data to language knowledge necessary to write a note of explanation to Managing Director
Background knowledge	International business, finance, UK business culture; temporary knowledge from input data

ability is implicit in the task, since apparently the test taker is expected to draw information from the input data relevant to the need for a bank loan and present it factually. Finally, it is apparent that knowledge of some idioms, figures of speech and cultural references is part of the construct, since some examples of each of these are to be found in the input data and prompt. In terms of background knowledge necessary for completing this task, the test taker will need some prior knowledge of international business, British business practices, and finance in order to understand the input data, but most of the necessary information for writing the note to the Managing Director comes from the input data itself. The test taker must engage an appropriate business discourse domain and use his or her strategic competence to relate the background knowledge to his or her language knowledge in comprehending the input and writing the note. Readers should remember the distinction, though, between the construct to be measured, which is a statement about the features of specific purpose language ability required to carry out a test task, and the criteria for correctness, which are those features the test developers actually intend to rate or score. As I discussed in Chapter 2, there is often a great difference between the construct to be measured and the criteria for correctness, which are influenced by such constraints as the temporal, financial, and human resources available for testing and the interests and requirements of the test sponsors.

Task characteristics of the OIBEC

We will begin the analysis of the task characteristics of the *OIBEC* with the rubric, as shown in Table 7.2.

Table 7.2. *Characteristics of the rubric* (OIBEC)

Objective	To assess candidates' ability to express themselves in writing clearly, concisely, and with reasonable accuracy, and to solve business and commercial problems involving finance, travel, business negotiation and company development
Procedures for responding	Write response in spaces provided in test booklet, using black or blue ink or ball-point pen
Structure	
Number of tasks	Six
Relative importance	Variable: tasks receive from 20 to 10 marks each
Task distinctions	Clear: each task is numbered and begins on a separate page
Time allotment	One hour and 35 minutes for all six tasks
Evaluation	Test takers are told that they will be tested on ability to write with clarity, conciseness, and reasonable accuracy, their ability to set out a business letter, and their ability to solve problems; they are given little information about criteria or procedures for scoring

Rubric

While most elements of the rubric are clearly spelled out, either in the syllabus and specimen material booklet or on the question paper itself, the evaluation criteria are not well-specified. Although candidates are told that the objective is to assess their ability to write with clarity, conciseness, and reasonable accuracy, their ability to set out a business letter, and their ability to solve problems, they are not given any details about criteria by which all these features will be judged. Of course, it is the case that the *OIBEC* is intended to be taken following a course of study – candidates are advised that a hundred hours of instruction are required before they submit themselves for examination – hence the identification of the information document as a syllabus, and the provision of a reading list, giving the titles and publishers of dozens of study materials. Still, it might be helpful to the candidates, and make interpreting performances more meaningful, to include some information about the criteria and standards by which the responses will be judged.

The characteristics of the input, expected response, relationship between input and response, and assessment are shown in Table 7.3.

Input

Given the nature of the task and the input data, it is not surprising that no setting information is given in the prompt or input data, although it would no doubt have added to the situational authenticity if some description of the company offices, staff, and facilities had been included. The purpose of the task is somewhat implicit: it is not really made clear what the function of the note might be, although this may be clear to those experienced in business. By the same token, the problem identification is also implicit: the test taker has to infer that he or she is to lay out the elements of the difficulty leading up to the planned meeting with the bank manager.

The input data itself is quite extensive: seven pages of prose and tabular information, some of it quite dense and complex. There are a number of pieces of information that should pique the interest of the candidates and help engage them in the task, including the fact that the younger members of the Kudos family, in their zeal to obtain a

Table 7.3. *Specific purpose test task characteristics (OIBEC)*

Input

Prompt
  Features of context

Setting	No information given
Participants	Finance Director and Managing Director of Kudos Tours
Purpose	Largely implicit: to write a note, as Finance Director, to the Managing Director, laying out the details of a deal to obtain replacement airline seats for a number of planned tours
Form/Content	Content based on input in Case Study materials
Tone	Implicit: personal but formal
Language	Standard business English
Norms	High-level executive to superior
Genre	Informational note
Problem identification	Implicit: 'Taurus Transport . . . are able to meet our needs, but at a price . . . We therefore need to find £1,945,200 urgently . . .'

Input data

Format	Case Study booklet combining narrative, tables, letters, and memos
Vehicle of delivery	Written
Length	Seven pages
Level of authenticity	
Situational	Fairly high level: good information about a 'company in trouble'
Interactional	Fairly engaging: candidates have three days to study Case Study materials

Expected response

Format	Written
Type	Extended: 50 lines provided for handwritten response

Response content

Language	clear, concise, accurate expression, business letter genre
Background knowledge	Interpretation of business financial charts, banking practice, office practices

Level of authenticity

Situational	Fairly high: common task in business world
Interactional	Fairly high

Table 7.3 *(cont.)*

Interaction between input and response

Reactivity	Non-reciprocal
Scope	Broad: seven pages of input data, with specific reference to two tables
Directness	Moderately direct: must use information in Case Study document, but some business-related background knowledge needed to interpret input data

Assessment

Construct definition	Information given in syllabus and specimen material booklet: able to 'express himself/herself clearly, concisely, and with reasonable accuracy,' 'demonstrate the ability to solve business and commercial problems,' 'set out a letter correctly,' and 'edit writing'; these criteria appear to be based on consultations with business specialists
Criteria for correctness	Little information provided; a pass mark of 60% is required for a Certificate, and of 75% for Distinction
Rating procedures	Little information provided; papers rated by trained examiners in Oxford

bank loan to enter a risky, profit-motivated deal, offered their own homes as collateral, followed by the news that the company they gave the money to has gone into liquidation. Their money is gone, at least for the moment, and they must raise more capital to meet existing obligations to clients, hotels, and transportation companies – a scenario of almost Dickensian proportions! We might assume that interactional authenticity, in particular, will be at a high level, given not only the narrative interest, but also the situational authenticity established by the tables and memos.

Expected response

The response task is to complete a note from the Finance Director to the Managing Director using the information provided in the prompt and the input data. Since 50 lines are provided for the response, this note potentially involves quite a lengthy piece of composition, incorporating a fair amount of information. The language required in the response is clearly that of business English, including technical and pan-technical vocabulary, the manipulative function of arguing for a substantial amount of new money, and knowledge of a formal business register, as from a subordinate to a superior. Background knowledge required for the response is fairly extensive, demanding an ability to read and interpret the financial tables in the input data and incorporating it into the note requesting more money. The interactional authenticity of the expected response will no doubt be fairly high, since the candidate will want to document carefully the case for going to the bank for a loan of nearly two million pounds.

Interaction between input and response

This is a non-reciprocal task, but of rather broad scope: the test taker must process seven pages of input data, including two tables. The response itself, as pointed out above, is also fairly broad in scope. The task is moderately direct, since most of the information to be used in the note to the Managing Director must be obtained from the input data. However, background information is necessary to interpret and select the most relevant points in the data in order to justify the new loan.

Assessment

Although not much information is available in the specimen material on the scope of the investigation into the target language use situation, it would appear that some consultations with experienced business professionals were carried out. In fact, the lack of information about precisely what the criteria for correctness are is a rather serious deficiency in the specimen material, in my view. The criterion of ability to solve business and commercial problems would appear to be somewhat similar in function to that of task fulfillment that was discussed in the *Japanese Language Test for Tour Guides* in Chapter 6. It is not clear precisely how this ability is to be assessed, but it certainly seems to require more than the rating of mere language ability, and thus to go somewhat beyond the weak performance hypothesis of ability to use language in the target situation that I discussed in Chapter 1.

Summary

The *Oxford International Business English Certificate* examination appears to be a fairly well-defined specific purpose test with a high degree of authenticity, particularly interactional authenticity. The input data is extensive and involves the test candidate with a complex business problem that forms the basis of the test tasks and no doubt engages an appropriate discourse domain. The test clearly reflects a development process that included consultation with specialists in international business and a concern with establishing an authentic context. In spite of a few features that could be more detailed, particularly the matter of evaluation criteria, there are many aspects of good test design evident in the *OIBEC* that LSP testers would do well to emulate.

We will now consider a number of other examples of LSP reading and writing test tasks, though in less detail. As we did in Chapter 6, we will look at tests for admission to academic and training programs, tests for certification as teachers, and tests for other vocational purposes.

Tests for admission to academic and training programs

International English Language Testing System (IELTS)

Recall from Chapter 6 that the *IELTS* is a test for academic admission purposes, jointly administered by the British Council, UCLES, and the International Development Programme of Australian Universities and Colleges. The academic reading sub-test takes about one hour and contains 40 items. There are three sections in the sub-test, each based on a separate reading passage on varying topics, and there is a variety of tasks accompanying each passage, including selected response, limited production, and extended response tasks involving filling in tables, completing summaries, and labeling diagrams. The reading passages, of extended length (i.e., ranging between approximately 600 and 1000 words), are found in a source book separate from the question paper and answer sheet. We will consider a set of tasks based on a passage entitled 'The Rollfilm Revolution,' a piece on the history of the development of photographic film.

IELTS *reading task*

Rubric

The rubric instructs the test takers as shown in Extract 7.5.

Extract 7.5

> *You should spend about 20 minutes on* **Questions 26–38** *which are based on Reading Passage 3 on pages 17 and 18.*

University of Cambridge Local Examinations Syndicate (1995b: 17)

This rubric thus contains information about time allotment and the number of questions. Each separate task in this section of the test contains its own rubric in addition to the general one above, and we will have a look at the task specific rubric below.

Input

A sample of the input text is shown in Extract 7.6.

Extract 7.6

> The introduction of the dry plate process brought with it many advantages. Not only was it much more convenient, so that the photographer no longer needed to prepare his material in advance, but its much greater sensitivity made possible a new generation of cameras. Instantaneous exposures had been possible before, but only with some difficulty and with special equipment and conditions. Now, exposures short enough to permit the camera to be held in the hand were easily achieved.

Ibid.

Although it could be argued that this passage is of a level of syntactic and semantic complexity appropriate for university-level reading, no reason is given as to why the test takers should want to read it, beyond the implicit assumption that since this is a language test they must read it!

The questions based on this input data are in three sections, the first being four statements about which the test takers must say whether they agree or do not agree, or that there is no information in the passage; the second set of questions requires the test takers to complete five labels on a diagram of a box camera; the third set of four questions requires the completion of a table. We will look at the second set in a bit of detail.

Following the presentation of the input data, there is a further rubric for the diagram completion task, as shown in Extract 7.7.

Extract 7.7

> *Complete the diagram below. Choose* **NO MORE THAN THREE WORDS** *from the passage for each answer. Write your answers in boxes 30–34 on your answer sheet.*

Ibid. (19)

This rubric provides some minimal information about evaluation criteria – no more than three words – and the procedure for responding. Taken together with the general rubric for the entire reading passage, the instructions are fairly informative, although there is no information on the objective of the reading module and very little on evaluation criteria.

Expected response

Test takers are provided with a diagram of a box camera with labels indicating the names and purpose of various components. Two names and three of the purpose labels are missing. The diagram is shown in Extract 7.8.

Extract 7.8

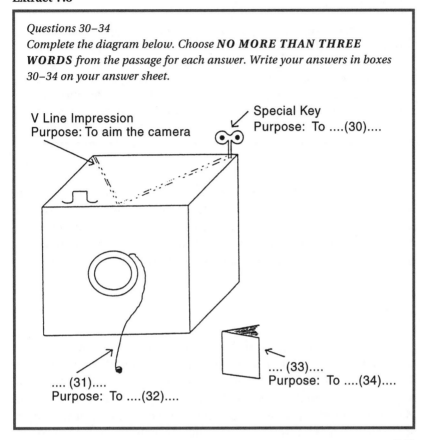

Questions 30–34
Complete the diagram below. Choose **NO MORE THAN THREE WORDS** from the passage for each answer. Write your answers in boxes 30–34 on your answer sheet.

V Line Impression
Purpose: To aim the camera

Special Key
Purpose: To ....(30)....

.... (31)....
Purpose: To ....(32)....

.... (33)....
Purpose: To ....(34)....

Ibid.

This is an example of the classic information transfer task, and appears to measure an ability to recognize information relevant to an established purpose or need. The level of authenticity is probably moderately high, since this type of task is a common one in language teaching workbooks and, we might suspect, in some content course materials, as well.

Interaction between input and response

The part of the input data relevant to this task concerns a new model box camera introduced in 1888 and is given in Extract 7.9.

Extract 7.9

> It was a small box, containing a roll of paper-based stripping film
> sufficient for 100 circular exposures 6 cm in diameter. Its operation was
> simple: set the shutter by pulling a wire string; aim the camera using the
> V line impression in the camera top; press the release button to activate
> the exposure; and turn a special key to wind on the film. A hundred
> exposures had to be made, so it was important to record each picture in
> the memorandum book provided, since there was no exposure counter.

Ibid. (17)

Although the input data as a whole is quite long, the portion of it relevant to this particular task is fairly narrowly defined, once the test taker has located it, and there is a quite direct relationship between the input and the expected response. Thus, this is perhaps not a task which engages communicative language ability to any high degree.

Assessment

Finally, the scoring criteria in this limited production task are largely implicit, beyond the injunction to use no more than three words from the passage. There is no information about the consequences of responding to item 30 'advance the film,' or to item 31 'pull-cord,' or to item 34 'count exposures.' No doubt these matters are dealt with in the instructions to raters, but it would be helpful to provide more examples to candidates concerning acceptable responses.

Summary

The *IELTS* reading sub-test appears to be closer to the general end of the specific purpose–general purpose continuum, as I noted in Chapter 6. The task types are varied and probably represent to some degree the kinds of skills university-level readers require to carry out their studies, and they no doubt allow score users to make inferences about the ability to locate relevant information in a text, in the case of this particular task. However, at the same time, the reading test passages and tasks are very decontextualized, and there is very little information provided to test takers to enable them to engage an academic discourse domain. Consequently, interpretations of performance will likely be rather limited in terms of their generalizability to real-world contexts.

IELTS *writing task*

The *IELTS* contains two writing tasks, one requiring the test takers to describe information in a diagram and the other to write an argument or discussion on a given topic. Since the second of these tasks consists of a rather straightforward prompt for a 40-minute essay, we will look at the first, somewhat more interesting, specific purpose task.

Rubric

The rubric for the *IELTS* writing task is shown in Extract 7.10.

Extract 7.10

WRITING TASK 1

You should spend about 20 minutes on this task.

The graph below shows radio and television audiences throughout the day in 1992.

Write a report for a university lecturer describing the information shown below.

You should write at least 150 words.

University of Cambridge Local Examinations Syndicate (1995c: 23)

Thus we see that time allotment and length are specified in the rubric, but no information is given about either the objective or the evaluation criteria.

Input

The rubric incorporates the prompt, and provides information about the content of the input (radio and television audiences), the addressee (a university lecturer), and the genre (a report). There is no information on the purpose for writing the report, however, thus detracting somewhat from the authenticity of the task. The input data itself, as shown in Extract 7.11, appears to be a fairly representative example of the type of graph a student might find in a textbook on communication studies or various other fields in the social sciences.

Extract 7.11

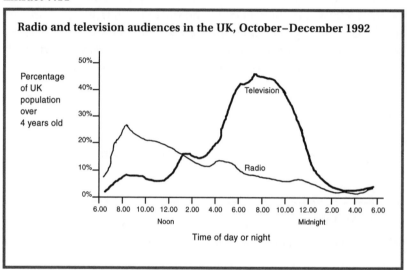

Radio and television audiences in the UK, October–December 1992

Ibid.

Expected response

Writing a report for a university lecturer is a moderately authentic response task, although, as suggested above, information about purpose and about evaluation criteria would make the task potentially more interactionally authentic.

Assessment

The *IELTS* band descriptors (see Chapter 6, pp. 148–149) mention accuracy, appropriacy, and expression, but there is little other information in the specimen material packet about the assessment of writing. The *IELTS* does have an extensive examiner training program, however, for both the speaking and writing modules, and the assessment criteria are based on studies of the communicative needs of university-level students.

Summary

Overall, this appears to be a reasonably authentic academic writing task, although it could be enhanced by an explicit statement of a field specific purpose for writing the report, and by some information on what aspects of writing will be evaluated. We are now ready to look at a writing sub-test from the *UETESOL*.

University Entrance Test in English for Speakers of Other Languages (UETESOL)

Recall from Chapter 6 that the *UETESOL* is produced and administered by the Northern Examinations and Assessment Board in the UK, and is, like the *OIBEC* examination, associated with a syllabus of study. The objective of the examination is to test academic skills 'in a context as close as possible to that likely to be encountered in an undergraduate course' (Northern Examinations and Assessment Board 1996c: 1), and is considered especially suitable for students intending to enter courses in science, engineering, business studies, and the social sciences, but not literary studies.

UETESOL *reading task*

There are two independent sets of reading tasks in the *UETESOL*, each set based on a different reading passage of 550–650 words. The reading section is presented in a Written English paper, including writing, editing, and reading skills. The input texts are presented in a question paper and the actual questions and places to respond are presented in an answer book. We will look at a passage and set of tasks from the February 1996 administration of the *UETESOL*.

Rubric

The instructions on the cover of the question paper are shown in Extract 7.12.

Extract 7.12

Time

2 hours 30 minutes + 15 minutes reading time

Instructions for candidates

Spend the first 15 minutes reading the questions. Do not begin writing until you are told to do so.

Write your answers in the answer book provided.

Answer **all** the questions in **all** the sections.

Information for candidates

Candidates are reminded of the need for good English and clear presentation.

There are three sections.

There are 30 marks for each section.

The use of dictionaries, either English or bi-lingual, is **not** permitted.

Northern Examinations and Assessment Board (1996d: 1)

Notice that candidates are told to read for 15 minutes and that they will be told when to begin their responses. This rubric will accommodate a strategy of looking at the tasks before reading the input texts; such a strategy would help test takers determine specific purposes for their reading. Note, too, that test takers are given two and a half hours to complete the two sets of reading tasks and two writing tasks, but no information is provided as to the time allotment for individual tasks, apart from the 15 minutes provided for reading through all the input prompts and data in the question paper. There are additional instructions for each reading passage in the question paper; for example, question 3B, shown in Extract 7.13.

Extract 7.13

> **Question 3B** (12 marks)
>
> Read the two texts below and answer the questions on pages 12 and 13 of the answer book.

Ibid. (5)

Finally, the answer book contains still more instructions for responding to each of the three tasks: ticking the box beside the most appropriate title for the input text, writing T (True) or F (False) after each of six statements about the text, and writing the number of the paragraph supporting the answer as well. Extract 7.14 shows the instructions for task 3.

Extract 7.14

> **3.** Text 2 relates to the four maps below. It describes five air mass types which occur over the UK. Their names are given in the five boxes in the text. Match the air mass types to the maps and write the appropriate name(s) in the space above each map. Note that one map depicts two air mass types.

Ibid. (13)

This set of instructions blends rubric with prompt material and provides information about the problem to be addressed. The prompt itself, described below, also contains an indication of the number of marks to be assigned to the task, in this case, five.

Altogether, then, the *UETESOL* contains a great deal of information about the nature of the test task: the procedures for responding, the number of tasks and the distinction between them, the time allotment, and some information about evaluation criteria, including the number of marks each task is worth. The only additional information one might want would be a statement about what abilities the tasks are meant to assess.

Input

The input data for question 3B are two fairly authentic academic texts about weather in the United Kingdom, as reproduced in Extract 7.15.

Extract 7.15

Question 3B (12 marks)

Read the two texts below and then answer the questions on pages 12 and 13 of the answer book.

Weather in The United Kingdom

Text 1

1. The weather of the United Kingdom is ever changing: a fine, warm day can be followed by chill rain and fog, even in summer. Recurring inclement weather was how the Romans perceived the British Isles 2,000 years ago. In 1994, the summer started dry and hot in the Southeast, but finished wet, with extremely heavy thunderstorms over East Anglia on the last night of August. Why is British weather so notoriously changeable while more southerly latitudes, such as the Mediterranean, have more stable conditions, particularly during the summer?

2. The air passing over each region provides the basic characteristics of today's weather. Its properties are constantly being modified by the temperature and moistness of the surface over which it is passing, and the amount of radiation it is receiving from the Sun. So, for instance, in the summer, areas just inland tend to be cooler and cloudier than those further inland, due to the influence of the sea. However, the temperature, humidity, stability and cloudiness of the air mass have been imparted to it, perhaps days earlier, over some relatively uniform and distant part of the globe. These include the tropical or polar oceans, deserts, icecaps or snow-covered surfaces. Local weather and global geography are thus strongly coupled.

3. The British Isles lie in a battle zone of competing air masses with air of tropical and polar origin separated by the polar front. During the winter, the front tends to push further south more often than in summer, allowing air with different properties to spread across the country. Depending on the pressure patterns and the position of the polar front, these air masses can dominate a region's weather for periods ranging from 12 hours to a few weeks.

4. One way of thinking of a locality's climate is in terms of the frequencies of various air masses, or weather types. For example, northwest Scotland tends to lie north of the polar front during winter so that the frequency of Polar maritime episodes then is much greater than in southeast Britain, which experiences more of a mix of Polar maritime, Tropical maritime and Polar continental. These air mass frequencies at a given location will evolve with the seasonal fluctuation of the battle between polar and tropical air.

5. In the longer term, one potential consequence of global warming over the British Isles is not merely a change in temperature, but more an alteration in the frequencies of individual air masses. Thus, if the greenhouse effect becomes a reality instead of a threat, Britain may experience more episodes of Tropical maritime and Tropical continental air in the next century than at present.

Text 2–Air Mass Types

Polar continental (Pc)

A winter air mass formed over Europe. It brings very cold, dry air when persistent easterly flow is experienced and occasionally brings heavy snow to eastern counties, as it acquires moisture over the North Sea.

Tropical continental (Tc)

A summer air mass formed over Africa or southern Europe. Very dry and warm air is brought to the British Isles by southerly winds. It is associated with summer high pressure, haze and air-pollution and drought, such as was experienced in southeast Britain in 1994. Thunderstorms occur after sufficient moisture has been collected for mid-level instability. An unstable frontal boundary between Tc and Tm air sometimes leads to very heavy thunderstorms.

Polar maritime (Pm)

Air encountered after the passage of a cold front or before the arrival of a warm front. It originates over the North Atlantic and is therefore usually cool and moist. However, the lack of airborne particles over the ocean gives good visibility, except in showers induced by instability triggered by passage over warmer waters near the UK. Generally associated with westerly or northwesterly winds.

Tropical maritime (Tm)

Typically encountered in warm sectors of frontal systems or during prolonged southwesterly flow. It originates in the tropical North Atlantic and is therefore warm and moist. Mist and low cloud are frequently associated with this air mass, due to the reduction of the air's temperature to its dewpoint–the temperature to which a parcel of air must be cooled before clouds form–as its passes over the cooler seas near Britain.

Arctic maritime(Am)

This air mass forms over the Norwegian-Greenland Sea and brings very cold air to Britain during prolonged northerly wind episodes. It is common during the winter, although occasionally experienced in summer as well. The air is very dry, cold, and feels raw. In winter it often brings snow to northern Scotland and the East Anglian coast.

Ibid. (5)

As we saw with the *IELTS* tasks, there is no field specific purpose, or even measurement purpose, provided for reading these texts. This would enhance the interactional authenticity of the input data to match the already high level of situational authenticity.

The prompt for task 3 is shown in Extract 7.16.

Extract 7.16

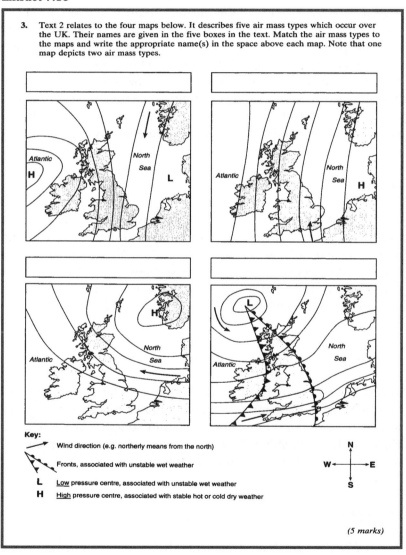

3. Text 2 relates to the four maps below. It describes five air mass types which occur over the UK. Their names are given in the five boxes in the text. Match the air mass types to the maps and write the appropriate name(s) in the space above each map. Note that one map depicts two air mass types.

Key:

Wind direction (e.g. northerly means from the north)

Fronts, associated with unstable wet weather

L   Low pressure centre, associated with unstable wet weather

H   High pressure centre, associated with stable hot or cold dry weather

N
W ◄─┼─► E
S

(5 marks)

This appears to be a highly interactional task, requiring the fairly intensive engagement of linguistic, strategic, and background knowledge. Being able to match the maps with the written descriptions in text 2 demands quite complex interpretation of the text, dealing with some technical and pan-technical terminology, such as *easterly flow*, *high pressure, mid-level instability, unstable frontal boundary*, and *maritime*, and a certain amount of geographical background knowledge such as the location of the Norwegian–Greenland Sea, Scotland, and East Anglia, for example. Test takers must also use information from the prompt to interpret certain parts of the input text, as indicated in the key, including the descriptions of fronts and low and high pressure. One must wonder, however, whether all that is really required to do this task is to pay attention to the wind direction arrows; if validation research showed this to be the case, it would substantially lower the potential for interactional authenticity.

Expected response

The limited production responses for this task probably reflect a fairly high level of interactional authenticity, though with a caveat with regard to the arrows, as suggested above. Note that the prompt indicates that one map depicts two air mass types, so test takers have to write two names in one box. It is not clear whether writing the full name is required, or whether the abbreviation will do.

Interaction between input and response

This is a task of fairly broad scope, with quite a bit of reading to do, moving between the input text and the prompt. It is also quite direct, in that most of the information needed to complete the task is included in the text, although, as I suggested above, some amount of background knowledge is required as well.

Assessment

The *UETESOL* syllabus document (Northern Examinations and Assessment Board 1996c) says that the test takers will need to 'scan for particular information, extract, summarise and manipulate information, make inferences, and apply the information to the solution of a related problem' (p. 2) in the reading section of the test. The authors point out that care has been taken to ensure that, since this is a reading test, heavy use is made of graphical and tabular frameworks for responses to avoid merging reading and writing ability, and we see this illustrated in the present example. Candidates may be asked to produce short written responses from time to time, if the nature of the task seems to require this rather than a table or graph, but in such cases, 'marks will be awarded for the content of the answers rather than the accuracy of language' (p. 3).

Summary

Here we see reading tasks that are likely to be rather high on the scales of both situational and interactional authenticity, requiring test takers to do a fair amount of reading and to move back and forth between question prompts and texts to complete rather complex tasks. The tasks are intrinsically interesting and challenging but, in addition, the test developers have provided a good amount of information to the test takers about the nature of the tasks and how they are to accomplish them.

UETESOL *writing task*

The writing skills part of the *UETESOL* consists of two parts: (1) a short description of a process, a report on a procedure, or a set of instructions for a simple task from information presented in graphic, tabular, or verbal form; and (2) a more extended interpretation of information, including compare and contrast, cause and effect, drawing conclusions, or making hypotheses.

Rubric

The rubric for the writing tasks is pretty much combined with that for the reading tasks: two and a half hours are provided, but no suggestions for how long to spend on each task. There is no information about what the objective of the writing tasks might be, apart from the general reminder of the need for good English and clear presentation. Nor are the test takers told anything about evaluation criteria. The instructions specific to the writing tasks are in the form of prompts, and these include information about length: 'Write between half to three quarters of a side' or 'You should write about a side to a side and a half.' Test takers are provided with space in the answer book to write their responses: pages (or sides) with about 30 lines each.

Input

Question 1B provides the prompt shown in Extract 7.17.

Extract 7.17

You have been asked to compile a guide to some of the fungi* in Britain. Using the information in the table below and the illustrations on page 5, classify the fungi into 3 or 4 groups as you think appropriate. Describe the common features and variations within each group.

* fungi – more than one fungus

You should write about a side to a side and a half.

Northern Examinations and Assessment Board (1996e: 4)

Thus, the prompt provides information about the purpose of the task, form and content, and the problem to be addressed, namely classification. There is no indication of the audience for the guide, and therefore it is not clear whether the guide is for novice students, professionals, or the general public. This could influence how test takers approach the task and how score users might interpret performance. For example, a guide for amateur mycologists who want to collect fresh mushrooms to eat would be quite different from one intended for professionals interested in classification schemes, and different again from a guide for students who need to learn to identify various fungi. These considerations would lead to differences in such characteristics in the writing as form and content, tone, norms of interaction, and genre. This is a point I have raised a number of times in this book: the more completely and precisely specific purpose contextual information is provided for the test taker, the more effectively inferences can be made about specific purpose language ability underlying performance on the task. This is particularly true of extended response tasks such as the one under discussion here since the writer has quite a complex task to carry out and interpreting his or her performance on it would be greatly facilitated by knowing beforehand what contextual characteristics he or she was working with.

The input data is reproduced in Extracts 7.18 and 7.19.

Extract 7.18

Question 1B (20 marks)

You have been asked to compile a guide to some of the fungi* in Britain. Using the information in the table below and the illustrations on page 5, classify the fungi into 3 or 4 groups as you think appropriate. Describe the common features and variations within each group.

* fungi – more than one fungus

You should write about a side to a side and a half.

Name	Colour	Good to eat ⊖ Unpleasant ⊕ to eat Poisonous ⊛	Time of Year	Location	Height	Diameter
(a) Fly agaric	red/yellow	⊛	July-Oct	under birch trees	up to 20cm	up to 15cm
(b) Ramaria flavia	yellow	⊖	July-Sept	mixed woodland	15-20cm	10-15cm
(c) Panther cap	brown	⊛	July-Oct	mixed woodland	up to 15cm	up to 12cm
(d) Parasol	brown	⊖	July-Sept	grassy areas	up to 40cm	up to 30cm
(e) Yellow stereum	yellow	⊕	all year	on dead birch trees	–	2-10cm
(f) Ramaria opsis	violet	⊕	Aug-Oct	grassy areas	1-2cm	–
(g) Destroying angel	white	⊛	June-Sept	mixed woodland	up to 15cm	3-10cm
(h) Birch bracket	brown	⊕	all year	only on birch trees	–	20-30cm
(i) Death cap	yellow	⊛	July-Oct	under oak trees	12-15cm	up to 15cm
(j) Field mushroom	white	⊖	June-Sept	grassy areas	4-8cm	up to 10cm
(k) Yellow stainer	white	⊛	July-Oct	mixed woodland	up to 15cm	up to 15cm
(l) Yellow antler	yellow	⊕	July-Jan	on dead oak trees	3-7cm	–
(m) Sulphur bracket	yellow	⊖	May-Oct	on oak trees	–	10-15cm
(n) Horse mushroom	white	⊖	June-Sept	grassy areas	up to 10cm	up to 20cm

---

Ibid. (4)

Extract 7.19

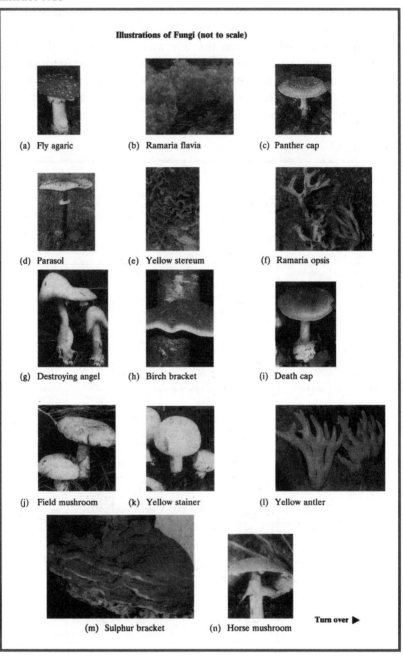

Illustrations of Fungi (not to scale)

(a) Fly agaric

(b) Ramaria flavia

(c) Panther cap

(d) Parasol

(e) Yellow stereum

(f) Ramaria opsis

(g) Destroying angel

(h) Birch bracket

(i) Death cap

(j) Field mushroom

(k) Yellow stainer

(l) Yellow antler

(m) Sulphur bracket

(n) Horse mushroom

Turn over ▶

Ibid. (5)

These input data have the appearance of fairly authentic textbook material in a botany class. The material is moderately complex, and the test taker must cope with a fairly extended amount of information.

Expected response

This is clearly a fairly complex task: the test taker must decide upon a focus for classification, then summarize the features of items within each class. There are a number of possible classification strategies – color, edibility, season, location, size, or appearance. Of course, each of these would require a different type of descriptive approach, and some are more defensible than others. The student who chose an appropriate classification strategy might carry out the writing task more satisfactorily than another candidate who writes equally well but who chose a less effective classification scheme. In other words, the language of the expected response is potentially fairly complex, and interpretations of performance could take both facets – communicative language ability and knowledge of classification categories – into account.

Relationship between input and response

The relationship between the input and the response is fairly direct, since most of the information needed to complete the writing task is in the input data. However, the actual classification task depends to some degree on background knowledge of classification strategies, and it is this aspect of the task that both adds interactional authenticity and makes it a bit more difficult to interpret the performance, since the score user would not know whether a weak performance was due more to poor writing or to lack of experience with classification, particularly in the case of candidates for admission to university as undergraduates.

Assessment

There is information in the syllabus document (Northern Examinations and Assessment Board 1996c) about assessment criteria. For example, concerning the second, more complex, writing task, the criteria shown in Extract 7.20 are discussed.

Extract 7.20

> Answers of about 300 words will be required. As candidates are required to develop a logical piece of writing which interprets the information provided, it is clearly important that they avoid any attempt to describe extensively all the information provided. Candidates should be able to compare and contrast, show cause and effect relationships, draw conclusions, make hypotheses and produce other such patterns of discourse. They should be able to paragraph their writing and to use a variety of means to create coherence at the intersentential and inter-paragraph level. They should be able to produce sentences of a complexity consistent with the formal register.
>
> Candidates will be expected to write grammatical prose with due regard to word order, subject/verb agreement and appropriate use of tense and voice.

Ibid. (2)

This information is addressed to teachers so that they might develop courses to prepare candidates for the examination, and is no doubt fleshed out considerably in materials for the training of the examiners who rate the performances.

Summary

This *UETESOL* writing task appears to be a moderately specific purpose measure of writing, requiring both language knowledge and academic background knowledge. The test developers have attempted to contextualize it by providing a plausible purpose for processing the input data and carrying out the task. The task itself is a complex one, requiring the candidates to compare and contrast fungi both within and between categories. In the prompt, more information could have been provided about audience and purpose, which would have made the possibilities for inferences about specific purpose language ability richer and more applicable to the target language use situation.

We now turn our attention to two examples of tests for the certification of teachers, the *English Language Skills Assessment* (*ELSA*), and the *Proficiency Test for Teachers: Italian*.

Tests for certification as teachers

English Language Skills Assessment (ELSA)

The *ELSA* was developed by the New South Wales Department of School Education and the Adult Migrant English Service in 1991–92 for the purpose of assessing the English language ability of applicants for employment as teachers who had qualified outside Australia and who came from a non-English-speaking background. After a review of the literature on defining language ability in the school context, and on procedures elsewhere for assessing the language ability of non-native-English-speaking teachers, the developers visited primary and secondary schools to gather information about the target language use situation: (1) they obtained samples of spoken and written discourse, and documents relating to school policy, curricula and administration; and (2) they conducted interviews with teachers, both native and non-native English-speakers, to obtain spoken and written texts to create a benchmark against which to measure performance, and with Department of School Education staff working with non-native-English-speaking teachers to obtain information on aspects of language competence which separated effective from non-effective teachers (McDowell 1995). As a result of their analysis, the test developers decided to attempt to measure the following micro-skills in the reading and writing tests:

Reading: understand literal and implied meaning
skim for gist
scan to extract specific information
read for overall comprehension
decode meaning within reasonable time
interpret text for attitude and style

Writing: convey exact meaning accurately and clearly
organize ideas in a clear logical structure
use register appropriate for task/situation

McDowell (1995: 18)

They also decided to treat reading and writing as integrated, rather than independent, skills and to test them together in a single sub-test. 'We had found that writing in the school context usually occurred in response to written input (notes from colleagues, letters from parents, memos from the department); reading texts of different genres and script types (including original printed format, reformatted text and handwritten text) could therefore double as authentic input for the writing tasks' (McDowell 1995: 20). The texts were taken from genuine school documents, newsletters to parents, newspaper articles on education, and academic papers. There are seven sections in the reading and writing paper, each containing different tasks. The reading tasks include multiple-choice comprehension items, short-answer questions, matching tasks, and error correction tasks. There are two writing tasks: a short-answer, limited production task and a longer direct writing task. Both are based on written input. We will look at the extended production task.

ELSA *reading and writing task*

Rubric

The rubric for the *ELSA* reading and writing task informs the candidates that the test contains seven sections and that they will have one hour and 35 minutes to complete the entire test. They are advised to spend no more than 55 minutes on sections 1–4 and no more than 40 minutes on sections 5–7. Test takers are also told that the task is designed to assess the ability to skim, scan, and select information from written texts, but are given no information about the writing evaluation criteria.

Input

The prompt and input data for the second section are shown in Extract 7.21.

Extract 7.21

Sandra has received the following handwritten note from the Deputy Principal. Read this note then turn over the page for further instructions.

AUSTRALIA STREET HIGH SCHOOL

10/12/92

Dear Sandra

Yesterday there was an unfortunate incident in the playground at morning recess, while you were on duty. Sally Mason of class 8R2 claims she was hit in the face by two Year 10 boys. She has severe cuts and bruises to the face and her parents are anxious to know what occurred. You were on playground duty at the time but do not appear to have filed a report. Are you able to say what occurred and who was involved in the incident?

Please let me have your written comments by return so that I can report to the parents.

Many thanks

J V Cutler

Adult Migrant English Service (1994: 4)

The context is defined in terms of the participants, purpose, topic, and function, but such characteristics as tone, norms of interaction, and genre are left to the imagination and background knowledge of the candidates. The test takers are given the prompt shown in Extract 7.22 containing ideas to include in their responses.

The situation is deliberately left somewhat vague, with the 'Ideas' box providing the only clues as to why the teacher did not report the playground incident. The test taker has to use background knowledge to realize that not all of the ideas should be used in the explanation. The prompt identifies to some extent the problem to be addressed, but it is really the input data, the note from the Deputy Principal, that provides that information, which must be inferred: 'You were on playground duty at the time but do not seem to have filed a report.' Thus, the problem is fairly contexualized, and the candidates must rely on their background knowledge about playground duty and the filing of reports on violent incidents to complete the task.

Extract 7.22

Imagine you are Sandra and write to the Deputy Principal explaining what happened. You may use some of the ideas below in your reply if you want. You may also use your own ideas.

IDEAS

Bad weather
Staff member away
Needed to help in toilet block
Not rostered on Wednesday
Called to telephone

Ibid. (5)

Expected response

The response is to be written in the space provided, about two-thirds of a page.

Relationship between input and response

The task is non-reciprocal, although the candidate is given some choice as to what approach to take in arguing his or her way around the problem. It requires processing a fairly broad amount of input and the expected response is also rather extended and is of moderate directness since it requires some use of background knowledge.

Assessment

The *ELSA* specifications document (Iles and McDowell 1994) includes a list of enabling skills for the writing sub-test, and includes such criteria as using a style and genre appropriate to the context, displaying discourse markers and coherent discourse, distinguishing relevant from irrelevant material, using an appropriate tone (Iles and McDowell 1994). These criteria cover many of those in the framework for defining the construct in an LSP test, particularly those involving the textual, functional, and sociolinguistic levels.

Summary

This task is an example of a moderately authentic, well-specified test task. It is fairly highly contextualized, requiring that the candidate be familiar with conventions of staff–administration report writing, and it requires a fair amount of plain ingenuity in getting out of what appears to be a tight spot. It certainly would seem to test the candidates' knowledge of the manipulative function of English, and perhaps the imaginative function as well. The developers of this reading and writing task have made a strong effort to provide specific purpose situational cues in the prompts and input data to help ensure that test takers engage appropriate discourse domains in interacting with the material.

Proficiency Test for Teachers: Italian

Reading task

I noted in Chapter 6 that the *Proficiency Test for Teachers: Italian* has two main functions: (1) to serve as a benchmark for teacher education by making the language requirements of the foreign language teacher explicit, and (2) to certify language teachers by helping determine whether those applying for employment in primary schools are proficient enough in the language to perform their duties as language teachers. The reading section of the test is intended to reflect the importance of the teaching of culture as well as language and focusses on 'extra-classroom use' of Italian (National Languages and Literacy Institute of Australia 1993: 8), whereas the speaking task we looked at in Chapter 6 was more classroom specific. Thus, the reading text is taken from a magazine or newspaper article and candidates are given a number of tasks to demonstrate their comprehension. The Italian teachers' reading task is included here because it is an example of good language testing practice and because it illustrates an interesting aspect of LSP assessment, that of more culturally oriented content which it is deemed necessary for language teachers to control and be able to explain.

Rubric

The instructions in the draft handbook inform candidates that they will have 55 minutes for the reading tasks. The general instructions are in English, as shown in Extract 7.23.

Extract 7.23

> In this section you are required to read a passage taken from an Italian newspaper or magazine on a topic of general interest and answer questions about its content. The questions test your ability to read both for detail and for overall meaning. Some items check your comprehension of the broad meaning of the text while others require attention to detail.

National Languages and Literary Institute of Australia (1993: 15)

Thus, candidates are given information about the objective and the time allotted, and some information about the criteria for correctness. The handbook also tells candidates that the sample text is considerably shorter than that in the actual test. There is also a rubric in Italian, reproduced in Extract 7.24.

Extract 7.24

> **Comprensione Di Testo Scritto**
>
> Leggere il brano nella pagina seguente e completare i vari compiti secondo le istruzioni date.

Ibid. (5)

Translation:

Comprehension of a Written Text

Read the passage on the following page and complete the various exercises according to the instructions given.

Each of the five reading tasks contains additional instructions in Italian specific to that task. For example, *Attività 2* has the rubric shown in Extract 7.25.

Extract 7.25

> *Dare brevi rispose in inglese alle seguenti domande scrivendo negli spazi appositi.*

Ibid. (6)

Translation:

> Give brief responses in English to the following questions writing in the spaces provided.

This rubric adds information on the procedure for responding.

Input

The reading text in this example is adapted from a magazine and contains six paragraphs. It concerns the theory that obesity is genetically based. The first paragraph is reproduced in Extract 7.26.

Extract 7.26

OBESI SI NASCE O SI DIVENTA?

Secondo il dottor Gian Franco Adami della Scuola di specializzazione di scienza dell'alimentazione dell'Universita di Genova ci può essere una predisposizione genetica, cioè innata, all'obesità. È quanto risulterebbe da uno studio effettuato in America su coppie di gemelli monocoriali (concepiti, cioè, dallo stesso ovulo) Anche nel caso di separazione e di affidamento a famiglie diverse, i gemelli nel corso degli anni sviluppano un peso che risulta poi uguale tra di loro.

Ibid. (4)

Translation:

IS ONE BORN OBESE OR DOES ONE BECOME OBESE?

According to Doctor Gian Franco Adami from the University of Genoa School of Specialization of Food Science, there may be a genetic predisposition, i.e., innate, towards obesity. These appear to be the findings of an American study of pairs of identical twins (conceived from the same egg). Even in the cases where the twins were separated and raised in different families, over the years they developed a weight that was more or less equal between them.

At the end of the passage, there is a note about the origin of the text, a popular magazine, reproduced in Extract 7.27.

Extract 7.27

Adattato da 'Troppo grassi per essere sani' La Fiamma 30/5/93

Ibid. (4)

This attribution of the text to an Italian publication helps authenticate it.

The prompts for this activity, shown in Extract 7.28, indicate the problem to be addressed.

Extract 7.28

---

4. Perchè le diete non funzionano, secondo il dottor Amati?

    (i) _____

    (ii) _____

5. A che cosa ci si riferisce quando nel brano si parla degli 'ideali che vengono proposti in continuazione' (paragrafo 4)

_____

_____

_____

You must answer all the questions given below. Ensure that all relevant details are included in your answers. Write down your answers in English in the answer book provided.

You may use a dictionary.

Ibid. (5)

Expected response

The rubric indicated that the candidates are to respond briefly in English in the spaces provided. There is no information about whether these responses are to be in full sentences, but the format of item 4 would appear to suggest that phrases would be acceptable. In any case, this is a limited production task.

Relationship between input and response

The scope of the task requires a rather broad amount of text to be processed and a limited response which is quite directly dependent upon the input.

Assessment

The criteria for correctness were derived from an analysis of actual candidates' papers, and a list of acceptable and unacceptable responses was compiled. The limited production tasks, as that in the example above, are double marked by trained examiners.

Summary

This reading section of the *Proficiency Test for Teachers: Italian* is intended to assess ability to comprehend authentic reading texts in an extra-classroom category. This category was regarded by the test designers' informants as relevant to their role as teachers of both culture and language (Elder 1993b). Since the focus of the reading section is on demonstrating comprehension, little information is provided about a specific purpose for reading the text, and the tasks are very assessment oriented. The interactive authenticity of the section might be enhanced by providing more discussion of the cultural objective.

Tests for other vocational purposes

Royal Society of Arts Certificate in Business Language Competence (CBLC)

The *RSA Certificate in Business Language Competence* is intended to assess communicative skills within a business context in languages other than English, including French, German, Italian, and Spanish. There are five levels of certification: Basic, Survival, Threshold, Operational, and Advanced. At each level there are five or six sections, called elements, covering such activities as listening, reading, telephoning, conversing, making presentations, and writing. There are a number of tasks in each section, and the input materials are what the test developers call 'simulated authentic' (Royal Society of Arts Examinations Board 1994a: 47), and indeed the materials do have a visually authentic look about them. Results in each section are rated either pass or fail and candidates must pass all sections to receive a full certificate. We will look at a German reading task at the Advanced Level.

CBLC *German reading task*

Rubric

The specimen materials inform test takers that the time allowed for the reading section is 60 minutes and that dictionaries may be used. There is more rubric material provided before the questions for this section.

There is no information in the specimen rubric about how many tasks there will be, although, of course, the test taker can look through the test booklet and find out. Information is provided in the specimen materials about assessment objectives, though it is not clear if this information is provided to actual candi- dates at the time of the test. The objectives are numbered and one must refer to the *CBLC* Syllabus (*Ibid.*), a 59-page document that appears to be addressed to course planners and instructors. At any rate, in the specimen materials, we are told that task 3 is intended to assess an ability 'to assess facts, ideas and opinions for a specific purpose from a range of documents on the same or related topics' (p. 47).

Input

There are three documents provided for task 3: a diagram and explanation, a diagram without explanation, and a newspaper article. The documents are all related to the economy of the former German Democratic Republic. The first document is reproduced as Extract 7.29.

Extract 7.29

Element 2

READING GERMAN

• *Reading Material* •

DOCUMENTS FOR TASK 3

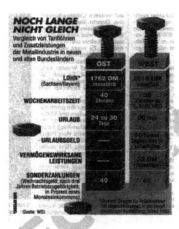

NOCH LANGE NICHT GLEICH
Vergleich von Tariflöhnen und Zusatzleistungen der Metallindustrie in neuen und alten Bundesländern

Quelle: WSI

Am 1. April dieses Jahres steigen die Löhne der ostdeutschen Metallarbeiter auf rund 80 Prozent der westdeutschen Tarife, ein Jahr später dann auf 100 Prozent. Für die Ostfirmen heißt das: rund 26 Prozent mehr Lohn ab April, und, nach Rechnung der Arbeitgeber, noch mal über 30 Prozent mehr im nächsten Jahr.

Die Betriebe im schwächlichen Osten dagegen, deren Produktivität notorisch hinter den Lohnkosten herhinkt (siehe Grafik), sollen bald um mehr als ein Viertel höhere Personalkosten verkraften. Dieter Kirchner, Hauptgeschäftsführer des Arbeitgeberverbandes Gesamtmetall, sagt schlimmste Folgen voraus: "Es wird noch weniger Arbeitsplätze geben. Und viele Betriebe werden dichtmachen müssen, die andernfalls eine Chance zum Überleben hätten."

Die Argumente sind bekannt: Die Arbeitgeber verweisen auf die immense Kostenbelastung, die Betriebe und Arbeitsplätze bedrohe. Allenfalls den Inflationsausgleich, also acht bis neun Prozent mehr Lohn, wollen sie vom 1. April an zahlen. Die Anpassung der Tariflöhne an das Westniveau soll um ein paar Jahre aufgeschoben werden.

Source: Der Spiegel

SAMPLE
CBLC GERMAN 2RM
ADVANCED

Royal Society of Arts Examinations Board (1994b: 13)

Notice that the diagram and text compare the economies of East and West Germany. The source of the document is given as *Der Spiegel*, a popular news magazine.

An English prompt is provided for task 3, as shown in Extract 7.30.

Extract 7.30

> You are on a business trip to the former East Germany. Because your company is interested in setting up business in Brandenburg, you have been asked to write a report in English for your company's magazine on the wage situation in the former GDR.
>
> Use the ideas, opinions and statistics contained in this material to write your report. In writing the report you should:
>
> (a) explain the differences between the wage level in the old and the new federal states
>
> (b) explain the point of view/aspirations of the trade unions
>
> (c) explain the former East German employers' situation and their aspirations
>
> (d) explain what is happening to wage levels in comparison with productivity.

Ibid. (15)

The input materials are fairly high in situational and probably interactional authenticity. The prompt provides a purpose, a genre, and an audience for the writing task, and there is quite a bit of specific information about what ideas to include in the report. The input data is fairly extended – the texts without the diagrams run to about 330 words – and there is a fair amount of information to process. The level of language appears not to be too technical, but of the type business people might be expected to need to comprehend.

Expected response

Notice that the response is to be written in English, the native language of the majority of test takers. As we see in the prompt above, the test takers are given quite a bit of guidance about what ideas to include in their response, and their task therefore is to find the required information in the documents and interpret it for the report. No information is given about the required length of the response apart from the overall 60-minute time limit for the whole section, but otherwise this appears to be a fairly situationally and interactively authentic task, requiring both language knowledge and specific purpose background knowledge.

Interaction between input and response

This is a relatively direct task since most of the material for the response must come from the input data, although some degree of background knowledge is probably necessary to interpret the material and organize it. Both the input and the response are fairly broad in scope and should represent a challenging task for the test takers.

Assessment

No information is available about how the assessment criteria were devised, but there was no doubt some research carried out about what skills and abilities are needed to conduct business in the target countries. In any case, there are detailed assessment objectives, performance criteria, and assessment guidance provided in the *CBLC* syllabus for each certificate level and each section of the tests. The guidelines state that the responses must contain all relevant information as specified in the prompt, and that factual details must be accurate. The main criterion for task 3 is that 'relevant facts, ideas and opinions [must be] selected and written down in English.' In other words, there appears to be no requirement that the report be organized in a certain way or even grammatically well-formed. This detracts somewhat from the interactional authenticity of the task, since it loses some of its communicativeness by not requiring the engagement of a report-writing discourse domain. The purpose of not requiring a report format and so on, is no doubt to keep the task focussed on reading in the target language and not contaminating it with writing; however, this does limit the interpretations that can be made of performance.

Summary

Overall, this is a well-specified specific purpose reading task with a fairly high degree of situational and interactional authenticity in the input, though to a slightly lesser degree in the response. The test developers were obviously attempting to maintain a degree of authenticity in the task by requiring a written response as opposed to a selected response task, for example, but also to limit the assessment of reading to the selection of facts, ideas, and opinions in the target language by not requiring an authentically formatted response.

Test of English for International Communication (TOEIC)

TOEIC was developed in 1979 by Educational Testing Service (ETS) in the US in response to requests from clients for a standardized test of English listening and reading in the context of international business (Educational Testing Service 1996). The test is now administered by an independent commercial subsidiary of ETS, the Chauncey Group. *TOEIC* is given world-wide, although the majority of test takers and score users are located in Asia, particularly Japan and Korea, and it is taken by over a million candidates a year. It consists of 100 multiple-choice listening comprehension items and 100 multiple-choice reading comprehension items. The reading sub-test has three sections: sentence completion, error recognition, and comprehension of short texts. Candidates are given 75 minutes to complete all three parts. We will take a look at an example of a short text reading comprehension task.

TOEIC *reading task*

Rubric

The rubric for the task reproduced in Extract 7.31 shows the thoroughness that is a hallmark of the ETS approach to language testing, giving very complete instructions and a sample problem to help ensure that candidates are familiar with the test method and response procedure before beginning the test task itself.

Extract 7.31

> This is a test of your ability to use the English language. The total time for the test is approximately two hours. It is divided into seven parts. Each part of the test begins with a set of specific directions that include sample questions. Be sure you understand what you are to do before you begin work on a part.
>
> You will find that some of the questions are harder than others, but you should try to answer every one. There is no penalty for guessing. Do not be concerned if you cannot answer all of the questions.
>
> Do not mark your answers in this test book. You must put <u>all your answers on the separate answer sheet</u> that you have been given.

Educational Testing Service (1982: 43)

Candidates are given detailed instructions for blackening the letter of the correct multiple-choice response on their answer sheet as well as an example. They are told how to correct a mistakenly marked response, and are even given a reason why it is important to mark their answers carefully:

Extract 7.32

> . . . so that the test-scoring machine can accurately record your test score.

Ibid.

The rubric for this test is quite complete, in other words, in terms of objective, time allotment, distinction between tasks, and response procedures. What is missing from both this and the specific rubric for the reading comprehension section, shown in Extract 7.33, is any detailed information about evaluation criteria: what aspects of English knowledge the test is designed to measure. The test takers are simply told that the objective of the test is to measure their ability to use the English language. The rubric for the reading comprehension section of *TOEIC* (see Extract 7.33) is similarly detailed in terms of procedures for responding.

Extract 7.33

PART VII

Directions: Questions 161–200 are based on a variety of reading material (single sentences, paragraphs, advertisements, and the like). You are to choose the one best answer, (A), (B), (C), or (D), to each question. Then, on your answer sheet, find the number of the problem and mark your answer. Answer all questions following a passage on the basis of what is stated or implied in that passage.

Ibid. (30)

This is followed by a six- or seven-line sample paragraph and a single multiple-choice question, with the correct answer already marked. Then, there is a short explanation of why the answer is the best one.

Input

There are 15 separate texts for the candidates to read, with 2–5 questions about each. The passages in the version of *TOEIC* available for review include a letter reminding a magazine subscriber to pay the subscription, a notice advertising a communications equipment exhibition, an agreement form for a personal background investigation, a notice to airline passengers about lost luggage claims, a book review, and so on. The reader, in other words, must abruptly switch topic and genre up to 15 times during this part of the test – probably not becoming communicatively engaged in any of the texts. An example of the input data and questions is shown in Extract 7.34.

It is unlikely that much business-related background knowledge would be needed to read this text and answer the questions correctly, and the task would appear to be quite close to the general end of the specificity continuum. The input text itself has a fairly realistic ring to it, although an actual notice would no doubt include contact information – an address, phone and fax number, at least. There also appears to be a typo in the third line: 'may remedy delinquency.' The first question requires inferencing ability, while the second requires the knowledge that 'balance overdue' and 'holding up payment' add up to a bill not being paid.

Extract 7.34

Questions 199–200 refer to the following notice.

> When an account runs a little past due, we find that most of our patients appreciate a brief note from us, reminding them of the fact, so that they may remedy delinquency. This statement shows a balance overdue, according to our records. Unless you have some special reason for holding up payment, your check will be appreciated. If you have insurance to cover this charge and have not notified us of the fact, kindly let us know at once.

199. Who has sent out this notice?

(A) A criminal lawyer
(B) A doctor
(C) A banker
(D) An insurance broker

200. Why was this notice sent out?

(A) Because the bill had not yet been paid.
(B) Because the insurance did not cover the charges.
(C) Because the checking account had insufficient funds.
(D) Because the prescription was incomplete.

Ibid. (42)

Expected response

TOEIC employs a machine-scored response format in which the test taker marks his or her chosen response on a separate answer sheet. An effort is made in the rubric to ensure that test takers understand how to do this and how to change a mistakenly marked choice.

Interaction between input and response

The task is, of course, non-reciprocal. In terms of scope, there is a moderate amount of information to process in reading the text. Question 199 assumes some minimal background knowledge to make the required inference, and is thus somewhat less direct than question 200, which requires a search of the text for the reason for the notice.

Assessment

The producers of *TOEIC* say that the test is intended to measure 'the everyday English skills of people working in an international environment. The scores indicate how well people can communicate in English with others in business, commerce, and industry. The test does not require specialized knowledge or vocabulary' (Educational Testing Service 1996: 1). The scores are based on the number correct out of 100 items, and are converted to a scale from 5 to 495 points. The *TOEIC examinee handbook* (Educational Testing Service 1996) provides some information about the relationship between *TOEIC* scores and various types of jobs, such as employees in a hotel, a defense company, and an international electronics company. However, there is no information about what specific abilities *TOEIC* is intended to measure or the criteria for correctness. Such information is no doubt included in the detailed test specifications, which is a proprietary ETS document.

Summary

This is a good example of a well-constructed norm-referenced traditional multiple-choice test task, with no doubt high reliability, but extremely limited in the inferences it will allow about language knowledge. *TOEIC* attempts to focus on largely decontextualized aspects of language knowledge, in spite of its business and commercial appearance. Although the *TOEIC examinee handbook* states as a particular emphasis communication in business, commerce, and industry, it is unlikely that the reading tasks engage the test takers in genuinely communicative behavior or in genuinely specific purpose language use, and the test would be placed near the general end of the specificity continuum discussed in Chapter 1.

Occupational English Test (OET)

As described in Chapter 6, the *OET* is a performance test for assessing the English abilities of applicants for licensure to practice medical professions in Australia. The writing sub-test of the *OET* is a specific purpose writing task in which the input consists of approximately one-and-a-half pages of case-history notes or other clinical records from the test takers' particular branch of medical science. The task is to write a letter of referral to a fellow professional, informing the colleague of the patient's history and requesting further examination and treatment. We will look at a task designed for physicians.

OET *writing task*

Rubric

Candidates are told to read the case notes and complete the writing task that follows them.

Input

Extract 7.35 is an example of input for the writing task.

Extract 7.35

MEDICAL PRACTITIONERS

Time allowed: 40 minutes

Mrs. Lyons is a patient in your general practice. Read the case notes below and complete the writing task that follows.

CASE NOTES   Mrs Harriet Lyons 84 yo woman

14/5/88
PH:
- osteoarthritis ®hip → THR 1985
- hypertension × 20 yrs
- Type II diabetes × 15 yrs
- recurrent UTIs
- dementia × 10 yrs

Medications:
- Daonil 5 mg bd
- Aldomet 500 mg bd
- Indocid 25 mg tds

Brought in by daughter, with whom she lives.
Increasingly difficult to cope with her.
- urinary incontinence for last week. ?dysuria.

	• abdominal pain.
	• No fevers / sweats / loin pain.
	• More confused than usual. Refusing to eat.
	• No vomiting, diarrhoea.
O/E:	Afebrile. Confused.
	Mild suprapubic tenderness.
	Urine: protein +++ RBS +++ glucose 1/2%
Assessment:	Worsening mental state 2° to UTI.
	As MSU impossible to obtain,
	R̽ with Amoxil 500 mg tds × 7 days
21/5/88	No more incontinence. Confusion improved.
12/6/88	Found wandering in the street by neighbours. Becoming increasingly vague. No other specific symptoms. Daughter very tearful. Reassured.
4/7/88	Found lying next to bed by daughter. Tripped over rug on way to toilet. Incontinent.
	Behaviour becoming more difficult lately; emotional outbursts, refusing to co-operate.
	Unsteady gait recently.
O/E:	Confused.
	BP 149/75 lying 110/60 standing.
	Bruise on ®hip. Movements good.
	No other injuries noted.
Assessment:	Postural hypertension 2° to Aldomet.
For:	↓ to 250 mg bd.
21/7/88	Gait has improved, but mental state continuing to be a problem. Daughter feels that she 'just can't cope any more' without outside help. Thinks that 'a nursing home might be best for everyone' and request specialist opinion.
For:	Refer to Dr Chalming (geriatrician) re improved medical management and/or placement.

McNamara (1990: 491)

Notice that there are a number of abbreviations and symbols used in the text, as well as highly technical terminology and the names of various medications, and a relatively high degree of profession specific background knowledge is required. There is obviously a heavy dependence on reading ability to carry out this task, and the test designers clearly see reading and writing as 'a single aspect of the Occupational English Test' (McNamara 1990: 211). There is in the

OET a separate reading sub-test, but it is not field specific and each professional group takes the same one.

The prompt for this writing task is shown in Extract 7.36.

Extract 7.36

WRITING TASK

Using the information in the case notes, write a letter of referral to Dr Chalming. The main part of the letter should be 12–15 lines long.
Do not use note form in the letter; expand the case notes where relevant into full sentences.

Ibid.

Note that the prompt incorporates elements of the rubric and actually provides little contextual information. Clearly, the candidates are expected to have knowledge about such aspects of the task as form and content of a letter of referral, and norms of interaction between professional colleagues.

Expected response

As the prompt indicates, candidates are expected to be concise while at the same time using good letter-writing form, including complete sentences. It is likely that this task has a high degree of situational and interactional authenticity in spite of the lack of explicit contextual information in the prompt. The form and content of the input data is likely to provide a high level of situational authenticity by itself.

Relationship between input and response

The input data to be processed is very broad in scope, and the task of summarizing the information into a 12–15-line letter would appear to be a major challenge. The test taker is dependent upon the input data for much of the factual content of the letter of referral but must also employ a high level of background information and language knowledge in order to complete the task.

Assessment

The writing task is rated by means of a scale, as illustrated in Figure 7.1.

Figure 7.1 OET writing scale

```
┌─────────────────────────────────────────────────────────────────┐
│  OVERALL TASK FULFILLMENT                                         │
│                                                                   │
│        Completely satisfactory  _|_|_| |_|_|_  Unsatisfactory     │
│                                                                   │
│  APPROPRIATENESS OF LANGUAGE                                      │
│                                                                   │
│                 Appropriate  _|_|_| |_|_|_  Inappropriate         │
│                                                                   │
│  COMPREHENSION OF STIMULUS                                        │
│                                                                   │
│                    Complete  _|_|_| |_|_|_  Incomplete            │
│                                                                   │
│  CONTROL OF LINGUISTIC FEATURES                                   │
│  (GRAMMAR AND COHESION)                                           │
│                                                                   │
│                    Complete  _|_|_| |_|_|_  Incomplete            │
│                                                                   │
│  CONTROL OF PRESENTATION FEATURES                                 │
│  (SPELLING, PUNCTUATION)                                          │
│                                                                   │
│                    Complete  _|_|_| |_|_|_  Incomplete            │
└─────────────────────────────────────────────────────────────────┘
```

McNamara (1990: 212)

Each scale is intended to represent a range of ability from native or near-native speaker to elementary, and the middle of each scale is meant to indicate minimum ability to carry out professional writing tasks. Raters are instructed to place a cross in one of the six boxes in each category to locate the candidate's performance, and are reminded that the first category carries more weight than the others in computing the results, and the mark for overall task fulfillment is added to the average of the marks in the other four categories (McNamara 1990: 212). It is not clear from this scale whether much emphasis is placed on control of the genre of letters of referral, but it is certainly the case that background knowledge is an implicit part of the construct since comprehension of the stimulus is one of the rating categories. However, background knowledge is not being explicitly assessed in the *OET* writing test.

Summary

Like the *OET* speaking task we looked at in Chapter 6, this sample task from the *OET* writing sub-test is a prototypical example of both the best in LSP testing practice and the problems associated with highly field specific instruments. The writing task is highly contextualized and requires a good deal of specific purpose background knowledge to process, and so is both situationally and interactionally authentic. At the same time, non-specialist raters apparently find it difficult to judge the quality of the response owing to their unfamiliarity with the conventions of the genre of letters of referral. In fact, McNamara found it to be 'somewhat problematic owing to the very specific kind of text required to be produced in the test: the content, purpose and organization of such texts were unfamiliar to non-specialist raters' (1990: 405). This raises the issue of the value of indigenous assessment criteria that I discussed in Chapter 5: even if, during the analysis of the target language use situation, we are able to discover specific purpose criteria for assessing communication within the target domain, it may not be at all easy to convert these into a rating scale which non-specialists can use. I will return to this problem in the next chapter.

Portfolio assessment

Before concluding this chapter, I want to discuss one additional aspect of the assessment of specific purpose writing (and other skills as well), that of portfolio assessment. Since portfolio assessment is somewhat different in nature from the types of assessment I have discussed so far in this book, I decided to discuss the topic separately here. The use of portfolios, particularly in the assessment of reading, writing, and speaking, is a growing trend and certainly has potential applications in LSP assessment. Portfolio assessment is one means of alternative assessment and refers to the 'purposeful, selective collection of learner work and reflective self-assessment that is used to document progress and achievement over time with regard to specific criteria' (Kohonen 1997: 15). Already, portfolio assessment is used in many specific purpose areas, for example in mathematics (Asturias 1994), chemistry (Phelps 1997), physics (Slater 1994), teacher training (Dubetz *et al.* 1997), and English for academic purposes (Spath Hirschmann and Traversa 1997). Collaboration between LSP practitioners and instructors in the specific purpose content areas is a productive approach to the assessment of specific purpose language development in a specific discipline, since the same portfolio of work could be used for the dual purposes of assessing learning in the specific purpose field and progress in the acquisition of field specific language ability. Criteria for assessing specific purpose language use could be developed in cooperation with the field specific content instructor and thus reflect the indigenous criteria established within that discipline.

The most usual practice in portfolio assessment involves the learner in preparing his or her own portfolio, sometimes in collaboration with the instructor, sometimes not, placing in it examples of various types of language performances, including drafts and revisions as well as finished products. For example, Spath Hirschmann and Traversa (1997: 58) describe an EAP reading portfolio at the University of Buenos Aires as containing the following:

- the texts read by the learners during the semester;
- the reading exercises the learners carried out;
- learners' think-aloud written reflections on the reading process;
- the oral discussions between the instructor and reader / reading group on text content and reading process;
- a final written summative essay;
- a final instructor–reader / reading group conference.

One can easily see that the preparation and submission of a portfolio of work undertaken by a student in an LSP situation could include examples of all sorts of specific purpose language use in both academic and vocational situations. For example, an academic writing portfolio would contain copies of writing assignments and the student's responses to each one. Often, multiple drafts are included, providing a record of the revision process. A speaking portfolio would contain taped samples of a learner's presentations and interactions, as well as any documentation associated with the spoken performances. In vocational training and internship programs, a portfolio of samples of actual work undertaken might be used to document progress and readiness for employment or promotion.

As Cohen (1994) points out, a portfolio produces, in effect, a set of multiple measures of writing, providing a depth and breadth of coverage not usually possible with conventional tests. Moya and O'Malley (1994) suggest five positive characteristics of portfolio assessment procedures:

- comprehensive: both depth and breadth of work is represented
- predetermined and systematic: careful planning is essential
- informative: work must be meaningful to teachers, students, staff and parents
- tailored: work included must relate to the purpose of the assessment
- authentic: work should reflect authentic contexts, in and out of the classroom

Kohonen (1997) compares standardized testing with alternative assessment practices along 10 dimensions and concludes that alternative assessment, including portfolio assessment, 'entails a movement towards a culture of evaluation in the service of learning' (p. 14) and sees the portfolio as an interface between learning and evaluation. Perceived advantages of portfolio assessment include the potential for a more comprehensive, process-oriented assessment of long-term progress in writing, and learners becoming more self-critical and reflective about their own work (Savitch and Serling 1997), and more publicly accountable for their own progress (Herter 1991).

The characteristics of specific purpose language ability and test tasks discussed in this book can offer a way of organizing and evaluating LSP portfolios. For example, the characteristics of the rubric, particularly the specification of the objective, procedures for responding, structure, and evaluation criteria and procedures, should be stated clearly before the student begins creating the portfolio. The characteristics of the input, particularly the features of the LSP context, are all relevant for prompting the assignments that will be included in the portfolio. Indigenous assessment criteria reflect the realities of how communicative performances are judged in LSP situations, and should be stated clearly in the instructions for assembling the portfolio. Using these criteria as a basis for evaluating the portfolio itself is an obvious advantage of employing the framework advocated in this book, since inconsistency across raters and over time and the lack of validity evidence are frequent points of criticism in portfolio assessment, as is discussed below.

Portfolio assessment is not exempt from a concern for the qualities of good testing practice as discussed in Chapter 5. Problems with portfolio assessment include the fact that there is very little research evidence to support the claims made by its proponents and the acknowledgement that there are difficulties in maintaining consistency in assessments across individuals and over time (Madaus *et al.* 1997; Brown and Hudson 1998). Indeed, Hamp-Lyons and Condon (1993) report that assessors need training to standardize assessment criteria just as raters do in more traditional testing. Hamp-Lyons (1993) points out in this regard that grades assigned to portfolios tend to cluster close together and thus lose much discriminatory value in showing differences between more and less proficient writers (cited in Cohen 1994). Demonstrating the validity of interpretations of portfolio assessment is also a problem: the criteria used to determine validity must reflect the holistic nature of language development, must be sensitive to individual student differences, and must accurately reflect student progress (Moya and O'Malley 1994; Brown and Hudson 1998). Another problem is that portfolio assessment can be very time-consuming for assessors – there is a great amount of material to process – and, given the time involved, samples a less representative portion of performances than can a form of assessment that elicits a greater variety of tasks (Madaus *et al.* 1997). In spite of these problems, however, portfolio remains a popular form of alternative assessment, and, for certain purposes, the advantages appear to outweigh the disadvantages. For example, in LSP situations in which the language instructor and the content area instructor work closely together, portfolio assessment would appear to be an efficient means of assessing student performance in both spheres, since a single portfolio could be used for both purposes.

Portfolio assessment techniques offer a powerful means of LSP assessment that can have the additional benefit of empowering learners and second language users (Pollari 1997), but it must be remembered that portfolio, and other alternative means of assessment, must reflect the qualities of good testing practice in the same way that other assessment instruments must (Brown and Hudson 1998). For more discussion of the use of portfolio assessment, see Weigle (forthcoming).

Conclusion

What have we learned about LSP tests of reading and writing through this examination of example tasks? We have considered tasks covering a wide range of specificity, a range of input types, including tables and photographs, an extended case study, and very realistic texts, the provision of situationally relevant purposes for processing the input data, and response types ranging from the highly realistic, situationally authentic, and genre specific to extremely limited response task. We have seen generally less variety in assessment criteria, most tests employing fairly linguistically oriented, traditional categories. As I discussed in Chapter 6, the development of communicative, specific purpose assessment criteria is emerging as one of the most vexing and problematic aspects of LSP testing, and will no doubt be the focus of much research and development activity in years to come. Another area of research involves investigations of the properties of portfolio assessments, particularly in terms of reliability, fairness, and validity.

....

CHAPTER EIGHT

LSP test development and technology

Introduction

In Chapter 5 I discussed the problem of moving from an empirical analysis of the field specific target language use situation to test task specification. In Chapters 6 and 7 we looked at a number of existing field specific tests and considered the processes by which they were developed. In this concluding chapter I will discuss further crucial aspects of field specific test development, namely operationalization, piloting, revising, and validation. I discuss these important facets of test development in this chapter rather than in Chapter 5, because they deal with the whole test as opposed to individual tasks, which was the focus of earlier discussions of test development.

Operationalization refers to the application of the qualities of good testing practice discussed in Chapter 5 – validity, reliability, authenticity, impact, and practicality – to inform our decisions about precisely how the characteristics of the TLU situation can be converted into test tasks. For example, not all TLU tasks will be appropriate to the testing situation because they may not provide us with useful information about the language abilities we wish to measure, or they may require specialized information that not all the test candidates can be expected to have. In such cases, the tasks will need to be modified for use in the test.

However, no matter how careful test developers may be in making the transition from TLU task characteristics to test task, it is not until the tasks are **piloted**, tried out on live test takers, that it can be seen how well they work – whether the instructions are clear and complete, the time allotted is appropriate, the context is clear and appropriate, the input data is at the required level of specificity, and the expected response is in fact obtained. I will briefly discuss various approaches to analyzing the results of trial testing, as they apply in the case of field specific tests, and consider the revising of tasks in the light of information gained from such evidence.

Finally, in the discussion of test development, I want to look more closely at the types of evidence that might be collected for the construction of what I will call a **validity mosaic**, following Butler (1995): evidence that interpretations of test performance are appropriate for the intended purpose(s) of the test. As we will see, there are a number of approaches to obtaining validity evidence, each of them providing a slightly different viewpoint on interpreting performance, but all of them adding up to a more and more complete picture of what we may confidently say the test is measuring and of how we may interpret performance on it.

A second major theme of this concluding chapter is a consideration of how advances in technology, mostly related to computer applications, may be exploited in the measurement of field specific language ability. It is important for LSP testing practitioners to think seriously about the applications of computer technology in the development and delivery of their tests since it offers a great potential for enhancing the qualities of good testing practice, particularly in terms of validity, authenticity, and practicality. For example, computers can provide a platform for delivering multimedia input that is richer and more varied in content than is possible on paper; there is a capability for delivering input data that contains more task features in target situations where computer technology is the norm, thus helping ensure the engagement of specific purpose language ability; and computer delivery can offer greater accessibility for test takers and, over time, cost efficiency in scoring and reporting results. As Frank Smith put it in a keynote address at the 1983 convention of the Teachers of English to Speakers of Other Languages, the issue appears not to be whether we want computers in our work:

> The tide is already seeping under the doors and climbing up the walls. The question is how computers are to be employed and what the consequences will be.
>
> Smith (1984: 12)

In the discussion I will attempt to take note of both the 'promise' and the 'threat' of computer technology in specific purpose language testing, looking particularly at how some of the potentialities of the World Wide Web, computer adaptive testing, and computer assisted techniques might be exploited in the enhancement of specific purpose language tests. I will also consider the use of electronic corpora of specific purpose language data in LSP testing, although, as we will see, there is not at present a great deal of useful material. And finally, I will briefly survey other technological developments of potential use in LSP testing: multimedia applications, including the use of compact disks and digitally generated sound.

Lastly, to conclude the book, I will revisit some of the major themes and consider some important issues that will influence the future of specific purpose language testing.

LSP test development

Operationalization

So far in this book I have discussed the development of field specific tests mainly at the level of task, because this level is the most crucial in engaging a field specific discourse domain in the test takers. Clearly, however, we need to begin to think in terms of the whole test, the combined set of tasks that will give us as complete a picture as possible of the test taker's field specific language ability. In Chapter 5, in the discussion of the specifications document, I outlined the information necessary for describing the content of the test: its organization, including the number of tasks, the time allocated for each, the length of text or other input data required for the task, and the specification of the characteristics of the tasks in terms of the framework for describing the language characteristics and the task characteristics in the TLU situation (Tables 5.1 and 5.2). The operationalization stage of test construction involves moving from these rather theoretical descriptions to actual test materials, including the following steps:

- preparing the rubric, which involves making decisions about the sequence of the various tasks and their relative importance, and the

writing of the instructions containing all the information the test takers will need to work through the test
- producing the input materials, including a prompt which provides contextual information and identifies the problem to be addressed, and presenting the input data in an appropriate format
- devising a method of recording the expected responses
- preparing materials to guide the scorers/raters in carrying out their tasks

It should be pointed out that different scholars think of specifications and operationalization in different ways. Bachman and Palmer (1996), for example, distinguish the two by placing all discussion of test organization and item/task characteristics in the operationalization stage, which they refer to as producing a blueprint for the test, leaving only the more theoretical discussion of test purpose, description of the TLU domain, construct definition, and plan for evaluating test usefulness in the specifications document. Others (e.g., Alderson *et al.* 1995; Heaton 1990; Hughes 1989; McNamara 1996; Weir 1990, 1993) organize the two stages much the way I have done here, with the specifications containing all the information needed to produce the test/tasks and the operationalization stage referring to the actual production of test materials.

No matter how the two stages of test development are characterized, it is important to remember that the process of making the transition from TLU characteristics to test task characteristics and then to the production of test materials will always be constrained by what Weir (1990) refers to as basic considerations in test design. I will discuss how these considerations and qualities affect the development of field specific tests. In this book, I have combined a number of these considerations and I referred to them in Chapter 5 as the qualities of good testing practice: principles for ensuring that the tests we produce are as good as we can make them in terms of validity, the interpretations we make of test performance; reliability, the consistency and accuracy of the measurements; situational authenticity, the relationship between the target situation and the test tasks; interactional authenticity, the engagement of the test taker's communicative language ability; impact, the influence the test has on learners, teachers, and educational systems; and practicality, the constraints imposed by such factors as money, time, personnel, and educational policies.

Qualities of good testing practice

I introduced these qualities in Chapter 5, and looked at an example of how they can be evaluated in a practical test development project. Here, we need to consider briefly how the qualities constrain the transfer from TLU situation to test task in the development process. We would like to be able to simply transplant the TLU tasks into the test situation, and in some cases that is possible. For example, we saw in the *ELSA* writing task, the letter which formed the input data was a very realistic example of the type of note a teacher might receive from an administrator, and the writing task itself, composing a short note in reply, was reasonably authentic in terms of the interaction between language ability and the context: situation, participants, purpose, topic, function, tone, and norms of interaction. In this case, the qualities of testing practice did not impinge much on the operationalization of the test. In most cases, however, consideration of the qualities of good testing practice will limit what test developers can do in moving from TLU tasks to test tasks. Some possible examples are given below.

> *Validity:* The TLU domain might include a task requiring partici-
> pants to suggest ways that students might get help with home-
> work when they need it, but newly arrived candidates for
> teaching positions would not have that knowledge.
> *Reliability:* A particular task in the TLU domain, for example
> instructing a client to have a seat in the waiting room, might
> be so brief that by itself it would not allow for a reliable
> measure of ability.
> *Authenticity:* A task in the TLU domain is authentic by defini-
> tion, but testers may not be able to duplicate it effectively in
> the test domain. For example, I discussed the use of air traffic
> control radar screens in Chapter 6; further, it may not be
> possible in the test situation to duplicate reciprocal/adaptive
> tasks from the target situation, such as interaction with col-
> leagues in a research lab.
> *Impact:* A TLU task may be so specific, narrowly focussed, and
> predictable that it would lead language instructors to teach the
> task rather than the language ability underlying it. For
> example, the TLU task of transferring a phone call could lend
> itself to the construction of teaching materials that focussed on
> the memorization of a small number of routinized expressions.

Practicality: The TLU domain might include the writing of a term paper, but time constraints in the testing domain would not allow for that whole task to be carried out, or computer use might be an important aspect of the TLU task, but costs prohibit their use in the testing situation.

Clearly, these qualities limit to some degree what the test developer is able to do when moving from the TLU situation to test tasks, and this can be viewed negatively: if only we did not have to pay attention to these pesky qualities of good testing practice, we could develop a really true to life field specific test. One danger in field specific testing is the tendency to assume that simply because our test tasks are based on a careful assessment of the target language use situation, they will necessarily exhibit the desirable qualities of good tests. As Linn *et al.* (1991) point out, 'simply because the measures are derived from actual performance or relatively high-fidelity simulations of performance, it is too often assumed that they are more valid than multiple-choice tests' (p. 16). They remind us that evidence must be sought to support interpretations of performance on even the most authentic of assessments. Reference to the qualities of good testing practice, then, rather than playing a dampening role in field specific testing, is necessary to the development of what is essentially a measurement device which must display accepted standards for good measurement.

Guidelines for scoring

As Weir (1993) points out, 'Even if examiners are provided with an ideal marking scheme, there might be some who do not mark in exactly the way required' (p. 26). In most specific purpose tests, the candidates must use specific purpose background knowledge to at least some extent; consequently, scorers will need guidance on how to recognize and interpret factual errors in assigning a rating for performance of the task. Another aspect of scoring involves clear, precise definitions of characteristics that are to be considered in assigning a score. For example, in the *TEACH* test, one of the criteria for rating communication skills is teacher presence; there is no doubt a wide range of views on how this quality is realized, and it is necessary to define and exemplify it so that raters can recognize and evaluate it.

Those who are experienced with language testing, particularly in cases where more holistic rating of language performance is done, will view Weir's caution above as an understatement. Alderson *et al.* (1995) remind us that 'if the marking of a test is not valid and reliable, then all of the other work undertaken earlier to construct a "quality" instrument will have been a waste of time' (p. 105). The issue of validity in rater guidelines centers on whether the intended features of the construct to be measured are reflected in the criteria raters apply when they make their judgements of the performance. The issue of reliability refers to the consistency with which raters apply these criteria. It is only by means of carefully constructed rater guidelines and training that the test developers can insure that the qualities of good testing practice will be realized in scoring.

The preparation of guidelines for scoring is important in all testing, but it may be even more important in field specific testing, where an added dimension is that raters may be unfamiliar with the technical content of the test and consequently have a difficult time judging the quality of a response. I discussed this issue in Chapter 6 with regard to the *Occupational English Test* (McNamara 1990), but it is certainly worth mentioning again here. Rater guidelines should deal not only with such issues as acceptable responses and variations on them and the relative weighting of tasks from the point of view of the construct to be measured, but also with acceptability and coverage of the content from the point of view of subject specialists. For example, imagine a task in which the candidates are to describe the steps necessary for carrying out a titration experiment in a chemistry lab. How are raters to deal with a situation in which a candidate's language abilities are adequate but where the actual steps described would not result in a successful titration? There may well be variation in the raters' own background knowledge such that some of them would recognize the error in content and some others would not. This alone would result in a certain amount of inconsistency in rating if those raters who knew about titration lowered the scores of those candidates who got it wrong while the less chemically astute raters did not. As a second example, it may be that the language of the response is so technical that raters simply cannot capture the gist or follow the organization of the discourse and consequently would find it very difficult to make a judgement on such construct characteristics as the appropriateness of vocabulary, rhetorical organization, cohesion, functional knowledge, register, or cultural references. I have discussed similar issues in Chapter 5 as an important concern in the development of field specific test tasks, and noted that it is essential to involve subject specialists early and often in the development process to help the testers understand the field specific discourse domains they must work with. However, it is just as important to communicate that information to the raters to assist them in making judgements about the quality of the language performance of the test takers.

Piloting and revising

No matter how carefully we put our test together, and no matter how experienced we and our colleagues may be in the business of language testing, the best way to determine how well we have done our job is to actually give the draft test to other people, both informally and under test conditions, to see how clear the instructions are, how appropriate the content is, how difficult the tasks are. Even language testing experts disagree wildly about what a task or item is testing or how difficult it is. Alderson (1993) reports on three studies in which professional testers and experienced English teachers were abysmally poor at agreeing on identifying what skills were being tested, how difficult items and sub-tests were, and whether test takers would receive a distinction, credit, pass, or fail. Alderson concludes: 'It is essential to investigate and establish the reliability, validity, and accuracy of professional judgements in language testing and to identify alternative procedures and sources of information in cases where judgements have been found unsatisfactory' (p. 56). It is these 'alternative procedures and sources of information,' the piloting (also called trialling) of draft tests, that I will discuss briefly here, particularly as they affect field specific tests. We can identify two steps in piloting, one rather informal and brief, which I will call informal piloting, and the other, more systematic, time-consuming, and expensive, which I will call formal piloting.

Informal piloting

In this stage of test development we need to give our draft test to a small number of colleagues, students, and subject specialist informants, both native and non-native speakers of the target language, to get feedback from them on such matters as the appropriateness of test content, approximate level of difficulty of tasks and of the whole test, the clarity of the instructions, the appropriateness of time allowed for tasks, and the likelihood of obtaining the expected responses. A surprising number of problems almost always arise at this stage – mechanical, conceptual, and factual oversights that are often caused by the test developers not having sufficient grasp of the intricacies of the field specific material they are working with, but also involving relatively simple failures to make instructions and prompts sufficiently clear. Comments and suggestions from this small group of advisers should be used to revise the test as appropriate. As I suggested above, while this appeal to experts has its value, we cannot depend on them for reliable, final analyses of task difficulty or content validity. Therefore, I will next discuss the more formal piloting operation.

Formal piloting

This stage of development, which involves giving the draft test under formal test conditions to a relatively large group of trial candidates, and scoring it with raters trained according to the procedures developed earlier, will vary in scope and thoroughness depending on the availability of human and material resources. Generally, the higher the stakes dependent on test performance, the more important it is to find the resources necessary for thorough piloting. The purposes of formal piloting are to confirm (or disconfirm) the judgements made by reviewers during informal piloting, to evaluate and refine our methods for training administrators and raters, to carry out analyses of performance on tasks and items, and to conduct other quantitative and qualitative studies that will inform our concern for the qualities of good testing practice, particularly, at this stage, validity and reliability.

In piloting a specific purpose test, it should be clear that the trial candidates must be representative of the target test population to the greatest extent possible. In development of test specifications, I included an analysis of the characteristics of the language users and test takers, and this information should be used as a guide to selecting the trial population. As suggested above, the size of the trial population will vary with a number of factors, but certainly it is the case that the larger the group, within the constraints of the quality of practicality, the better.

Once the trial population has been selected and the pilot test administered, there are basically two types of analyses that should be conducted: quantitative analyses and qualitative analyses, which I will discuss below. Once again, reference should be made to the specifications document, which includes our outline of a plan for evaluating the qualities of good testing practice: the pilot test analyses should conform to that plan as much as possible. The qualities of validity, reliability, authenticity, impact, and practicality are all possible subjects of pilot test analysis, bearing in mind, of course, that findings from the pilot studies will be preliminary, and will often result in the revision of the draft test: the plan for evaluating the qualities of good testing practice can be implemented in earnest only after the test becomes operational. Still, information gained in the piloting stage will be invaluable to the later evaluation program.

Quantitative analysis

There are numerous statistical, quantitative techniques for analyzing the test performance of groups of test takers. Which ones are appropriate for any given test will be determined by whether the test is norm-referenced or criterion-referenced, and whether it contains objectively scored tasks, such as multiple-choice, true–false, error-recognition, or subjectively scored tasks, as in writing and speaking tests. Typical techniques of quantitative analysis which might be employed include classical item analysis, used mainly for determining the degree to which selected response tasks efficiently discriminate among test takers; item response theory (IRT) analysis, a technique useful for matching the difficulty of multiple-choice items with varying ability levels among test takers; standard distribution statistics, including the mean, standard deviation, and standard error of measurement; classical test and sub-test reliability estimates, including such procedures as the split-half, Kuder-Richardson, and Cronbach's alpha methods; inter-rater and intra-rater reliability estimates, to see to what extent raters are consistent across time; generalizability theory techniques, for determining the relative effects of differing sources of variance in test performance; intercorrelations and factor analysis among tasks, sub-tests, and whole tests, for the purpose of determining what abilities are being measured; and structural equation modeling, for the investigation of relationships among both observed variables and unobserved, theoretical constructs underlying test performance. Readers can consult a number of publications concerning these and other procedures, including Alderson *et al.* (1995), and Brown (1991 and 1992).

Qualitative analysis

Similarly, there is a wide variety of useful information to be gained from qualitative analyses of pilot test performance. Qualitative methods generally focus more on the individual than on groups, and on verbal rather than numerical data. Techniques such as observations, questionnaires, interviews, verbal report, and think-aloud studies can be used with the trial candidates to gain information about the quality of the test rubric, the instructions, time allotment, and the prompt, the appropriateness and level of the content, the process of responding to tasks, and general satisfaction with the format of the test. The language produced in test performances is also subject to qualitative linguistic analysis to compare the features of the test language with those of language in the TLU situation. Again, there are a number of published sources of information about qualitative analysis which readers may wish to consult, including Cohen (1994), and Brown and Hudson (1998).

Revisions in test content, structure, and format should also be made after what Bachman and Palmer (1996) call the 'logical evaluation of usefulness,' by which they mean the systematic, largely qualitative review of what I have termed the qualities of good testing practice. For example, in Chapter 7, I was a bit critical of the *IELTS* writing task prompt for failing to provide a specific purpose for the writing task. The prompt simply tells the test taker to write a report for a university lecturer describing the information shown below, and I suggested that this detracted from the quality of authenticity. We might revise the prompt as follows to provide a reason for carrying out the writing task: Write a report for a university lecturer describing the information shown below, which the lecturer requires for a class on radio and television advertising. Now, whether such a modification is in line with the aims of the test developers is something only they can judge, but the example suggests how the analysis of the qualities of good testing practice can guide the revision process.

Revision thus needs to be carried out as a result of both qualitative and quantitative studies of the test qualities. At the conclusion of the studies the draft test should be revised in the light of the findings, and, if necessary, piloted and analyzed again: there is no guarantee that instructions which have been rewritten for clarity, that tasks which have been revised with regard to level of difficulty or content, or that amended scoring guidelines and procedures will in fact be any more effective than the original versions. Eventually, however, all the revisions that can be made will have been made, and the test will be ready for operational use with the intended test population. The next step in the testing process is that of validation, and I will now turn to a discussion of this important aspect of field specific testing.

The validity mosaic

Validation is a process of gathering evidence to support the claim that a test measures certain abilities or attributes in certain contexts for certain purposes. Simply put, validation is an exercise to determine that a test measures what its developers intend it to measure. Validity is about interpretations of test scores in the light of the purposes for which the test was developed. Therefore, the key question is not whether a test is valid but, rather, for what purposes it is valid. We have seen, for example, that the *TEACH* test for prospective international teaching assistants has as its stated purpose providing 'evidence of prospective teaching assistants' oral English proficiency in a classroom in their own field of study.' Now, what evidence might we want to see in order to accept or reject this claim? Obviously, there are a number of possibilities: (1) we might simply look at the format of the test and try to determine to what extent it looks like an appropriate measure of English ability in a field specific classroom; (2) we might examine the content of the prompts and input data to determine to what extent they appear to represent the field; (3) we could ask judges to evaluate the tasks in terms of the skills or abilities they seem to measure and compare these judgements with the construct to be measured as described in the test specifications document;

(4) we could ask the test takers, by means of a questionnaire, an interview, or a think-aloud, to provide information about how they tackled each task and what reasoning processes they employed as they responded; (5) we would want to know something about the consistency of ratings of the responses: whether raters appear to agree with each other, and with themselves, about assigning scores to performances; (6) we could take a look at the relationship between performance on the test and performance in an actual classroom in the candidate's field of study, including the students' evaluation of the international teaching assistant; (7) we would want to see whether there were some tasks on the test that are systematically biased against some test takers owing to gender, ethnic or cultural background, or cognitive style; (8) we could compare performance on the *TEACH* with performance on another test with a similar purpose; (9) we could study what effect the very existence of the test had on the teaching of English to prospective international teaching assistants and whether the levels of ability assigned to various performances on the test reflected what is known about the process of second language acquisition; and (10) we could carry out a study of the interaction between the abilities we intended to test and the methods we employed to measure them.

It should be clear from these brief examples of possible approaches to validation that validation is not a once-and-for-all event but rather a dynamic process in which many different types of evidence are gathered and presented in much the same way as a mosaic is constructed: each piece of ceramic or glass is different, sometimes only slightly, sometimes dramatically, from each other piece, but when they are assembled carefully, indeed artfully, they make a coherent picture which viewers can interpret. The process of validation is much like this, presenting many different types of evidence which, taken together, tell a story about the meaning of a performance on our test. It is for this reason that I employ the term validity mosaic to characterize the process, bearing in mind that validation is a mosaic that may never be completed, as more and more evidence is brought to bear in helping us interpret performances on our tests, and as changes occur in the purposes of testing, the abilities to be assessed, the contexts of testing, and generalizations test developers want to make.

One way to summarize the multifaceted issue of validation might be to recall Merrill Swain's expression 'bias for best,' which essentially calls for testers to create conditions in their tests which will make it possible for test takers to demonstrate their performance and thus allow for the most positive interpretations of their language ability. All the pieces of information which might make up the validity mosaic – consideration of the format, content, abilities being measured, response processes, scoring consistency, generalizability of performance, systematic bias, relationship to other tests, impact on teaching and learning, and the interaction between test taker abilities and measurement methods in a test – are focussed on demonstrating that the interpretations we make of test takers' performance are justified, fair, accurate, and meaningful.

I would like to turn now to a consideration of the use of technology in LSP testing, including the World Wide Web, computer adaptive and computer assisted tests, computer-based collections of genuine spoken and written texts, and multimedia applications. In this discussion, I will emphasize both the promise and the threat of the use of technology in test development and delivery, for technology can both enhance and detract from our goal of developing tests that are valid, reliable, authentic, and practical, and which will have a beneficial impact on learners, teachers, and educational programs.

Technology and LSP testing

In his plenary address at the 1983 convention of Teachers of English to Speakers of Other Languages (TESOL), a talk entitled 'The promise and threat of microcomputers for language learners,' Frank Smith observed that 'Computers are incredibly powerful devices, capable, I think, of destroying both literacy and teachers if they are not used intelligently' (Smith 1984: 1). Similarly, Michael Canale, at the 1985 Language Testing Research Colloquium (LTRC), asked:

> should we view the computer as just another tool or appliance that is simply to be mastered and put to use, or should we view it as a language or medium that is capable of generating unanticipated goals and images . . .?
>
> Canale (1986: 31)

How far have we come since the 1980s in using technology intelligently? What unanticipated goals and images have been generated? As Charles Alderson observed, rather depressingly, in 1996, 'computers have been used in language testing for a long time, but more recent developments in the use of computers to deliver language tests threaten to compromise the validity of the instruments by encouraging users to employ test methods of questionable value' (Alderson 1996: 249). He goes on to note that the ease with which computers can present and score multiple-choice items threatens to inhibit test developers from seeking new and more valid ways of assessing language proficiency and language learning. In this section of the chapter I will consider some aspects of technology that have been suggested as being of potential value to the LSP testing enterprise: the use of the World Wide Web and the Internet, computer adaptive testing, computer assisted language testing, the use of computer-based corpora of field specific discourse, and multimedia applications.

Resources for LSP testing on the World Wide Web

As far as I have been able to ascertain, at the time of writing there is only one example of an LSP test on the World Wide Web – unhappily, not a very good one. There is a *TOEIC*-like practice test on-line, sponsored by Dai-job, a Web-based recruiting service for foreign companies in Japan (Dai-job On-line). The English test (see http://www.testden.com/scripts/dai/demo/demo.asp) contains 60 multiple-choice items based on the format of *TOEIC* incomplete sentence and error-spotting tasks. The content of the items is business-related, but like *TOEIC* itself, no specific purpose background knowledge is required for responses. Unlike *TOEIC*, however, the Dai-job items are not well written and contain some typographical errors. The test taker does get immediate feedback on his or her performance, in the form of a score, a brief analysis of the correct responses, and a paragraph-length profile of his or her English language abilities. This test is worth having a look at as an essay in Web-based assessment, but unfortunately it is not a good example of either LSP testing or even of Web-based testing techniques.

A European group is engaged in a project to produce a foreign languages assessment system, which they call the *Vocational Language Assessment On-line* (V-LASSO), for use on the Internet (see http://www.access.be/leonardo/eng/index.htm). The project is being developed by five partner organizations in four countries under the sponsorship of the European Commission, and although at the time of writing it is not clear to what extent this project will result in specific purpose assessment instruments, it is worth following its development. The project is scheduled for completion in 1999.

There are, however, a number of more general tests and informational resources that can be exploited in the development of specific purpose language tests. The first site that should be accessed is the Resources in language testing page (Fulcher On-line (a)): http://www.surrey.ac.uk/ELI/ltr.html. This page contains links to over 80 language assessment related sites, including private and commercial organizations, government resources, testing associations, centers and councils, universities, and tests on-line. While none of the current on-line tests are LSP tests, they do illustrate both the potential and the limitations inherent in Web- and computer-based language testing. For example, the University of Surrey has a number of quizzes on-line that test students' comprehension of texts in a course on academic and technical writing. Extract 8.1 shows a sample item from the quiz on academic/technical style.

Extract 8.1

> You will already have learned that two features of academic/technical style are that (1) it is formal, and (2) it is impersonal. The following are 10 sentences taken from the abstract of a thesis on the use of drama in tourism. Some sentences are in appropriate academic style and some are inappropriate, as they are too informal/personal. For each sentence, decide whether they are appropriate or inappropriate.
>
> 1
>
> The aim of the research was to weigh up the strengths and weaknesses of live drama in the tourism market and look at how far its organisation and marketing have been successful.
>
> • Appropriate
> • Inappropriate

Fulcher (On-line (b))

The students respond by clicking on one of the dots, and after they have completed the 20-item test, it is scored immediately and they are given feedback on each item, as shown in Extract 8.2.

Extract 8.2

> 1
>
> 0 out of 1
>
> The aim of the research was to weigh up the strengths and weaknesses of live drama in the tourism market and look at how far its organisation and marketing have been successful.
>
> Appropriate was wrong
>
> A correct answer was Inappropriate
>
> This sentence is actually inappropriate, because the phrasal verbs 'weigh up' and 'look at' are rather informal, and should be replaced with more formal equivalents, such as 'evaluate' and 'examine' or 'consider'.

Ibid.

Quizzes such as this illustrate both the advantages and the limitations of on-line tests: the test taker receives instant feedback, which can be as extensive as the developer wishes, but the format is rather conservative and appears to be limited to various types of selected response tasks. Fulcher provides links to some 13 sites that contain examples of Web-based language tests, and these are worth exploring to see the kinds of tasks that have been devised for delivery on-line. There are also on-line templates for developing one's own Web-based tests; for example, the on-line QuizCenter at the University of Hawaii: http://motted.hawaii.edu/et_tools/quizcenter/. This is a free service provided to educators who wish to make their own on-line quizzes.

An example of a Web site that seems exploitable in the service of LSP testing is MedWeb, an experimental project at the University of Birmingham, in the UK (http://medweb.bham.ac.uk/caa). MedWeb contains three types of automated assessment activities: a searchable clinical case database, a searchable multiple-choice question database, and a preset test list. The clinical database contains a number of short clinical cases, each of which is read on-line, with accompanying pictures and other visual information. A question is asked about each case and responded to in a dialogue box. The test taker can then check his or her answer against a model answer provided. There are cases in neurology, ophthalmology,

Extract 8.3

MedWeb (On-line: http://medweb.bham.ac.uk/cases.markcase.fcgi$97)

obstetrics, and general medicine. A set of questions in neurology is shown in Extract 8.3.

The model response for this task is shown in Extract 8.4. The multiple-choice question database consists of sets of multiple-choice

Extract 8.4

MEDWEB CASE DATABASE - A NEURORADIOLOG...   HTTP://MEDWEB.BHAM.AC.UK/CASES.MARKCASE.FCGI

MEDWEB CASE DATABASE - A NEURORADIOLOGICAL SPOT DIAGNOSIS

REVIEW THE PRESENTATION

RESULTS OF QUESTION 1

YOU ENTERED ROCKS IN HEAD

A MODEL ANSWER WOULD HAVE INCLUDED

THE CT SCAN DEMONSTRATES HYDROCEPHALUS. NOTE HOW MARKEDLY DILATED THE VENTRICULAR SYSTEM IS, IN THIS PARTICULAR CASE THIS IS DUE TO AQUEDUCT STENOSIS.

THE DEPARTMENT OF NEUROLOGY HOME PAGE

[CHOOSE A DIFFERENT CASE] [COMPUTER ASSISTED ASSESSMENT HOME]

[MEDWEB HOME] [FEEDBACK] [SEARCH] [EXIT]

PAGE AUTOMATICALLY GENERATED 29/1/98; 6:38:40 PM BY MEDWEB

Ibid.

items in one of three areas: medical, dental, or business. After choosing a subject area and entering a search term, such as histology, a set of test items will appear. The test taker can respond to the questions, which will be marked and a report returned. An example of a histology question is shown in Extract 8.5. Finally, the preset test list contains sets of questions on business and finance, pre-clinical bio-medical science, and general medicine. After choosing an area, the test taker selects a specific topic, such as anatomy, and will be given a set of questions, as shown in Extract 8.6.

Extract 8.5

MedWeb (On-line: http://medweb.bham.ac.uk/http/caa/newdb/mcq.
GetMCQs.fcgi)

Visitors to the MedWeb site have suggested other content areas and have submitted sample items which are also accessible at the above site. For example, there are several sets of items in business, as shown in Extract 8.7.

It seems likely that this type of technology and content could be adapted to field specific language testing. For example, the focus in a language test might be upon comprehension of the information in the table, as in Extract 8.8.

Extract 8.6

MedWeb Quiz Bank Question   HTTP://MEDWEB.BHAM.AC.UK/HTTP/C...GETMCQGROUP.FCGI$PUBLIC?ANATOMY

Respiratory questions

ALL THESE QUESTIONS ARE OF A GENERAL UNDERGRADUATE STANDARD SUITABLE FOR ANY BIOMEDICAL STUDENT.

ENTER YOUR ID (OPTIONAL) [_____] (E.G. YOUR EMAIL ADDRESS OR STUDENT ID NUMBER)

1. WHICH NERVE IS COMMONLY DAMAGED DURING DISLOCATION OF THE SHOULDER?

○ A MEDIAN NERVE
○ B RADIAL NERVE
○ C AXILLARY NERVE
○ D MUSCULOCUTANEOUS NERVE

2. PAINFUL ARC SYNDROME CAN BE CAUSED BY CALCIUM DEPOSITS IN THE TENDON OF WHICH MUSCLE?

○ A DELTOID
○ B SUPRASPINATUS
○ C SUBSCAPULARIS
○ D TRAPEZIUS

3. WHICH ONE OF THE FOLLOWING MUSCLES DOES NOT FORM PART OF THE ROTATOR CUFF?

○ A INFRASPINATUS
○ B TERES MINOR
○ C TERES MAJOR
○ D SUBSCAPULARIS

4. WHICH OF THE FOLLOWING STATEMENTS IS INCORRECT ABOUT THE MOVEMENT OF PRONATION?

○ A THE THUMB IS MOVED LATERALLY
○ B THE RADIUS CROSSES OVER THE ULNA
○ C THE PALM OF THE HAND IS TURNED TO FACE POSTERIORLY
○ D IT IS PARTIALLY MEDIATED BY PRONATOR QUADRATUS

5. AT THE ELBOW, WHICH OF THE FOLLOWING NERVES IS FOUND WINDING AROUND THE MEDIAL EPICONDYLE?

MedWeb (On-line: http://medweb.bham.ac.uk/http/caa/mcq.
getmcqgroup.fcgi$public?anatomy)

Extract 8.7

Capital Budgeting

1. The Yonan Components Corporation, maker of electronic components, is considering replacing a hand-operated machine used in the manufacture of electronic components with a new fully automated machine. Assume straight line depreciation and a marginal tax rate of 34%. Given the information in the following table, what is the initial outlay for the project?

Existing Situation		*Proposed Situation*	
Two Full Time Machine Operators	$24,000.00	Fully Automated Machine	
Machine Cost	$40,000.00	Machine Cost	$55,000.00
Annual Maintenance Cost	$6,000.00	Annual Maintenance Cost	$6,000.00
Annual Defects Cost	$5,000.00	Annual Defects Cost	$2,500.00
		Installation Fee	$6,000.00
Machine Life	10	Machine Life	5
Current Machine Age	5	Current Machine Age	–
Current Salvage Value	$10,000	Current Salvage Value	$ –
Expected Salvage Value	$ –	Expected Salvage Value	$ –

- ☐ $51,000
- ☐ $47,600
- ☐ $61,000

MedWeb (On-line: medweb.bham.ac.uk/http/caa/newdb/mcq. getmcqgroup.fcgi$business?capbudg)

Extract 8.8

Areas in which the proposed situation would result in increased costs include which of the following (tick as many as apply):

- ☐ Machine cost
- ☐ Annual maintenance cost
- ☐ Annual defects cost
- ☐ Machine operators
- ☐ Installation fee

Another possibility would be a writing task in which the candidates were asked to produce a report, comparing and contrasting the existing and the proposed situations. The Web technology would allow for the report to be forwarded electronically to the examiners, who could rate it, write comments on it, and return it directly to the test taker. Educational Testing Service is currently employing a similar system for the rating of essays produced in the computer-based *TOEFL* examination (Educational Testing Service 1998).

It remains to be seen whether the use of the World Wide Web will result in any test tasks that correspond more closely to a TLU situation than the examples here appear to. It seems unlikely, for example, that the tasks and test methods exemplified here bear much relationship to what students of medicine need to do in their daily work outside the test situation. In other words, these test tasks are currently being driven by the technology rather than by an analysis of TLU tasks. On the other hand, McNamara (1990) defended the use of multiple-choice reading comprehension tasks in the *OET* because they reflected the dominant testing format in the assessment of professional competence in several of the professions using the *OET*. Perhaps Web-based tasks could be used as vehicles for LSP tests based on a similar argument; however, so far, Web-based tests have largely failed to live up to their potential for enhancing situational and interactive authenticity.

Computer adaptive testing and LSP tests

In existence since the mid-1980s, **computer adaptive language tests** (CATs) involve the presentation by computer of test items at or near each test taker's level of ability from a bank of items of known difficulty, thus making for greater efficiency in testing. It is important for LSP testers to consider CAT techniques since they potentially offer advantages in terms of accessibility, scoring efficiency, and overall testing time; however, they are also associated with concerns about validity and authenticity, which need to be taken into account. CATs are based on a theory of test performance known as item response theory, which has itself been criticized as potentially unsuitable for the analysis of language test performance. I will briefly discuss both these concepts in the context of specific purpose language testing.

Like Web-based tests, computer adaptive tests are usually multiple-choice tests, since selected response items are most amenable to the methods used to calculate the relationship between item difficulty and test taker ability, and, for this reason, CATs tend to be fairly uninteresting for field specific language test developers, who tend to prefer more complex performance assessments. However, because computer adaptive techniques are being used more and more in language testing, a brief discussion of the topic is appropriate here.

In a typical CAT, a test taker is presented with a multiple-choice question of medium difficulty. If he or she gets that item right, the next one presented will be of greater difficulty; if that one is answered correctly, an even harder one is presented; when the test taker misses a question, the next item is slightly easier, and so on. Eventually, the computer gets a fix on the test taker's ability level and presents only items at that level until a predetermined degree of reliability has been achieved, and the test ends. In theory, CATs are more efficient than tests in which the items are presented in a fixed order in that the test takers are not given questions that are either far too difficult or far too easy for them, and thus contain fewer questions than a standard paper and pencil test. Furthermore, the score is available immediately, possibly with feedback about what items had been missed and what the correct answers were.

Computer adaptive testing was made possible by the development of **item response theory** (IRT), which is based on the assumption that 'an individual's expected performance on a particular test question, or item, is a function of *both* the level of difficulty of the item and the individual's level of ability' (Bachman 1990: 203; emphasis in original); the probability can be calculated that a test taker of a given ability will correctly answer an item of a given difficulty. Items in CATs are selected nowadays not just according to their IRT statistical properties, but according to a complex set of constraints, including, for example, content variety, question type, and total number of items. Moreover, it may be that measurement theory can be adapted to deal with such complex performances in language testing (see, for example, Bennett *et al.* 1991, and Bachman and Eignor 1997 for discussion of possible advances), and if so, then the future of CATs in field specific language testing may be a bright one. Educational Testing Service is developing the next generation of the *Test of English as a Foreign Language* (*TOEFL*), in a project known as *TOEFL 2000*, as a more specific purpose test of academic English (Chapelle *et al.* 1997), and is intended to employ the most up-to-date technology, including computer adaptive methods. This project will no doubt be a test case for the use of computer adaptive testing techniques in specific purpose language testing. A brief demonstration example of a computer adaptive test on the World Wide Web can be found at http://access.blueshoes.com/taaltest/index.htm.

Certainly, item response theory has already proven to be useful in validation studies of more complex communicative tests. For example, McNamara (1990) employed IRT analysis in studying the characteristics of the *Occupational English Test*. In another study, this time of a more conventional multiple-choice placement test, Henning (1990) investigated specialization bias with regard to test takers' fields of study, a topic of interest to field specific test developers, using IRT techniques. Henning, by the way, found no evidence that the content of any type of input data (e.g., reading, listening, and error detection passages) produced specialization bias (i.e., those test takers whose field of study was related to the content of the passage fared no better than those whose field was not related to the content; this aspect of specificity was discussed in Chapter 2).

Computer assisted LSP testing

If computer *adaptive* language tests seem not very interesting to field specific test developers, the more general notion of computer *assisted* tests may be of more interest and utility. **Computer assisted language testing** (CALT) techniques, in which input is delivered and/or responses are recorded by means of computers, or in which computers assist raters and scorers, are potentially of great use to LSP testers. Computers can provide test takers with some measure of control over the testing process by allowing them to explore the testing environment in ways somewhat analogous to the use of computers in non-test situations. For example, in computer assisted tests, candidates (and test administrators, of course) can vary the topics, participants, purposes, genre, channels, and codes in simulations of real-world tasks. Computers have also been used to prompt and score open-ended writing tasks and speaking tasks. For example, Corbel (1995) reports on a computer program that assists novice raters using the Australian Second Language Proficiency Ratings by focussing their attention on key aspects of test taker responses. It is likely that a similar program could be developed to assist raters in dealing with specific purpose content. Another example of such computer assistance is *PhonePass*, a telephone delivered and computer scored test of speaking ability (Ordinate On-line). Test takers dial a telephone number and are instructed to carry out a number of speaking tasks. Their performances are scored by a speech recognition and analysis program. *PhonePass* is a test of general spoken English, but the technology could no doubt be adapted to LSP testing, by incorporating sensitivity to specific purpose vocabulary, for example.

Alderson (1991) outlines the many possibilities of computer assisted language testing, including (1) providing immediate feedback to test takers on the current task before they progress to the next one, perhaps offering an opportunity for a second attempt at the task; (2) providing a variety of on-line help, simulating TLU on-line writing and research tasks employing task specific dictionaries, grammatical information, and translations; and (3) providing detailed analysis of test takers' progress through complex tasks, thus offering the possibility for useful diagnostic information. In a more recent paper, he argues for a broadly based concept of computer assisted language testing, making use of the advantages of computers – speed, memory, patience, and accuracy – in test construction and delivery, response scoring and analysis, test analysis, and the reporting of results (Alderson 1996). At Lancaster University, work is progressing on the development of a computer-based language testing system. Called *LUCAS* (Lancaster University Computer Assessment System), the software contains examples of non-multiple-choice and non-adaptive item types and is set up so that users can devise their own computer assisted test items (Alderson and Windeatt 1995). Chapelle (1998) has developed a theoretical framework for computer applications in language testing, citing examples of computer assisted tests of listening comprehension, writing, and reading comprehension with open-ended (or constructed response) items. Work such as Chapelle's should go some way toward stimulating research and development activity in this important area of language testing. Clearly, computer assisted language testing holds great promise for the development of field specific tests. It remains for us to begin to explore such applications in ways that reflect the use of such technology in specific academic and professional contexts.

Corpora of field specific discourse

A potentially useful tool for the investigation of TLU contexts is the use of computer databases of **corpora** of field specific discourse, both written and spoken. An electronic corpus is an on-line text that can be analyzed for its discourse properties by means of a number of corpus analysis tools, including concordancers, which assist in analyzing word frequency, phrases, and collocations, and parsers, which tag and analyze texts for various grammatical properties. The following is an example of a tagged text from a news report, analyzed in Biber *et al.* (1998). The untagged sentence is 'A move to stop Mr Gaitskell from nominating any more labour life peers is to be made at a meeting of labour MPs tomorrow.'

Tagged sample
A ^at++++
move ^nn++++
to ^to++++
stop ^vbi++++
Mr ^npt++++
Gaitskell ^np++++
from ^in++++
nominating ^xvbg+++xvbg+
any ^dti++++
more ^ap++++
labour ^nn++++
life ^nn++++
peers ^nns++++
is ^vbz+bez+aux++
to ^to++++
be ^vb+be+aux++
made ^vpsv++agls+xvbnx+
at ^in++++
a ^at++++
meeting ^nn+++xvbg+
of ^in++++
labour ^nn++++
MPs ^npts++++
tomorrow ^nr+tm+++
. ^.+clp+++

In this example, each word in the sentence appears on a separate line with a space after each word, and the tag beginning with ^. The + marks separate different 'fields' of information about each word. The information is mainly about grammatical classes, such as indefinite article (at), singular common noun (nn), infinitive marker (to), infinitive verb (vbi), and so on. The tag for 'made' identifies the word as a passive verb form (vpsv) in the first field, used as an agentless passive (agls) in the second, and as a past participle form (xvbnx) in the third. Some tags contain semantic information as well: 'tomorrow' is identified as an adverbial noun (nr), but also as referring to time (tm) in the second field. From such an analysis of a corpus, LSP test developers could derive a list of key vocabulary and sentence and word structures. In the present example, for instance, information about verb forms most often employed and key political vocabulary such as nominating, life peers, and MPs, would emerge, as would expressions such as 'a move to stop' and compounds such as 'labour life peers.'

The analysis of large numbers of texts such as this can add rich detail to our understanding of the linguistic properties of specific purpose speech and writing, and is very similar to some of the earliest specific purpose language research in register analysis (e.g., Barber 1962). Although early work in register analysis received much criticism for its relatively limited approach to the study of grammar and vocabulary, more recent work has extended the scope of inquiry into rhetorical and discourse analysis. In fact, in recent years, thanks in large part to the growing capability of computers to store and analyze large corpora, there has been a renewed interest in analyzing the grammatical and rhetorical features of specific purpose texts (Dudley-Evans and St John 1998). Understanding how grammar, technical and pan-technical vocabulary, and rhetorical structure are employed in the service of communication in specific purpose contexts is a fundamental goal of LSP test developers, and computer assisted corpus linguistics offers us a powerful research tool.

Alderson (1996) speculates that corpora, particularly of written texts, might also serve as a rich source of data for text compilation and selection in language tests and sees the possibility that test constructors could specify in the test specifications the types of texts they required in terms of content, syntax, level of vocabulary, and so on, and the computer could search corpora for suitable texts. Alderson also discusses the potential use of corpora in the presentation of texts for learners to make judgements about such aspects as source and genre of the text, or the gender and sociolinguistic status of the author; serving as 'reference points against which candidate responses could be compared' (p. 256), for example, and also when norming the test or reporting results. So, as a source of real-world input texts likely to be useful in various facets of LSP test development and use, computer-based corpora would appear to be of great potential benefit. The problem, from the LSP point of view, is the availability of sufficient specific purpose corpora, and the paucity of specific purpose language corpora is a major gap in the resources available for LSP test development, which suggests an area of research that needs attention. At the time of writing, two projects are under way to collect corpora of spoken and written academic texts in North America, one at the University of Michigan English Language Institute (for information see http://www.lsa.umich.edu/eli/micase/micase.htm) and one sponsored by Educational Testing Service in connection with the *TOEFL 2000* development project mentioned above.

Multimedia applications

I should not leave this discussion of technology in language testing without briefly mentioning the possibilities offered by multimedia hardware and software. It is now possible to integrate CD-ROM, video, audio, and the processing power of computers to deliver tests that feature interaction among the various components. An early example of such an integrated system in language teaching is the well-known *Montevidisco* project at Brigham Young University in the 1980s (Gale 1983). This system made use of videodisc technology, connected to a computer and cassette recorder, to allow the student to take a simulated trip to a Mexican village, encountering authentic cultural and linguistic situations to which he or she was expected to respond, either orally or in writing. The student controlled movement through 28 major contextual sequences, including a market, a hotel, a drug store, a taxi, a bullfight, a hospital, and a cantina (which female students were not allowed to visit), interacting with local residents. Recent advances in computerized multimedia technology make such innovation much easier, cheaper, and more accessible than in the past. Language testers have not so far made much progress in adapting this type of technology to the goals of measurement, although there has been some development activity. For example, Briggs (1993) has employed video technology in the testing of international teaching assistants, using real-life academic contexts as the input data; Marsden (1990) reports on the use of videotapes of authentic everyday situations in placement testing; and Zuskin (1993) developed a video-prompted discourse completion test. Once again, these seem to be essays in the use of technology in language testing which might stimulate field specific testers in the development of more complex performance tasks, prompted and mediated by multi-media technology.

Pitfalls of technology

Finally, field specific testers need to consider well the possible pitfalls of the use of technology in test delivery. Language testing that is driven by technology, rather than technology being employed in the service of language testing, is likely to lead us down a road best not traveled. For example, we need to ask, as has been asked in the case of the *Montevidisco* project, in what sense surrounding the test taker with computer, keyboard, monitor, CD player, audio recorder, micro-phone, and speakers could be considered an authentic communi-cative situation. Videotapes, compact disks, and computer programs are not real life, however much they may attempt to display authentic situations, except insofar as their use in the test situation reflects their use in the TLU situation. For example, delivery of videotaped scenes of a teacher at work in a classroom or of a supervisor talking to an employee on a shop floor are no doubt an improvement over formats in which test takers are instructed to imagine the same situations, but such input delivery formats should not be considered to be substi-tutes for the real thing. The problem here is not so much a matter of unrealistic testing techniques as it is one of caution in the interpret-ations that are made based on performance on tests enhanced by technology. This is clearly a validity issue.

The same is true of the use of item response theory in the develop-ment of computer adaptive tests. Canale pointed out years ago (Canale 1986) that the assumption of unidimensionality required by IRT 'threatens to be trivializing and compromising' (p. 34), forcing us to ignore the well-documented influence on reading performance, for example, of world knowledge and cultural background, language and gender differences, and general reasoning skills and reading styles. McNamara (in press) suggests that 'the typical item format of CAT tests may be at odds with the new and promising approaches to reporting performance on reading tests in terms of the cognitive demands of tasks' (p. 11). In fact, McNamara argues that the use of CAT techniques may represent a conservative force in language testing, not only in item format, but in its focus on psychometric and technological issues to the exclusion of consideration of the nature of communicative abilities and their assessment. We have seen that both computer adaptive and Web-based tests tend to use a multiple-choice format, and the challenge to test developers is to devise creative ways of employing technology that reflect language use in target situations.

In this regard, note that the future of test delivery seems headed in the direction of computer-based formats involving, for example, the on-screen delivery of reading texts and the presentation of listening texts in digital form. I have emphasized a number of times in this book that changing any of the situational characteristics of the input has the potential to change the performance they are meant to elicit, and, consequently, the interpretations we might make of the performance. This is certainly true of the delivery format of the input data. Researchers have shown, for example, that speaking assessments elicited in live interviews are qualitatively different from those elicited by means of tape-recorded input (Shohamy 1994; O'Loughlin 1997). Similarly, as McNamara (1997b) points out, 'a performance test of reading from a screen may be justified in its own right (replicating real world tasks in the age of the computer), it is not a substitute for a reading test delivered in a more conventional manner' (p. 137). In the computer-based *Test of English as a Foreign Language* introduced in 1998 (Educational Testing Service 1998), for example, test takers must use a mouse to scroll through the reading texts on the screen. As many who do computer word processing can attest, reading in this way involves a different sort of skill than that required by reading the same text printed on paper. There is great potential here for research not only into the effect such technology has on language processing and performance, but also into the kinds of interpretations we can make about the nature of specific purpose language knowledge based on performance.

In conclusion, the challenge to field specific language testers with regard to the use of technology in their work centers on understanding how to balance the use of technology in tests to reflect the use of technology in the target situations with the natural desire to use technology to enhance the delivery and scoring of tests. Part of the task of describing the TLU situation will necessarily include an analysis of the use of technology, and the concomitant use of technology in the test situation should ideally reflect that analysis. Of course, it is also true that it is tempting to make use of interactive video and other innovative technology to provide authentic input and contextualization cues. We need to be cautious, however, and make every attempt to understand and control for the test method effects associated with these technological resources.

Conclusion

To conclude this book, I want to comment on four particularly interesting but troublesome issues in LSP testing: the nature of the input, engaging communicative language ability and specific purpose language ability, devising TLU-relevant assessment criteria, and the use of general vs specific purpose language tests.

The nature of the input

One aspect of the input in the LSP tests we looked at was the use of extended input data from genuine sources, as in the *ELSA* reading and writing task, for example. The level of realism associated with both the length and the source of the input data would seem to be worth the effort involved in obtaining and presenting such material. A second aspect of the input in tests employing roleplays is that provided by the interlocutors in such tests as the *OET* and the *Japanese Language Test for Tour Guides*. In each of these example tasks, much of the interactional authenticity depends on the skill of the interlocutor at playing his or her role convincingly. I noted, with reference to the *OET*, that in some medical training and examining, highly trained professional actors are employed as standardized or simulated patients, but that in the case of the *OET*, interlocutor training is much less emphasized than is rater training. It has also been found that interlocutor competence can be a source of bias in the rating of the test takers' performance (McNamara and Lumley 1993). Thus, the training of interlocutors in roleplay tasks is a very important aspect of LSP speaking performance testing.

Another point highlighted by the analysis of the input in the sample tasks is the fundamental problem brought about by the fact that LSP testing necessarily involves simulation: no matter how many contextual and other situational characteristics the test task shares with the target language use situation, the inescapable fact is that, using *PELA* as our example, there is no airplane, just as there is no patient in the *OET*, no irate Japanese tourist, no inquiring business client, no classroom full of eight-year-old learners of Italian. This is not merely a problem of attempting to ever more faithfully represent the characteristics of the TLU situation; the very nature of the LSP testing enterprise means that there will always and inevitably be a reduction in the dynamic interplay between the test taker and the characteristics of the test task, because a test is, by definition, a controlled and contrived environment. We must construct our tests, and present input, in as realistic a way as we can reasonably contrive, but in the end we must remember, with humility, that at best we can only make inferences about the state of a test taker's language knowledge, communicative language ability, or specific purpose language ability, based on our observation of the test taker's performance on our test tasks, and that this is not the same as observing the test taker performing tasks in the target language use domain.

Engaging communicative language ability

The second aspect of LSP testing that our analysis of the sample tasks has illuminated centers around engaging communicative and specific purpose language ability in our tests. I noted that some tasks may not engage communicative language ability since they do not appear to require much in the way of negotiation of meaning or the creation of discourse, as in the case of the tasks we looked at in the *IELTS* and *UETESOL* listening sub-tests, for example. These are tasks which require only that the test takers listen or read for specific information in the input data and then mark appropriate answer choices. In communicative language testing, of which LSP testing is a part, test tasks should be designed to engage both the test taker's language knowledge and his or her strategic competence for an identifiable communicative purpose; tasks in which the test taker is to search for specific information and tick answer choices are unlikely to engage communication strategies. This is a matter of empirical research, of course, as would be conducted in validation studies, but from the perspective of the theoretical foundations for LSP testing that I outlined in the first four chapters of this book, we need to do our best to engage the test takers in communicative language activity in our test tasks. Along these same lines, we also saw in various examples that it is quite possible to devise test tasks that display a high level of situational authenticity, by employing many characteristics of the target language use situation, but much less interactional authenticity, owing to a failure to engage the test takers in a communicatively purposeful activity. One way of avoiding this, as we saw in the Italian teachers test, and the *ELSA* reading and writing task, is to provide specific purpose reasons for doing the test task beyond the purpose of the test itself. Recall that in the Italian teachers test, the prompt told test takers to give a set of oral instructions as if to a group of learners, and in *ELSA*, test takers were asked to imagine that they were the recipient of a request from their supervisor and to respond accordingly. Again, it is the input that is the source of most of the contextual information that test takers need in order to engage appropriate discourse domains in performing tasks upon which score users will base their interpretations of specific purpose language ability. It is essential that a wide variety of information is presented to ensure that test takers will get the right end of the stick and produce a test performance interpretable as evidence of specific purpose language ability.

Devising TLU-relevant assessment criteria

Another aspect of LSP testing that has emerged from our look at some example tasks is the importance of including assessment criteria that are derived from the analysis of the target language use domain. We saw in the case of the *OET*, for example, that although the indigenous assessment criteria, encompassing ability to understand colloquial language and cultural references, ability to take case histories from patients and present them to colleagues, and ability to explain medical ideas in language patients could understand, the actual scoring criteria that emerged from this analysis were very linguistically oriented, and included such features as intelligibility, fluency, comprehension, appropriateness, and resources of grammar and expression, and have since been shown not to capture aspects of communicative language ability that medical professionals deemed to be important. In the Italian language teachers' test, there was an attempt to include TLU-relevant classroom communicative competence criteria, including teacherliness and metalanguage, both concepts grounded in the context of the target language use domain. Similarly, in the *Japanese Language Test for Tour Guides*, the evaluation category of task fulfillment includes such industry-relevant criteria as enthusiasm, empathy, ability to make something sound interesting, persuasiveness, and awareness of clients' needs or desires. The inclusion of such TLU-relevant criteria raises the question of whether raters need to be experienced in the TLU domain in order to assess test takers' performances, and this question deserves the attention of language test researchers. There is some evidence that if the rating guidelines are sufficiently clear, however, trained raters who are not experienced in the TLU domain can effectively rate TLU-related criteria (Brown 1995).

Another issue concerning assessment criteria is that there is a distinction between the engagement of specific purpose background knowledge in the test task and the overt assessment of it in the scoring criteria. For example, we saw in the *OET* and *TEACH* speaking tasks and in the *OIBEC* writing task that it was likely that a high level of specific purpose knowledge was needed to successfully carry out the test tasks, but in none of the tests was the quality of the specific purpose content assessed. In fact, a clear distinction is often made between the assessment of communication ability and the assessment of professional knowledge and skill. As I discussed in Chapter 2, specific purpose background knowledge is a part of the construct of specific purpose language ability, and in specific purpose language tests, some level of background knowledge will be necessary to respond to test tasks. So, even though tests such as the *OET*, *TEACH*, and *OIBEC* do not overtly assess background knowledge, they certainly engage such knowledge, and are therefore prototypical examples of LSP tests.

The use of general or specific purpose tests

One final observation is worth making as a result of the analysis of LSP tests: one well-known specific purpose test of medical English, the Professional and Linguistic Assessments Board (PLAB) *Use of English* component, was phased out in January 1998. A new PLAB assessment procedure, called the *Objective Structured Clinical and Oral Examination (OSCOE)*, has been devised to test clinical skills, including 'the ability to communicate effectively with patients, relatives, medical colleagues and other health workers' (General Medical

Council 1995). The non-field specific *IELTS* will be used as a kind of gatekeeping, preliminary assessment. In a similar way, in the US, the Educational Council for Foreign Medical Graduates is increasingly using the *Test of Spoken English*, a general purpose test, as a prerequisite for admission to the licensing examination, during which more specific purpose speaking skills would be assessed. I have also noted the gradual move in the *ELTS/IELTS* program toward less and less field specificity: recall the discussion in Chapter 2 of Clapham's study in which she found that only when a text was highly field specific did test takers' field of study appear to affect their performance. In addition, McNamara (1997a) has questioned the value of LSP tests, particularly in the area of the simulation of TLU tasks and of assessment criteria, and wonders whether the only real reasons for simulating TLU tasks in LSP tests are face validity and the potential for beneficial washback. Where do these trends and concerns leave us in the field of specific purpose language testing?

I argued in Chapter 1 that there are two fundamental reasons for engaging in LSP testing: language performances vary with context, and specific purpose language is precise. It is appropriate that I conclude the book by returning to this argument in the context of the apparent trend toward more general purpose testing. There are many situations in which there is very little doubt that a specific purpose test is the most appropriate instrument to use in making judgements about language users' abilities to perform communicative tasks in specific purpose TLU contexts. Many of these, perhaps most, will be small-scale educational, professional, and vocational programs in which test developers are asked to produce instruments to assess specific purpose language ability of relatively small numbers of test takers in very specialized situations. Here I think the *TEACH* test is a prototypical example: a testing situation unique to North America, and carried out in the context of a single university (although the test format has been exported to other institutions). Other LSP testing situations are larger scale but still directed at quite specific purposes, as in the case of the *OET*, *ELSA*, the *Japanese Language Test for Tour Guides*, the *Proficiency Test for Language Teachers: Italian*, or the *PELA* test for air traffic control. Still other situations will call for LSP tests to address the needs of test takers on a very large scale, as we have seen with the *IELTS*, *UETESOL*, *OIBEC*, and *TOEIC*. In each case, a key factor seems to be that the test designers and test users want to be able to interpret performance on the test as evidence of specific purpose language ability, including both language knowledge and specific purpose background knowledge, in target language use situations. It seems to me, that viewed from this theoretical perspective, there will always be a place in the language testing field for LSP tests. There may be many situations where more general tests will be preferred; for example, where novices are being tested and there are no guarantees that test performance will be due mainly to communicative language ability and not to a lack of specific kinds of background knowledge. Or it may be that for reasons of practicality and efficiency, tests more toward the general end of the specific purpose continuum will be desirable. But, as I have tried to argue throughout this book, if we want to know how well individuals can use language in specific contexts of use, we will require a measure that takes into account both their language knowledge and their background knowledge, and their use of strategic competence in relating the salient characteristics of the target language use situation to their specific purpose language abilities. It is only by so doing, by carefully specifying as many of the characteristics of the situation and the individual as we can, that we can make valid interpretations of test performances. The field of specific purpose language testing has a rich and dynamic future, it seems to me, as we search for ways to understand more fully, and measure more accurately, the complex abilities language users require to function in specific purpose contexts where precision, clarity, range, and flexibility of language use are increasingly called for as requirements for participation in academic, vocational, and professional life.

Appendix: other LSP tests

Business English Performance Test (BEPT)

This test was developed at the English Language Center at Drexel University, in Philadelphia. It was designed to test the English skills needed by international students in a Master's degree program in business administration to participate in cooperative work experiences in US workplaces. The test takes about 30 minutes and consists of four tasks: a background interview, a roleplay in which the candidate makes a brief presentation and answers questions on it, and a two-part roleplay in which the candidate sets up an appointment with a client over the phone, and then meets the client face to face to present a business idea. The test taker's own résumé is the prompt material for the background interview, while authentic field specific materials are provided for the roleplay tasks. The tasks are rated in three categories by a panel of three or four trained evaluators: intelligibility (pronunciation and structure), range (vocabulary range in familiar and unfamiliar interactions), and discourse (quantity, quality, appropriateness, pacing, and rhythm). The raters do not evaluate business knowledge, but it is clear that such specific purpose background knowledge is necessary to perform well in the speaking tasks, since field specific input data are provided prior to the test such as an article on 'Marketing technology and health' and a 'Management staff benefit entitlement summary.'

For more information on the *BEPT*, contact: English Language Center, Drexel University, 229 N. 33rd. Street, Philadelphia, PA 19104, USA.

Cambridge Examination in English for Language Teachers (*CEELT*)

The *CEELT* was introduced in 1987 by the University of Cambridge Local Examinations Syndicate (UCLES) to provide a means of certifying the English language competence of teachers of English whose first language is other than English. The *CEELT* assesses speaking, listening, and reading and writing ability in three sub-tests, in the context of the language teaching classroom. The test is not intended to be a teaching qualification, since none of the components test a teacher's ability in practical classroom techniques or educational theory. The *CEELT* is offered at two levels, the first of which is somewhat above the Cambridge *First Certificate in English* level, and the second roughly equivalent to the Cambridge *Certificate of Proficiency in English* (University of Cambridge Local Examinations Syndicate 1995a). The *CEELT* oral component comprises three tasks: reading aloud a 150–200-word set of classroom instructions, reading aloud a 200–250-word narrative or description suitable for classroom use (at Level I) or an extract from an informational text that could be read aloud to teaching colleagues (at Level II), and describing and commenting on a video clip of $2\frac{1}{2}$–4 minutes showing an extract from an EFL lesson. In the *CEELT* listening component, the test takers listen to an audiotape and complete three tasks. The aural texts used as the input may be extracts from EFL lessons, lectures, talks or broadcasts relevant to professional development, or discussions among two or three speakers on aspects of teaching and learning. The input segments run from three to ten minutes, with the lectures, talks, and broadcasts being the longest, and the entire listening test takes one hour. There are four reading/writing tasks within each *CEELT* level: two reading tasks, an error correction task, and a writing task.

For more information on *CEELT*, contact: University of Cambridge Local Examinations Syndicate, 1 Hills Road, Cambridge CB1 2EU, UK.

Certificate/Diploma in Spanish for Business

This set of examinations was produced by test developers at the University of Alcala, in Spain, and is administered by the Instituto de Formación Empresarial on behalf of the Chamber of Commerce and Industry of Madrid (Cámara de Comercio e Industria de Madrid). The examinations are syllabus-based, and the course in Spanish for Business is one of several offered by the Madrid Chamber of Commerce and Industry. There are three levels of Spanish for Business: Basic and Superior Certificates, and a Diploma. The test tasks at all levels cover reading comprehension, written expression, and oral skills. At the basic level, candidates are expected to demonstrate an ability to read popular printed material concerned with economic and commercial subjects, write business messages, notes and simple letters, and converse about economic and commercial topics, asking for clarification when necessary. At the superior level, the emphasis is on flexibility within and between registers and demonstrating an ability to communicate within the context of a Spanish business, including company organization, finance, and external relations. The diploma level requires a specialized knowledge of Spain's economy and commerce and their influence on Latin American countries. The candidates will need to read authentic documents such as manuals, statistical reports, and organizational diagrams, produce specialized written reports and summaries, and give oral presentations, defending a point of view in debates.

For more information on the Certificate and Diploma in Spanish for Business, contact: Instituto de Formación Empresarial, Calle Pedro Salinas, nº 11, 28043 Madrid, Spain.

Diploma in Public Service Interpreting (DPSI)

This diploma is offered by the Institute of Linguists, a professional language organization promoting language study and use in education, commerce, and the professions in the UK. It is one of a number of certification and training programs administered by the Institute, including a Diploma for International Communication, a Diploma in Translation, and a Bilingual Skills Certificate. The DPSI is intended to provide a national standard for interpreting, and is available in a large number of languages. Candidates must stipulate one of four public service contexts: English Law, Scottish Law, Health, and Local Government. The examination consists of three tasks: oral interpreting and sight translation, and written translation to and from English. Performance on the tasks requires a familiarity with both the target and source cultures and a knowledge of procedures and terminology in the chosen professional service context. The topics covered within the public service contexts include, in the case of Law, the police, courts, probation, and lawyers; in Local Government, housing, education, environmental health, and social services; and in Health, residential and community health care. The oral interpreting task is assessed on the basis of eight criteria: meaning, omission, cultural references, fluency, vocabulary, syntax, presentation, and manner; the oral sight translation task is assessed on completeness, accuracy, appropriateness of expression, and speed of delivery; and the written translation task is assessed on accuracy, completeness, stylistic appropriateness, and presentation.

For more information on the *DPSI*, contact: Institute of Linguists, 24a Highbury Grove, London N5 2DQ, UK.

Listening Summary Translation Examination (LSTE) – Spanish

This specific purpose test was developed for the US Federal Bureau of Investigation (FBI), aimed at testing whether bilinguals' language skills are adequate for monitoring conversations in Spanish (when legally authorized to do so) between individuals suspected of illegal activities and for writing an English summary of the content. A textbook example of an occupational LSP test development project, it is being carried out by Second Language Testing, Inc. and the Center for Applied Linguistics on behalf of the FBI. The researchers first analyzed actual tape-recorded conversations of the type the candidate translators would deal with to determine general situational features such as frequent topics, tone, use of nicknames, colloquial expressions, and code words. They then produced 'summary specifications' for the test, based on the analysis of the tapes, and also developed brief scenarios outlining the gist of simulated conversations to be used in the test. The *LSTE – Spanish* consists of two sub-tests: 40 multiple-choice comprehension items based on eight to nine recorded telephone conversations. This is a screening exercise designed to eliminate candidates who fail to meet even a minimal level of competence deemed necessary to perform the second task, which requires test takers to write summaries of three recorded conversations. The conversations increase in length from one to three minutes, and test takers are allowed to take notes. They are told what kind of information should appear in an effective summary, including the overall topic and details such as names, dates, times, places, or amounts. The summaries are rated by means of a checklist containing the key expected information, and points are awarded for each piece of information appearing in the summary.

For more information on *LSTE – Spanish*, see Scott *et al.* 1996.

References

Abraham, R., and Plakans, B. (1988). Evaluating a screening/training program for nonnative speaking teaching assistants. *TESOL Quarterly* 22, 505–508.

Adult Migrant English Service (1994). *Exemplar for ELSA Test.* Sydney: AMES, New South Wales.

Alderson, J. C. (1991). Language testing in the 1990s: how far have we come? How much farther have we to go? In S. Anivan (ed.), *Current developments in language testing.* Singapore: Regional Language Centre, pp. 1–26.

Alderson, J. C. (1993). Judgments in language testing. In D. Douglas and C. Chapelle (eds.), *A new decade of language testing research.* Arlington, VA: TESOL, pp. 46–57.

Alderson, J. C. (1996). Do corpora have a role in language assessment? In J. Thomas and M. Short (eds.), *Using corpora for language research.* London: Longman, pp. 248–259.

Alderson, J. C., Clapham, C., and Wall, D. (1995). *Language test construction and evaluation.* Cambridge: Cambridge University Press.

Alderson, J. C., and Windeatt, S. (1995). Is there an interest in innovative items? *Language Testing Update* 17, 58–59.

Associated Examining Board (AEB). (1984). *Test in English for Educational Purposes.* Aldershot, UK: AEB.

Asturias, H. (1994). Using students' portfolios to assess mathematical understanding. *Mathematics Teacher* 87.9, 698–701.

Bachman, L. F. (1990). *Fundamental considerations in language testing.* Oxford: Oxford University Press.

Bachman, L. F. (1991). What does language testing have to offer? *TESOL Quarterly* 25.4, 671–704.

Bachman, L. F., Davidson, F., and Milanovic, M. (1991). The use of test method characteristics in the content analysis and design of English proficiency tests. Paper presented at the 13th Annual Language Testing Research Colloquium, Princeton, March.

Bachman, L. F., and Eignor, D. (1997). Recent advances in quantitative test analysis. In C. Clapham and D. Corson (eds.), *Language testing and assess-*

ment. *Encyclopedia of Language and Education*, Volume 7. Dordrecht, NL: Kluwer Academic Publishers, pp. 227–242.

Bachman, L. F., and Palmer, A. S. (1996). *Language testing in practice*. Oxford: Oxford University Press.

Barber, C. (1962). Some measureable characteristics of modern scientific prose. Reprinted in J. M. Swales (ed.), 1988, *Episodes in ESP*. Hemel Hempstead: Prentice Hall International.

Bennett, R., Enright, M., and Tatsuoka, K. (1991). Developing measurement approaches for constructed-response formats. Unpublished document, Educational Testing Service, Princeton, NJ.

Bialystok, E. (1990). *Communication strategies: a psychological analysis of second language use*. Oxford: Blackwell.

Biber, D., Conrad, S., and Reppen, R. (1998). *Corpus linguistics: investigating language structure and use*. Cambridge: Cambridge University Press.

Bley-Vroman, R., and Selinker, L. (1984). Research design in rhetorical/grammatical studies: a proposed optimal research strategy. *English for Specific Purposes* 82/83, 1–4, and 84, 1–5.

Briggs, S. (1993). Using 'real-life' academic challenges for evaluating communicative skills in English. Paper presented at the annual Language Testing Research Colloquium, Cambridge, August.

Brown, A. (1993). The role of test-taker feedback in the test development process: Test-takers' reactions to a tape-mediated test of proficiency in spoken Japanese. *Language Testing* 10.3, 277–303.

Brown, A. (1995). The effect of rater variables in the development of an occupation-specific language performance test. *Language Testing* 12.1, 1–15.

Brown, G., and Yule, G. (1983). *Discourse analysis*. Cambridge: Cambridge University Press.

Brown, J. D. (1991). Statistics as a foreign language – Part 1: What to look for in reading statistical language studies. *TESOL Quarterly* 25.4, 569–586.

Brown, J. D. (1992). Statistics as a foreign language – Part 2: More things to consider in reading statistical language studies. *TESOL Quarterly* 26.4, 629–664.

Brown, J. D., and Hudson, T. (1998). The alternatives in language assessment. *TESOL Quarterly* 32.4, 653–676.

Butler, F. (1995). Electronic-mail communication. 12 December.

Canale, M. (1986). The promise and threat of computerized adaptive assessment of reading comprehension. In C. Stansfield (ed.), *Technology and language testing* (pp. 29–46). Washington, DC: Teachers of English to Speakers of Other Languages, pp. 29–46.

Canale, M., and Swain, M. (1980). Theoretical bases of communicative approaches to second language teaching and testing. *Applied Linguistics* 8, 67–84.

Carroll, B. J. (1980). *Testing communicative performance.* Oxford: Pergamon Press.

Carroll, J. B. (1968). The psychology of language testing. In A. Davies (ed.), *Language testing symposium: a psycholinguistic perspective.* London: Oxford University Press, pp. 46–69.

Cazden, C., John, A., and Hymes, D. (1972). *The functions of language in the classroom.* New York: Teacher's College Press.

Chapelle, C. (1998). Construct definition and validity inquiry in SLA research. In L. Bachman and A. Cohen (eds.), *Interfaces between second language acquisition and language testing research.* Cambridge: Cambridge University Press, pp. 32–70.

Chapelle, C., and Douglas, D. (1993). Interpreting second language performance data. Paper presented at Second Language Research Forum, Pittsburgh, PA, March.

Chapelle, C., Grabe, W., and Berns, M. (1997). *Communicative language proficiency: definition and implications for TOEFL 2000.* TOEFL Monograph Series Report Number 10. Princeton, NJ: Educational Testing Service.

Chomsky, N. (1965). *Aspects of the theory of syntax.* Cambridge, MA: MIT Press.

Clapham, C. (1993). Is ESP testing justified? In D. Douglas and C. Chapelle (eds.), *A new decade of language testing research.* Alexandria, VA: TESOL Publications, pp. 257–271.

Clapham, C. (1996). *The development of IELTS: a study of the effect of background knowledge on reading comprehension.* Cambridge: Cambridge University Press.

Clark, J. (1972). *Foreign language testing: theory and practice.* Philadelphia, PA: Center for Curriculum Development, Inc.

Cohen, A. (1994). *Assessing language ability in the classroom.* Second Edition. Boston, MA: Heinle and Heinle.

Corbel, C. (1995). Exrater: a knowledge-based system for language assessors. In G. Brindley (ed.), *Assessment in action.* Sydney: National Centre for English Language Testing and Research.

Corder, S. P. (1983). Strategies of communication. In C. Faerch and G. Kasper (eds.), *Strategies in interlanguage communication.* London: Longman, pp. 15–19.

Dai-job (On-line). *English test.* Tokyo: Dai-job.com. Available at http://www.testden.com/scripts/dai/demo/demo.asp

Davidson, F., and Lynch, B. (1993). Criterion-referenced language test development: a prolegomenon. In A. Huhta, K. Sajavaara, and S. Takala (eds.), *Language testing: new openings.* Jyväskylä, Finland: Institute for Educational Research, University of Jyväskylä, pp. 73–89.

Davies, A. (1990). *Principles of language testing.* Oxford: Blackwell.

Denzin, N. (1996). *Interpretive ethnography: ethnographic practices for the 21st century.* Thousand Oaks, CA: Sage Publications.

Dorr-Bremme, D. W. (1990). Contextualization cues in the classroom: discourse regulation and social control functions. *Language in Society* 19, 379–402.

Douglas, D., and Myers, R. (in press). Assessing the communication skills of veterinary students: whose criteria? In A. Kunnan (ed.), *Fairness and validation in language assessment.* Cambridge: Cambridge University Press.

Douglas, D., and Selinker, L. (1985). Principles for language tests within the 'discourse domains' theory of interlanguage. *Language Testing* 2, 205–226.

Douglas, D., and Selinker, L. (1993). Performance on general versus field-specific tests of speaking proficiency. In D. Douglas and C. Chapelle (eds.), *A new decade of language testing research.* Alexandria, VA: TESOL Publications, pp. 235–256.

Douglas, D., and Selinker, L. (1994). Research methodology in context-based second language research. Chapter 6 in E. Tarone, S. Gass, and A. Cohen (eds.), *Methodologies for eliciting and analyzing language in context.* Northvale, NJ: Erlbaum, pp. 119–131.

Dubetz, N., Turley, S., and Erickson, M. (1997). Dilemmas of assessment and evaluation in preservice teacher education. In A. Goodwin (ed.), *Assessment for equity and inclusion.* London: Routledge, pp. 197–210.

Dudley-Evans, A., and St John, M. J. (1998). *Developments in ESP: a multidisciplinary approach.* Cambridge: Cambridge University Press.

Educational Testing Service (1965). *Test of English as a Foreign Language.* Princeton, NJ: Educational Testing Service.

Educational Testing Service (1982). *Test of English for International Communication. Form 3EIC2.* Princeton, NJ: Educational Testing Service.

Educational Testing Service (1986). *Test of Spoken English.* Princeton, NJ: Educational Testing Service.

Educational Testing Service (1996). *TOEIC examinee handbook.* Princeton, NJ: Educational Testing Service.

Educational Testing Service (1998). *Information bulletin for computer-based testing.* Princeton, NJ: Educational Testing Service.

Elder, C. (1993a). How do subject specialists construe classroom language proficiency? *Language Testing* 10.3, 235–254.

Elder, C. (1993b). The Proficiency Test for Language Teachers: Italian, Volume 1: Final report on the test development process. Melbourne: NLLIA Language Testing Centre, University of Melbourne.

Elder, C. (1993c). The Proficiency Test for Language Teachers: Italian, Volume 2: appendices. Melbourne: NLLIA Language Testing Centre, University of Melbourne.

Ellis, R., and Roberts, C. (1987). Two approaches for investigating second language acquisition in context. In R. Ellis (ed.), *Second language acquisition in context*. London: Prentice-Hall, pp. 3–29.

Erickson, F., and Shultz, J. (1981). When is a context? Some issues in the analysis of social competence. In J. Green and C. Wallat (eds.), *Ethnography and language in educational settings*. Volume 5, *Advances in discourse processes*, R. Freedle (ed.). Norwood, NJ: Ablex.

Fagundes, R. (1989). Strategies used in the SPEAK test: a discourse analysis. Unpublished master's thesis. Iowa State University, Ames.

Flowerdew, J. (1989). Unpublished transcription of a physics lecture delivered 21 December 1986, Sultan Qaboos University, Yemen.

Frankel, R., and Beckman, H. (1982). IMPACT: an interaction-based method for preserving and analyzing clinical transactions. In L. Pettigrew (ed.), *Explorations in provider and patient transactions*. Memphis, TN: Humana.

Fulcher, G. (On-line (a)). Resources in language testing page. Available at http://www.surrey.ac.uk/ELI/ltr.html

Fulcher, G. (On-line (b)). Thesis writing: quiz 6. Available at http://www.surrey.ac.uk/ELI/sa/thesis6.html

Gale, L. (1983). Montevidisco: an anecdotal history of an interactive videodisc. *CALICO Journal* 1, 42–46.

General Medical Council (1995). Changes to the PLAB test. London: General Medical Council.

Gumperz, J. J. (1976). Language, communication and public negotiation. In P. R. Sanday (ed.), *Anthropology and the public interest*. New York: Academic Press, pp. 273–292.

Hamp-Lyons, L. (1993). Components of portfolio evaluation: ESL data. Paper presented at the annual AAAL Conference, Atlanta, April. (Cited in Cohen 1994.)

Hamp-Lyons, L., and Condon, W. (1993). Questioning assumptions about portfolio-based evaluation. *College Composition & Communication* 44.2, 176–190.

Heaton, J. (1990). *Classroom testing*. London: Longman.

Henning, G. (1990). National issues in individual assessment: the consideration of specialization bias in university screening tests. In J. DeJong and D. Stevenson (eds.), *Individualizing the assessment of language abilities*. Clevedon, UK: Multilingual Matters, pp. 38–50.

Henning, G., and Cascallar, E. (1992). *A preliminary study of the nature of communicative competence*. TOEFL Research Report 36. Princeton, NJ: Educational Testing Service.

Herter, R. (1991). Writing portfolios: alternatives to testing. *English Journal*, January, 90–91.

Hornberger, N. H. (1989). *Tramitès* and *Transportès*: the acquisition of second language communicative competence for one speech event in Puno, Peru. *Applied Linguistics* 10, 214–230.

Huckin, T. and Olsen, L. (1984). On the use of informants in LSP discourse analysis. In A. K. Pugh and J. M. Ulijn (eds.), *Reading for professional purposes*. London: Heinemann, pp. 120–129.

Hughes, A. (1989). *Testing for language teachers*. Cambridge: Cambridge University Press.

Hymes, D. (1971). Competence and performance in linguistic theory. In R. Huxley and E. Ingram (eds.), *Language acquisition: models and methods*. London: Academic Press, pp. 3–24.

Hymes, D. (1972). On communicative competence. In J. B. Pride and J. Holmes (eds.), *Sociolinguistics*. Harmondsworth: Penguin, pp. 269–293.

Hymes, D. (1974). *Foundations in sociolinguistics: an ethnographic approach*. Philadelphia: University of Pennsylvania Press.

Iles, D. and McDowell, C. (1994). *English Language Skills Assessment (ELSA): Revised specifications*. Sydney: Adult Migrant English Service of New South Wales.

Institute of Air Navigation Services (1994). *PELA: a test in the Proficiency in English Language for Air Traffic Control. Information package*. Luxembourg: Institute of Air Navigation Services.

International Civil Aviation Organisation (ICAO) (1985). *Rules of the air and air traffic services*. Doc. 444–RAC/501.12. (Cited in Teasdale 1993.)

Iowa State University, Graduate College (no date (a)). *Instructions for preparing for the TEACH test*. Xerox. Ames, IA: Iowa State University.

Iowa State University, Graduate College (no date (b)). *Laboratory exercise 11, Events in the cardiac cycle*. Xerox. Ames, IA: Iowa State University.

Iowa State University, Graduate College (no date (c)). *TEACH rating sheet*. Xerox. Ames, IA: Iowa State University.

Iowa State University, Graduate College (no date (d)). *Guide for TEACH test student-questioners*. Xerox. Ames, IA: Iowa State University.

Jacoby, S. (1998). Science as performance: socializing scientific discourse through conference talk rehearsals. Unpublished doctoral dissertation, University of California, Los Angeles.

Jacoby, S., and McNamara, T. (in press). Locating competence. *English for Specific Purposes* 18.3.

Johns, T., and Dudley-Evans, A. (1980). An experiment in team-teaching of overseas postgraduate students of transportation and plant biology. *ELT documents 106: team teaching in ESP*. London: British Council. Reprinted in Swales 1985, pp. 140–153.

Kohonen, V. (1997). Authentic assessment as an integration of language learning, teaching, evaluation and the teacher's professional growth. In A. Huhta, V. Kohonen, L. Kurki-Suonio, and S. Luoma (eds.), *Current developments and alternatives in language assessment: proceedings of LTRC 96*. Jyväskylä, Finland: University of Jyväskylä, pp. 7–22.

Kramsch, C. (1993). *Context and culture in language teaching*. Oxford: Oxford University Press.

Lewkowicz, J. (1997). Investigating authenticity in language testing. Unpublished doctoral thesis, University of Lancaster.

Linn, R. L., Baker, E., and Dunbar, S. B. (1991). Complex performance-based assessment: expectations and validation criteria. *Educational Researcher* 20.8, 15–21.

Lumley, T. (1998). Perceptions of language-trained raters and occupational experts in a test of occupational English language proficiency. *English for Specific Purposes* 17.4, 347–368.

Lynch, B., and Davidson, F. (1994). Criterion-referenced language test development: linking curricula, teachers, and tests. *TESOL Quarterly* 28.4, 727–744.

Madaus, G., Raczek, A., and Clarke, M. (1997). The historical and policy foundations of the assessment movement. In A. Goodwin (ed.), *Assessment for equity and inclusion*. London: Routledge, pp. 1–34.

Marsden, B. (1990). BBC/British Council English language video test. Paper presented at the annual TESOL Convention, San Francisco, March.

McDowell, C. (1995). Assessing the language proficiency of overseas-qualified teachers: the English Language Skills Assessment (ELSA). In G. Brindley (ed.), *Language assessment in action*. Sydney: NCELTR, pp. 11–29.

McNamara, T. (1989). ESP testing: general and particular. In C. Candlin and T. McNamara (eds.), *Language, learning, and community*. Sydney, NSW: National Centre for English Language Teaching and Research, Macquarie University, pp. 125–142.

McNamara, T. (1990a). Assessing the second language proficiency of health professionals. Unpublished Doctoral Dissertation, Department of Linguistics and Language Studies, University of Melbourne.

McNamara, T. (1990b). Item response theory and the validation of an ESP test for health professionals. *Language Testing* 7, 52–76.

McNamara, T. (1996). *Measuring second language performance*. London: Longman.

McNamara, T. (1997a). Problematising content validity: the Occupational English Test (OET) as a measure of medical communication. *Melbourne Papers in Language Testing* 6.1, 19–43.

McNamara, T. (1997b). Performance testing. In C. Clapham and D. Corson (eds.), *Language testing and assessment. Encyclopedia of language and education*, Volume 7. Dordrecht, NL: Kluwer Academic Publishers, pp. 131–140.

McNamara, T. (in press). Computer adaptive testing: a view from outside. In M. Chalhoub-Deville (ed.), *Development and research in computer adaptive language testing*. Cambridge: Cambridge University Press.

McNamara, T., and Lumley, T. (1993). The effect of interlocutor and assessment mode variables in offshore assessments of speaking skills in occupational settings. Paper presented at Language Testing Research Colloquium, Cambridge, UK, and Arnhem, NL, August.

MedWeb. (On-line). *Medweb*. Birmingham, UK: University of Birmingham, School of Medicine. Available at http://medweb.bham.ac.uk/caa

Moya, S., and O'Malley, J. M. (1994). A portfolio assessment model for ESL. *The Journal of Educational Issues of Language Minority Students* 13, 13–36.

National Languages and Literacy Institute of Australia Language Testing Centre (1992). *The Japanese Language Test for Tour Guides. Handbook for candidates*. Melbourne: National Languages and Literacy Institute of Australia.

National Languages and Literacy Institute of Australia Language Testing Centre (1993). *Proficiency Test for Teachers: Italian. Draft handbook for candidates*. Melbourne: National Languages and Literacy Institute of Australia.

North, B. (1994). *Scales of language proficiency, a survey of some existing systems*. Strasbourg: Council of Europe CC-LANG (94) 24.

Northern Examinations and Assessment Board (NEAB) (1996a). *University Entrance Test in English for Speakers of Other Languages. Listening Skills*. Audiotape, 19 June. Manchester: NEAB.

Northern Examinations and Assessment Board (NEAB) (1996b). *University Entrance Test in English for Speakers of Other Languages. Listening Skills*. Answer Book, 19 June. Manchester: NEAB.

Northern Examinations and Assessment Board (NEAB) (1996c). *Syllabus for 1997 and 1998 UETESOL*. Manchester: NEAB.

Northern Examinations and Assessment Board (NEAB) (1996d). *University Entrance Test in English for Speakers of Other Languages. Written English*. Question Paper, 28 February. Manchester: NEAB.

Northern Examinations and Assessment Board (NEAB) (1996e). *University Entrance Test in English for Speakers of Other Languages. Written English*. Question Paper, 19 June. Manchester: NEAB.

Oller, J. (1979). *Language tests at school*. London: Longman.

O'Loughlin, K. (1997). The comparability of direct and semi-direct speaking tests: a case study. Unpublished doctoral dissertation, University of Melbourne.

Ordinate (On-line). *PhonePass*. Menlo Park, CA: Ordinate Corporation. Available at http://www.ordinate.com

Perdue, C. (1984). *Second language acquisition by adult immigrants: a field manual*. Rowley, MA.: Newbury House.

Phelps, A. (1997). Portfolio assessment in high school chemistry: one teacher's guidelines. *Journal of Chemical Education* 74.5, 528–531.

Pollari, P. (1997). Could portfolio assessment empower ESL learners? Portfolios in the teaching of English as a foreign language in Finnish upper secondary school. In A. Huhta, V. Kohonen, L. Kurki-Suonio, and S. Luoma (eds.), *Current developments and alternatives in language as-*

sessment: proceedings of LTRC 96. Jyväskylä, Finland: University of Jyväskylä, pp. 37–54.

Rea-Dickins, P. 1987 Testing doctors' written communicative competence: an experimental technique in English for specialist purposes. *Quantitative Linguistics* 34, 185–218.

Royal Society of Arts (RSA) Examinations Board (1994a). *CBLC – Certificate in Business Language Competence: syllabus*. Coventry, UK: RSA.

Royal Society of Arts (RSA) Examinations Board. (1994b). *CBLC – German. Certificate in Business Language Competence. Sample assessment material*. Coventry, UK: RSA.

St John, M. (1990). UET(O) to UETESOL: the revised JMB examination in English for academic purposes. *Language Testing Update* 8, 10–14.

Sajavaara, K. (1992). Designing tests to match the needs of the workplace. In E. Shohamy and A. Walton (eds.), *Language assessment for feedback: testing and other strategies*. Dubuque, IA: Kendall/Hunt, pp. 123–144.

Savitch, J. and Serling, L. (1997). 'I wouldn't know I was smart if I didn't come to this class'. In A. Goodwin (ed.), *Assessment for equity and inclusion*. London: Routledge, pp. 141–162.

Scott, M., Stansfield, C., and Kenyon, D. (1996). Examining validity in a performance test: the Listening Summary Translation Exam (LSTE) – Spanish version. *Language Testing* 13.1, 83–109.

Selinker, L. (1979). Interlanguage. *International Review of Applied Linguistics* 10, 209–231.

Shohamy, E. (1994). The validity of direct versus semi-direct oral tests. *Language Testing* 11, 99–123.

Skehan, P. (1984). Issues in the testing of English for specific purposes. *Language Testing* 1, 202–220.

Slater, T. (1994). Portfolios for learning and assessment in physics. *Physics Teacher* 32.6, 370–373.

Smith, F. (1984). The promise and threat of microcomputers for language learners. In J. Hanscombe, R. Orem, and B. Taylor (eds.), *On TESOL '83: the question of control*. Washington, DC: Teachers of English to Speakers of Other Languages, pp. 1–18.

Spath Hirschmann, S., and Traversa, A. (1997). When a portfolio programme adopts the portfolio. In A. Huhta, V. Kohonen, L. Kurki-Suonio, and S. Luoma (eds.), *Current developments and alternatives in language assessment: proceedings of LTRC 96*. Jyväskylä, Finland: University of Jyväskylä, pp. 55–70.

Spolsky, B. (1973). What does it mean to know a language? Or, how do you get someone to perform his competence? In J. Oller and J. Richards (eds.), *Focus on the learner: pragmatic perspectives for the language teacher*. Rowley, MA: Newbury House, pp. 164–176.

Spolsky, B. (1986). A multiple choice for language testers. *Language Testing* 3, 147–158.

Spolsky, B. (1995). *Measured words: the development of objective language testing.* Oxford: Oxford University Press.

Swales, J. (1981). Aspects of article introductions. *Aston Research Reports* 1. Birmingham, UK: University of Aston.

Swales, J. (1985). *Episodes in ESP.* Oxford: Pergamon Institute of English.

Tan, S. (1990). The role of prior knowledge and language proficiency as predictors of reading comprehension among undergraduates. In J. de Jong and D. Stevenson (eds.), *Individualizing the assessment of language abilities.* Clevedon, UK: Multilingual Matters, pp. 214–224.

Tarone, E. (1977). Conscious communication strategies in interlanguage: a progress report. In H. D. Brown, C. Yorio, and R. Crymes (eds.), *On TESOL '77: teaching and learning ESL.* Washington, DC: TESOL, pp. 194–203.

Teasdale, A. (1993). Authenticity, validity, and task design for tests of well-defined LSP domains. *Thames Valley University Working Papers In English Language Teaching* 2, 137–150.

Teasdale, A. (1996). Content validity in tests for well-defined LSP domains: an approach to defining what is to be tested. In M. Milanovic and N. Saville (eds.), *Studies in language testing.* Volume 3, *Performance testing, cognition, and assessment: selected papers from the 15th Language Testing Research Colloquium,* Cambridge and Arnhem. Cambridge: Cambridge University Press.

University of Cambridge Local Examinations Syndicate (UCLES) (1990). *International English Language Testing System. Module A. Specimen version.* Cambridge: UCLES.

University of Cambridge Local Examinations Syndicate (UCLES) (1994). *An Introduction to IELTS.* Cambridge: UCLES.

University of Cambridge Local Examinations Syndicate (UCLES) (1995a). *Certificate of Proficiency In English.* Cambridge: UCLES.

University of Cambridge Local Examinations Syndicate (UCLES) (1995b). *International English Language Testing System: specimen materials. Academic reading.* Cambridge: UCLES.

University of Cambridge Local Examinations Syndicate (UCLES) (1995c). *International English Language Testing System: specimen materials. Academic writing.* Cambridge: UCLES.

University of Cambridge Local Examinations Syndicate (UCLES) (1995d). *International English Language Testing System: specimen materials. Listening.* Text and audiotape. Cambridge: UCLES.

University of Cambridge Local Examinations Syndicate (UCLES) (no date). *CEIBT content and administrative information.* Cambridge: UCLES.

University of New Mexico – School of Medicine (1992). *State of the art assessment in medical education: a faculty development manual.* Albuquerque, NM: University of New Mexico – School of Medicine.

University of Oxford Delegacy of Local Examinations (1990). *OIBEC: executive level syllabus and specimen material.* Oxford: University of Oxford.

Upshur, J. (1971). Productive communication testing: a progress report. In G. Perren and J. Trim (eds.), *Applications in linguistics.* Cambridge: Cambridge University Press, pp. 435–442.

Weigle, S. C. (forthcoming). *Assessing writing.* Cambridge: Cambridge University Press.

Weir, C. (1983). Identifying the language needs of overseas students in tertiary education in the United Kingdom. Unpublished PhD dissertation, University of London.

Weir, C. (1990). *Communicative language testing.* New York: Prentice Hall.

Weir, C. (1993). *Understanding and developing language tests.* New York: Prentice Hall.

Widdowson, H. (1978). *Teaching language as communication.* Oxford: Oxford University Press.

Widdowson, H. (1979). *Explorations in applied linguistics.* Oxford: Oxford University Press.

Widdowson, H. (1983). *Learning purpose and language use.* Oxford: Oxford University Press.

Wilds, C. (1975). The oral interview test. In R. Jones and B. Spolsky (eds.), *Testing language proficiency.* Arlington, VA: Center for Applied Linguistics, pp. 29–44.

Zuskin, R. (1993). A video-prompted discourse completion test: the effects of gender and grammatical proficiency level on non-native speaker interpretations of context. Paper presented at the annual conference of the American Association for Applied Linguistics, Atlanta, April.

Index